OXBRIDGE ENTRANCE

D0541244

THE REAL RULES

Elfi Pallis

Tell Books
London

TELL BOOKS
Office 117
268 Belsize Road
London NW6 4BT
www.tellbooks.com

This edition published by Tell Books 2018

First edition published by
Tell Books in 2003

ISBN 978-0-9545944-97

Designed by www.anu-design.ie
Printed and bound by Clays Ltd, Elcograf S.p.A.

Contents

Acknowledgements

This book would not have been possible without generous help from a large number of people. First credit belongs to the many kind graduates who mapped out their varied routes towards Oxford or Cambridge. They also contributed what were often deeply moving tales and offered invaluable insights. I must further thank all those Oxbridge candidates I have mentored over time, who shared their fears, struggles and exhilarating moments.

Similar credit must go to the many state school teachers who found the time to proffer technical advice, success stories and educational frustrations. It is a measure of the awe in which the two universities are still held that most people in either group did not want to be named. This necessitated the use of pseudonyms, though the stories told are unchanged.

For academic guidance I am indebted to Deborah Eyre, Joan Freeman, Ruth Heilbronn, Keith L. Clark and Diane Montgomery. A number of current and former Oxbridge dons kindly talked me through their subject's general entry requirements. Among those were Richard Barnes, Peter Carey, Gabriel Dover, Françoise Friedman, Steve Hunt, Catherine Hood, William James, Avi Shlaim, Richard Partington, Claudio Scazzoccio, Richard Stone and Suke Wolton.

Iain Chalmers, Elizabeth Laird, David McDowall, Anne Rodford, Karl Sabbagh and Roger van Zwanenberg added further advice.

Thanks must also go to the members of ArRum, a London club for young Muslim professionals adhering to moderate forms of Islam. Despite busy lives, these graduates managed to convey to me an ethnic minority experience of the Oxbridge entrance process. Gregory Lewis generously gave me access to his research into black representation at Oxbridge. Black parents and staff at Dalston's Windsor Fellowship were welcoming and wise and opened their hearts to me.

Special appreciation must go to my editor, Liz Friend-Smith, whose tactful suggestions and love of precision were crucial in shaping this book. Lastly, Robert Smith provided moral support, literary help and the professional dramatist's sense of how to tell a story.

Naturally, none of the above is in any way responsible for the contents of this book.

The author and publisher are grateful to the following:

1. HarperCollins Publishers Ltd. for permission to reproduce an extract from *From the Land of Green Ghosts* by Pascal Khoo Thwe (HarperCollins, 2003)

2. Johnson & Alcock Ltd. for permission to reproduce an extract from *All Souls in My Time* by A.L. Rowse (Duckworth, 1993).

About the author

Elfi Pallis has for nearly two decades successfully mentored students aiming for Oxbridge. She also advises schools and parents on how to help bright young people from all backgrounds prepare for its challenging admissions process. As a journalist, academic researcher and media producer, she has created BBC programmes on education-related issues and still writes on it.

The author decided to research the Oxbridge entrance process after editing the London quarterly of the *National Association for Gifted Children* and running local workshops for poor but highly able pupils. She was shocked to find that even the brightest did not usually reach Oxbridge. After extensive research and interviews conducted with Oxbridge students, teachers and dons, she wrote *Oxbridge Entrance: The Real Rules,* now in its 9th, fully updated edition.

What sets this book apart is not just the detailed guidance it offers to readers of all ages and groups on the complex route towards Oxbridge success. Also unique is the impact is has had and continues to have on the admissions process. By both describing and evaluating each aspect of it, the author has helped to trigger wide-reaching reforms.

In 2006, Pallis went on to found *STATE SCHOOL TO OXBRIDGE*, an education initiative designed to raise the disappointing success rate of promising applicants through school-based workshops for teachers and students. She remains in constant touch with admissions tutors at both universities and is the parent of an Oxford graduate.

Since this book's first edition appeared in 2003, the author has received a steady flow of thank-you posts from delighted readers. Many insist they would never have got into Oxford or Cambridge without it. Some would not even have considered applying. After following its advice, though, all ended up thriving at Oxbridge both academically and socially.

*****

Follow Elfi Pallis on Twitter @oxbridgentrance

Read her Oxbridge blog at www.epallis.blogger.com

For her Oxbridge workshops see http://tinyurl.com/cceosch

1

Is there a road into Oxbridge?

They are two of the most stunning sights in Britain, yet the mere thought of Oxbridge makes people nervous. Who goes there and who should be going? Brainy and beautiful, but also looking quite expensive, Britain's two oldest universities send out a mixed message. Oxbridge dons, many of them world famous, say they want the "brightest and best" to join their bookish quest for great knowledge. Oxbridge bursars, tasked with balancing a different set of books, might prefer students undeterred by cost.

So, if you are young and bright but perhaps not rich, how do you know whether Oxford or Cambridge is for you? Or, if you are a parent who only graduated from the university of life, will they want your clever child there? What if your daughter is terrified of being interviewed by a roomful of plummy-voiced dons?

And, let's say the idea of Oxbridge grows on you, what exactly does it take to win a place?

Before you embark on finding out, take a mental tour around this very British institution. As you may know, there is not, in fact, any such place as Oxbridge, although it features in many families' dreams. The word, a blend of two town names, is a crucial part of its mystique. So are its turreted buildings, black-gowned students and bewilderingly complex entrance procedures.

There is, of course, far more to Oxford and Cambridge, as you will discover. Behind those ancient walls there are digitalized lecture halls, glass-domed libraries and state-of-the art labs in which masses of young and old people beaver away. Your teachers may have mentioned the academic record of the two universities, the great discoveries made there and the Nobel Prizes won.

If you are raising a bright, high-achieving teenager, Oxford and Cambridge can sound like a wonderful place for her, but also unreal or unwelcoming. And with so many richer, privately schooled pupils going there, how can you tell whether your state school educated daughter stands any chance at all?

The answer, on first sight, seems both positive and obvious. In recent years, Oxford and Cambridge have gone to great lengths to publicise that they invite applications from all sorts of talented young people. A Government-supported campaign run under a variety of names, but mainly known as Access, has resulted in every state school being contacted by at least one of the two universities. Millions of pounds, much of it taxpayer's money, have gone into promoting Oxbridge to a wider public and perhaps led you to consider this slightly awesome choice. Alternatively, you may have been told by your son's teacher that the promising lad ought to apply.

So, it's time to find out more. Oxford and Cambridge are certainly well worth exploring. Their most attractive features are far too little known.

Also, deciding to apply is not at all the same as getting in. To guide your teenager towards this aim, the book carefully lays out the long, tough and not that straightforward Oxbridge entrance process. It gives you the information absent from the official literature, then shows you how to do things right from the start, well before you fill in the application form.

Rather than simply sending off the girl and hoping for the best, this enables you to maximise her chances of acceptance. To that end, the book unpacks the qualifications and qualities that candidates must bring with them to succeed. There are chapters about A-level choice and grades, courses, colleges, academic interests, personal statements and Access schemes. Readers are taken through the key interview skills and the rigid entry rules of the Oxbridge medical schools. Minor mysteries too, like what to wear to your Oxbridge interview, are resolved.

Before embarking on this road, though, the book will tell you what is so different about Oxford and Cambridge, two universities 80 miles apart, yet so similar and so coordinated in their approach that their names have been fused. This way, you will be able to look beyond all those fears and myths that surround them.

Chances are, you will have heard discouraging stories. Some will be about the old- fashioned subjects studied there, which can worry a parent keen to ensure their offspring a good career. Others are about the strange way in which these subjects are taught.

Then there is the now considerable cost of sending a teenager to such a famous place. Does this really make sense? Could another, less famous, university near home not do the same job of teaching you Maths, History or Economics?

Most discouraging can be the doubts about whether Oxbridge really wants candidates like your son or daughter at all. You may have read about Oxford's Millenium rejection of Laura Spence, a Whitley Bay schoolgirl with five top A-levels and a strong working class accent. So, is all that publicity bumph a genuine invitation or just a professor's equivalent of "you really must come to dinner sometime?"

It is only when these questions are resolved in your mind that you and your teenager can hope to successfully negotiate Oxbridge Entrance.

WHAT MAKES OXBRIDGE SPECIAL?

Oxford and Cambridge are intellectual powerhouses, but what makes them that is a quite intangible factor. The two universities do not contain "all the best academics," as many of their graduates like to claim. Mental ability, a gift for teaching and the research skills which can lead an academic towards exciting new discoveries are also found elsewhere. At lots of British universities brilliant young academics inspiringly pass on cutting-edge knowledge to their students; professors, whose research has won them international acclaim, share their wisdom in seminars, lectures and laboratories.

What Oxbridge dons (as its academics are called) have, though, is time. Thanks to Government funding, which tops up the two universities' inherited wealth and that of individual colleges, their student-teacher ratio is far lower than anywhere else. This allows their dons to employ a leisurely, personalised teaching system, the tutorial. It was affectionately described by Robert Ranulph Marett, a Jersey lad who went up to Oxford in the autumn of 1894 and later became its Professor of the new science he had invented, Anthropology:

> Oxford bases her method strictly on the Socratic use of the dialectic, that is conversation, as a means whereby an older man engages with a younger man in a friendly interchange of views, with truth as their common object... a companion of maturer experience can greatly help him to think critically...though he must do so, not by laying down the law, but by showing the inquirer how to put to himself the right questions.
>
> *A JERSEYMAN AT OXFORD* by Robert Ranulph Marrett, 1941, OUP

Little has changed in this method since, although both conversation partners might be female these days and the subject under discussion Computer Science.

The tutorial is not, strictly speaking, unique to Oxford and Cambridge. Although most other universities allocate their students a tutor, their system is far less intensive. Half a dozen students might share one tutor, or a personal tutor might see the student only once a term.

Most learning outside Oxbridge takes place in large hall lectures and or in smaller year groups called seminars.

Oxbridge tutorials do more than guide a student "towards the truth". They make it possible for her to critically absorb a huge amount of information. Staff may also show great flexibility. Even a first year can satisfy her curiosity about a course-related subject by raiding the college library, writing an essay on what she found and discussing it with her tutor. If the student's tutor has not read a specific book mentioned by her, he may well do so for the purpose of discussion. He is not burdened by the needs of hundreds of other students, long teaching hours or piles of paperwork, as are even the most brilliant, committed academics elsewhere.

Although Oxbridge students have a huge range of lecture options, this group-based learning is not their main form of study. Much of their progress is expected to come from the conversations held with and work done for their individual tutor. It is a privileged learning system, but also one that puts great responsibility on the student. If she is keen, she will plough through mountains of written material, write long weekly essays and debate aspects of her course with her tutor and other students.

A student expecting to be jollied along is in for a shock. His tutor may not admonish him if he fails to pull his weight and although there are intermediate exams the lad must pass, they don't really count towards his degree; this is based on how he performs at his final exams, not on continuous assessment. Being told that "we are not here to teach you, you are here to learn" can be a liberating experience for a fast, inquisitive teenager.

The method works best for students who are quite independent-minded and willing to work hard. A student seeking firm guidance towards narrowly defined goals, on the other hand, might find it scary or confusing. It means mixing with adults and being treated like an adult while still allowing you to sleep until lunch - at least if you are an arts student.

The staff, meanwhile, have time left to attend to their own research. Thanks to this, and to fabulously equipped research facilities in all fields, even the youngest don can expect to quickly make his mark in a competitive academic world. And his fame, in turn, will reflect back on Oxbridge.

THE NETWORK
Oxford and Cambridge, though, are not just two high intensity learning and research centres. They also play another, equally important role in

British life as discreet power brokers. When making his first speech as Chancellor of Oxford in June 2003, former Conservative Minister Chris Patten expressed this by asking rhetorically: "What should Oxford University aim to be and to do? As yesterday so tomorrow, our task is to shape and create the future. It is as simple and audacious as that."

This is not an empty boast. Britain has some 120 universities, yet almost all its modern Prime Ministers studied at just two of them. So did most of those who determine what we see on TV or read in the papers. BBC Director-General Tony Hall is an Oxford graduate, as is Rupert Murdoch, the owner of a media empire that includes Sky TV, *The Sun* and Times Newspapers. Combative BBC presenters Mishal Husain and Emily Maitlis gained their degrees at Cambridge. Katharine Viner, the editor of *The Guardian*, a paper which snaps at the establishment's heels from the centre left, is yet another Oxford graduate. So is the editor of the rightwing *Economist*, John Micklethwait.

Oxbridge mass-produces judges, senior civil servants, politicians and most of the committee chairs appointed to pick the next great young artist or city boss. It also supplies the top level staff of many universities. Oxbridge dons pride themselves on their easy access to successful ex-students and the corridors of power.

As a result, the universities are, to many of their traditional students (not all!) a place for networking, for making useful, prestigious links that will last them a lifetime. "You might not remember me, but we were at Jesus in '99" is a meaningful phrase to any of its graduates. It is also a good way of asking for a job.

Meanwhile, successful ex-students drop in for college dinner and everybody who is anybody turns up as a speaker. An undergraduate who has impressed his tutor may meet famous scientists and authors, ennobled industrialists and enraged public campaigners. And because an Oxbridge qualification counts everywhere, a high proportion of graduates quickly emigrate to higher wage economies, which probably make their expensive education a net loss for the taxpayer.

But it is an ever-renewing circle. Junior politicians are launched onto an unsuspecting public from medieval quads and eventually return, in old age, as college wardens or university chancellors. History students become famous British novelists and teenagers studying lower life forms turn into property tycoons thanks to contacts made over a college drink. Most Oxbridge graduates eventually become parents who regard a place at Oxbridge as their kids' birthright and go ballistic when anybody suggests letting more outsiders in.

FUN CITY

The best reason for going to Oxbridge remains its lively academic atmosphere. This does not mean everybody is terribly academic, or even above-average bright. A handful of students, most of them male, will have been admitted to keep up the glorious reputation their college has enjoyed for a few hundred years in rugby or rowing and might leave with a poor degree but muscles that would be the envy of the Incredible Hulk.

The rest of the student body, though, can be pretty brainy. At Oxbridge it is OK to show off just how clever you are, to pepper your conversation with long, fancy words; to have frantic all-night arguments about crazy, complex ideas; and to develop the most obscure artistic tastes. Alternatively, it is fine to walk around with your nose permanently buried in a physics book.

Thanks to the superb leisure facilities, Oxbridge students need not even sacrifice other interests for the sake of nurturing their brains. Instead, they are encouraged to pursue them, often to a semi-professional level. Generous funding for student society means that an undergraduate is able to combine the most diverse activities: History with directing a musical, Geography with ballroom dancing, or Physics with water polo. To a smart all-rounder who used to be very careful "not to show off" in a mixed ability set, this can feel like paradise.

It can also, so potential candidates should be warned, feel like hell. The workload, if you want to get at least a middling degree, is quite shocking. Students learn to prioritise or collapse in a heap after too many sleepless, deadline-cursed nights. Courses can be too abstract for some tastes, tutor and tutee don't always hit it off and a student from an ethnic minority or working class background may pass several uncertain months before she considers herself at home. Still, the tears shed at graduation parties are real enough, and not just due to the champagne donated by parents whose money pit is about to become self-supporting.

WHAT ABOUT THOSE FEES?

Having glimpsed those immaculate lawns and ancient, high-maintenance buildings behind Inspector Morse on TV, you may well think that sending your daughter to Oxbridge is far too expensive. The announcement of new, trebled fees will have reinforced this view among many parents.

While studying at Oxbridge used to cost just over £3,000 a year, the same as anywhere else, English universities in 2012 gained the right to steadily increase their annual fees. Faced with deep, successive cuts in government funding, the top institutions did just that: they saw no other way of guarding their costly academic standards. By 2018, most UK universities were charging a whacking £9,250. As all their undergraduates live away from home, Oxford and Cambridge now looked like the most expensive option.

The thought of spending £27,750 upwards for three years of higher education, not including food or shelter, is already enough to make even a bald father's hair curl. How can you justify sending a boy somewhere so expensive, when he could study for a fraction of the cost in your home town?

A partial answer to the first question is that you won't be paying anything upfront. Instead, students are expected to raise the money for the new fees by borrowing.

The now privatised Student Loans Company will since 2018 lend your son the annual fee. A student only gradually starts to repay the money after university and at the very low interest rate of 3.1 per cent once he earns at least £21,000 a year (though this rises to 6.1 per cent once he earns £41,000 a year upwards). If he still owes anything after thirty years, the debt will be written off.

Oxbridge also actually gives money to poorer students in the form of substantial maintenance grants, listed on its Funding pages. Since 2018 Cambridge students whose parents are low earners are entitled to an annual grant of up to £3,500 and those at Oxford to up to £3,700, designed to cover food and rent. Needy students at both universities can also access college grants of between £200 and £2,000 and, at Oxford, may be given a Moritz Heyman Scholarship worth £3,000 in addition.

The scholarship was set up by Sir Michael Moritz, a computer billionaire who arrived at Oxford as a penniless teenage refugee. The £30m he donated to the university in 2012 are a little thank you for an invaluable education.

Family incomes have to be as low as £16,00 a year for a student to qualify for the totality of grants, but financial support is graduated according to family income.

Even the annual £9,250 fees are not cast in stone. Medical students, whose course lasts six years, do not have to pay fees for the last two, as the NHS does it for them. Moreover, both universities offer fee cuts to needy undergraduates. The amount is graduated by family income, but at Cambridge some reduction is offered even to the "squeezed middle".

Applicants who don't qualify for university support need not give up either. Many banks offer students interest-free overdrafts on current accounts, which pay for travel and new clothes.

If this still looks to you like a tax on cleverness, you are right. An Oxbridge course, though, can also be an investment. Generally, living away from home is likely to broaden your son's outlook. He may hear about careers never considered before, talk to and visit students whose parents do interesting, unfamiliar things. If your own family and friends all work in similar fields and so do the parents of his classmates, university can catapult him into a world of more varied options.

Also, the more desirable jobs are often obtained through personal contacts. Graduates tip off one another and academics make recommendations, but this only works for those who have established close links in the university years. Students who live at home and go to college simply to attend lectures tend to keep their old friends, rather than make new ones. They don't hang around after a lecture to chat. As a result the young man who is still out of work months after graduating will probably be the one his financially cautious parents kept at home.

This matters especially in a recession. Even a young idealist opting for teaching or charity work may find her Oxbridge skills valued. Top employers able to choose from a deluge of applicants often focus solely on their own pond. Several large companies announced after the economic crash of 2008 that they were now recruiting only graduates of five universities, headed by Oxford and Cambridge.

LIVING IT UP

As most potential university students come to realise, tuition fees are not the only item of expenditure you need to budget for. So, what about rental costs at Oxbridge?

Well, college rooms can cost £600 or more a month, depending on size and facilities, but you can shop around. Some of the oldest, grandest have the lowest rents, as they don't really need the money, or will help with costs. Thanks to generous university subsidies, most students live in during their entire course, and many pay no more weekly rent for a room in an historic building with a view "to kill for" than they would for a bedsit in some concrete maze. Their college covers the cost of internet connections and other maintenance bills. Also, since Oxbridge terms are much shorter than those at other educational institutions, there is less rent to pay.

Food too need not cost you an arm and leg at Oxbridge. Each college tries to ensure that a student eating in its dining room or cafeteria will pay no more for this than he would at most other universities. A good meal can be had for the cost of a ready supermarket dish. Outside the college gates, popular student haunts like Pizza Hut and McDonalds charge the same wherever you go.

Unlike in other university towns, students incur no travel costs, and there is a built-in night life. Every college has a bar, as well as a club room, the Junior Common Room (JCR), and many have their own theatre or a cinema society that shows recent films on a big, proper screen. Pints can cost very slightly more than in most redbricks, but university club nights, called Bops or Entz, cost less. Being smallish towns, either Oxford nor Cambridge can sustain any really flash clubs, so there is no need for dressing up (although your daughter might disagree). Students are also entitled to cheap tickets for gigs or shows in town.

Even those annual newspaper shots of students attending the college May Ball in full evening dress can be misleading. Dinner jackets and ball gowns are often hired or bought at the excellent local Oxfam shop, which circulates them among the student generations. And while May Ball tickets cost upwards from £90, depending on the college, they include dinner and all you can drink. There are also several ways of not paying: anyone willing to promote the event, clean up afterwards or do a couple of hours waiting at tables gets in for free. This is a popular option, since by that stage of the university year funds are often tight, and all the students I spoke to insisted that there was no stigma attached. Members of the May Ball organising committee, a post open to all comers, also get in for free in the subsequent year.

One female Cambridge don has run a protracted campaign to have the May Ball abolished, as she feels it gives outsiders quite the wrong impression of College life, but she is annually defeated by the student body. "We girls really like it, because it's a bit like being a princess for the day, and the men quite like what they see," Jess, who is the daughter of a train driver and the president of her college May Ball committee, told me with a giggle.

BARE ESSENTIALS

Text books, an essential of student life, cost the same at Oxbridge as anywhere else. However, only here can a student get by without ever buying a single one. Reading lists may be terrifyingly long, but no student has to make do without. The main university libraries of Oxford and Cambridge contain copies of every book ever published in the UK. Books are also available from other sources, so that any work mentioned in any course is normally available to all. An English student at Oxford, for instance, can find anything on his reading list or just mentioned by staff either at his college library or at the library of the university's English faculty or, if it is fairly obscure, at the university's reference library, the Bodleian. And, by the way, most of these lovely libraries are open 24 hours a day.

Of course, some people prefer owning books to borrowing, and there is no shortage of wealthy Oxbridge students who buy. Some do it because they to want underline, scribble in the margins and generally vandalise the printed page; but others just like to own everything mentioned in class. This has a very useful side effect. At the end of term three, these students often sell off their books (or at least the ones still in tolerable condition) for a fraction of the original price to people in the year below.

The expensive photocopying of key chapters, which is so common in other universities with a limited book supply, is almost unknown at Oxbridge.

What about the peculiar black outfits that you always see students wear on TV? Well, most students at Oxbridge, like elsewhere, live in sweatshirts and jeans. Formal occasions, such as exams or special dinners (which are a bit like wedding meals, including the long speeches), call for a dark suit or two-piece, plus a cap and gown, bought from a local shop, a graduate or, again, Oxfam.

Only very few colleges nowadays insist that students must wear formal dress for ordinary dinners, so gowns tend to last forever. The only unavoidable expense is the £13.99 white tie which male students have to wear with the suit. Apparently, whenever you try to borrow one, it always has ketchup on it.

For those seeking to recover from the wine flowing at these events, there is a choice of sports facilities which are truly amazing and totally free. In fact, there are few experiences for which you actually need to pay; one is membership of your university debating society, the Oxford or Cambridge Union. Joining these historic launch pads of government ministers and government critics currently costs £160 at Oxford, but only £99 at Cambridge for undergraduates who qualify for some university support. Alternatively, a student can pay £5 a night to attend a debate on an issue of the day. Only the drinking societies charge higher fees.

But what about student social life? Well, "Brideshead" it ain't, not any more. A student can go out every night of the week (though they'd better not, if they want to pass) without paying for anything. This is not say there is no high spending Hooray Henry set, dressed head to sun-bronzed toe in designer labels. If your son wants to keep up with them, he'll have to get a part-time job. There are quite a few of those in local shops or at colleges. The universities, although not keen on such distractions, also offer students work in the library, which is reassuring for non-drinkers.

CASH IN HAND, ALMOST

While Oxbridge will require your student daughter to pledge some of her future earnings, it is worth remembering that it may also give her money. Quite a lot of it, actually, as you can see from the sums mentioned earlier, and there is no shame in claiming it.

Some 1,500 Cambridge undergraduates receive a "Cambridge Bursary" each year because of low household incomes. A similar situation exists at Oxford. As explained, only the poorest get the full amount, but students whose parents earn around £42,000 still get something. Few other universities can afford to be so generous.

On top of this, Oxbridge is rich enough to have very substantial hardship funds. An undergraduate who has genuinely fallen on tough times will be directed towards the right application forms, especially in the crucial third year. Once in, no student has to leave Oxbridge because of genuine poverty.

This is not the only money set aside for student needs. There are bursaries designed to pay for a books, computers or travel. Others benefit students in certain fields, mostly within science. A struggling first-year may qualify for several hundred pounds just by coming from a specific region, or by having parents in a specific job: one Oxford bursary is for the children of grocers. If you have a fine singing voice and can read music, a Choral Scholarship can add £1,000 to your funding pot. You also get to take part in fabulous free trips abroad.

Lastly, there are quite a few smaller grants which reward achievement, often a good essay on a set topic. These are open to anyone. Information about all bursaries can be found through the university website.

Still unsure how you will pay for designer glasses? Well, the government since 2018 also offers students a yearly maintenance loan of up to £8,700 (which, alas, used to be a grant) in addition to any funding from university sources. While these sums have not been fixed forever, they are unlikely to change much in future years. If you are a UK resident, Student Finance England (SFE) will point you towards all the state support you are entitled to, at Oxbridge or elsewhere.

The important thing to realize is that once a student has been accepted, most of his basic financial worries can be resolved. Oxford and Cambridge today are pretty flexible societies. Students have similar, but not identical living standards. If your son is on a tight budget, he will not be shunned. There are always other students whose parents cannot pay them to keep up with the Chelsea set. Should your son wonder how he'll manage, I pass on some advice from a recent graduate: if you want your term money to last, don't smoke, and drink only at weekends.

THINKING AHEAD

So, while an Oxbridge education is no longer free or cheap, it is unlikely to be out of your reach. You should also know that many Oxbridge colleges are now busily raising money from rich ex-students, so they can further increase student grants.

Still, given that Britain is mainly governed by Oxbridge graduates, pulling up the free education ladder was a rotten thing to do. This is not to deny that studying at one of Britain's top universities can pay off. Employers, many of them products of the system themselves, love an Oxbridge degree, and many don't care which subject the applicant took. A degree in Classics was for some two hundred years seen as the ideal qualification for the post of Prime Minister. We have moved on only a little since: Margaret Thatcher's Oxford degree was in Chemistry; Tony Blair's, in Law. Conservative Prime Minister David Cameron graduated in Politics, Philosophy and Economics (PPE)), as did seven of his Ministers and the leader of the Labour opposition, Ed Miliband. Cameron's successor, Theresa May did Geography.

This is not to say that all Oxbridge graduates go into "sensible" careers. A few always drop out, or embark on wildly eccentric and quite unprofitable schemes, something perceived as a legitimate choice. This is, however, far less common than most people think. Anyway, should that solitary desert traveller ever feel like touching base and introducing his tribal friends to someone in Britain, his tutor will probably be delighted to oblige. He'll almost certainly know a chap who understands the visitors' dialect, has done research into their culture or might wish to discuss their national aspirations with them.

And should the traveller want to return to society or his studies in some way, the door is always open. Oxbridge graduates retain their opportunities whatever they do (even, it seems, if they commit treason). There is no excuse for any of them to say that he could not develop a career.

MIX AND MATCH

If it is the other students you are worried about, don't be. Oxbridge undergraduates these days come from a pretty wide range of backgrounds. Not that the mixing process always goes smoothly, especially at the start. Discovering that someone with a Scouse accent may have read more of James Joyce comes as a shock to many a public school boy. Nor do enough teachers tell their pupils that it is possible to have a deep love of British medieval history and yet not be white. Luckily, the brainier Oxbridge students tend to cotton on to these facts reasonably fast.

By the end of the first year, certainly, friendships have usually been formed that will cut across income, class or colour lines. Many of these will last a lifetime. Oxbridge graduates keep in touch and tend to employ, gossip about, and marry one another.

Telling your daughter this may still not be enough to remove her doubts about Oxbridge, especially if she attends a school that does not usually sends students there. Rather than give up, you might find it helpful to remember that at seventeen all adult suggestions sound bad. So does university in general. The girl is being asked to consider a long-term project, for a start, and at a moment at which the question whether she will have somewhere to go next Saturday night is far more urgent.

A more forward-thinking student may have her own ideas. Even if you're a bright, well-read young woman determined to become a TV chef, it is wise to research various career paths. Did you know that Nigella Lawson did Modern Languages at Oxford?

Parents may also need to address the most immutable of teenage emotions: fear of loneliness. Having looked though the prospectus and admitted that the course and facilities look pretty good, your teenager will turn to you and say firmly: "I can't possibly. None of my friends are going. It'll be horrible. All the other students will be from somewhere else. I'll be totally on my own."

This is not the moment to point out that one's best, lifelong friends are rarely the people one has smoked one's first fag behind the bike sheds with. Or that it is possible, maybe even exciting, to make friends with people different from yourself.

Instead, just deal with the basics. Firmly agree that your girl's current friends are great, and may well remain her friends for life. After all, she will see them in the extra-long Oxbridge holidays. Then remind her that she actually wanted to go out into the world and meet some new people. If you are bright, interested in ideas and/or academic subjects, Oxbridge is a great place to do just that.

And, of course, there will be ways in which she can hang out and meet people she is not already attending tutorials, seminars or lectures with: at the student common room or the bar, on the college sports field or the university drama society. Moreover, Oxford and Cambridge are small towns, and she will invariably bump into fellow students at Foot Locker, at the local Boots and in Tesco Metro.

BUT WILL I BE SNUBBED?

This is the real fear, the subtext behind many teenage hesitations. Your son may well be flattered by the idea of being thought academically bright enough to apply for Oxbridge, but worried that, once there, others will make him feel he does not belong.

You shouldn't sneer at such fears because they reflect an historic reality. When Roger Dataller, a South Yorkshire collier, went up to Oxford on a miners' scholarship in 1928, after years of preparation at night school, he encountered a world of petty snobbishness chronicled in his book *A Pitman looks at Oxford*.

In this world, students from private schools treated all others with total contempt. Even sport did not bridge the gap. "In my first term at Oxford I played soccer," a fellow working class student confided in Dataller soon after he arrived at the university. "Everything went swimmingly the first game. I played back. The other back was Lord - , son of - , He wasn't bad at first. He'd chat a little when play went up the field. Then he discovered who I was. Never spoke to me again..."

Until well into the 1970s, Oxbridge churned out embittered young men (and occasionally women) whose much longed-for Oxbridge education was won at the price of social agony and isolation. Their degree, they knew, would impress others enough to land them good jobs, but they would forever feel that they themselves had failed to impress. Oxbridge was a public school club, dominated by richer, more confident young people who all seemed to know one another and whose vocabulary, accent and manners made everybody else feel a clod.

But this was generations ago. Now Oxbridge is eager to emphasize its varied student body. At Oxford, I was encouraged to meet Gail, a student from the same region and social background as Roger Dataller. A quick, bubbly girl with a distinct Yorkshire drawl, she is writing a history of her local football club, Barnsley, as part of her course and describes going to Oxbridge as "the best thing I ever did."

Which is not to say that Oxbridge is a totally modern,

homogeneous place. It still has quite a few male, upper middle class customs, made more obscure by their incomprehensible Latin names, but they are not designed to trip up ordinary students. The university guides sent to all those accepted explain what students are expected to wear and do. Also, every newcomer is contacted in advance by a "college parent", a student from the year above. Not only will this student try to answer any worrying questions, but she will be at hand in the first week to guide the newcomer.

So, tell your daughter not be scared by popular misconceptions. Despite what you may have seen on TV (*Brideshead Revisited, The Glittering Prizes, Inspector Morse* and all those dramas about the Cambridge spies all have a lot to answer for), Oxbridge is no longer the homeland of the toff who specialises in put-downs. Not everyone is poor, but whenever I was there everyone was watching *The Big Bang Theory*.

THE NUMBERS GAME

Oxbridge admissions staff have not come quite as far as their students in adapting to a changing world. If your son is now thinking of applying, it may reassure him to know that the two universities, between them, in 2017 had admitted well over 3,000 state school students. This equalled 64 per cent of their British student intake, an unprecedented record.

It can be less reassuring to know that these are mostly middle class kids and that students from private schools, who teach eight per cent of British children, constitute most of the other 36 per cent. This makes Oxbridge a possible destination for a bright student from a state school, but not exactly a certain one.

Still, things used to be very much worse, so you may like to know what successive governments, keen on improving opportunities for all, did to move on from there. The story starts in 2001, when then Chancellor, Gordon Brown, described the earlier mentioned rejection of Laura Spence as "an absolute scandal". This was followed in January 2003 by the Labour government's announcement that it would, in three year's time, appoint a so-called Access Regulator, who would tie a university's Government funding to its success in admitting more students from disadvantaged backgrounds.

Much of this was aimed at the country's oldest universities, and when Education Minister Margaret Hodge visited Cambridge that February, she explained the need for a regulator by spelling out the current situation: "Let's not pretend that Cambridge is wonderful by letting people in on low incomes. Cambridge does not. Only 9 per cent come from the three lowest socio-economic groups.''

That remark went down like a lead balloon, and senior Oxbridge academics rushed to lobby the Minister's Oxbridge-educated superiors. Within days, Prime Minister Tony Blair told the Commons that pupils ought to gain places ''based on merit, not on their class background.'' By April 2003, the new Education Secretary, Charles Clarke, had promised that the regulator would not set external targets or quotas for university intakes.

In October 2004, Sir Martin Harris, like Charles Clarke a graduate of Cambridge, was finally appointed as Britain's first Access Regulator, or rather as Director of Fair Access. The change from the original job title proved to be significant. When journalists enquired what his organisation would do about the latest Oxbridge admissions figures, they were put right. Admissions, so staff at the Office of Fair Access (OFFA) explained, were altogether outside its remit. It only concerned itself with increasing applications.

It was to take another four years before it dawned on the government that OFFA could perhaps do more. In April 2008, Universities Minister John Denham announced that it would be given powers to scrutinise the admissions procedures of every university to check they were fair. The declared aim was ''transparency'', but the question of sanctions against offending institutions was yet to be resolved.

Nothing much happened until February 2011. The Tory-LibDem coalition now in power then decreed that, if universities wanted to charge the new, maximum fees, they would have to make greater use of the available contextual data, which recognised the achievement of disadvantaged pupils, and expand their Access activities. However, they would still set their own Access targets. If Oxbridge regarded a fifty-something per cent state school intake as entirely reasonable, that was that.

Britain's economic crisis, though, changed minds. With unemployment rising, there were mutterings that too many of our rich and powerful owed their jobs to private education and the Oxbridge place this had won them. Against this background, Cambridge (but state school) educated Universities Minister Vince Cable managed to push through the appointment of a new OFFA head with a new kind of CV in 2012.

Les Ebdon, a graduate of Imperial College, Professor of Chemistry and Vice Chancellor of the very new University of Bedfordshire, had long called for a better social mix of students at our top universities. In his new post, he argued that more flexible entry rules would boost social mobility. Institutions which failed to meet Access targets might even be fined.

Widely reported, these proposals led to Professor Ebdon being named by Debrett's in 2013 as one of the most influential people in Britain, but his influence on Oxbridge remained limited. While both Oxford and Cambridge instantly responded with a raft of new, state school geared initiatives, the percentage rise in the two universities' state school intake during his reign remained in single figures. In July 2017, OFFA was abolished altogether.

SO, CAN PEOPLE LIKE US REALLY GET IN?

The answer is yes, absolutely, but you would be unwise to rely on Oxbridge automatically recognising your daughter's ability, or on an effective Government intervention in favour of state school pupils. Candidates who get in tend to be not just bright, but also very clued up about the way in which the Oxbridge entrance process really works.

On the other hand, a lack of focused preparation harms many promising applicants. Even state school pupils described as outstanding by their teachers and offered academic enrichment activities each year fail to gain a place. Sometimes, they don't even get an interview.

As a result, state school pupils, and especially those from working class homes remain under-represented and under-appreciated at both universities, as do students from most minority ethnic groups. Still, this is not to say that you cannot improve the odds considerably. All you need to do is follow the advice in this book.

The best way to start is by treating an Oxbridge education not as a dream, but as a perfectly reasonable aspiration, no matter what you are earning and where your teenager goes to school. This does not mean it automatically goes to those who would most benefit from it. Oxbridge entrance is not actually an ability test, as the universities like to think, but nor is it a lottery. It is a snakes and ladders game based on a set of unwritten rules, known to all the parents who went there and to most public school teachers.

This book, based on dozens of interviews with Oxbridge academics, sixth form teachers, Oxbridge students and Oxbridge rejects, as well as on a study of the available literature, spells out those rules. Taking you through them step by step, it reveals the true road to the only two British towns known as one, Oxford and Cambridge. And, most importantly, it does not stop there: having taken you right up to the Oxbridge gates, it identifies the hidden forces which keep them as narrow as they are and suggests effective opening strategies.

MEASURING OXBRIDGE

Universities differ in lots of ways, some of which are particularly important when deciding where to apply. The quality of a university's teaching and research, the learning facilities available, the degrees obtained and the level of employment after graduation are generally regarded as key factors.

Most broadsheets, notably *The Times* and *The Guardian*, therefore publish annual university league tables based on these features. The Higher Education Funding Council of England (HEFCE) also publishes comparative records of university performance. On all these tables, both Oxford and Cambridge tend to occupy positions at or near the top.

There is another way of grading a university, which is by the company it keeps. Most universities are affiliated to one of three groups, *The 1994 Group, Million+* and *The Russell Group*. Of these, the Russell Group of twenty-four long established universities is the most eminent one. Its members employ staff with top qualifications, seek to maintain the highest academic standards and are internationally renowned for their achievements.

Oxford and Cambridge form part of this group, but also hold a special position due to their great age, reputation and huge financial resources.

Having said this, it is important to look out for variations by subject when it comes to university choice. Even an excellent university may not be at the top in, for example, physics, or may not specialise in a subject area which a student might be interested in, for example nuclear physics.

Moreover, the excellence of individual academics may not show up in a university's general rating. Outstanding researchers, university teachers, theoreticians and writers can be found in a great variety of places. While Oxbridge offers a great education, it should therefore never be seen as a talented student's only suitable destination.

2

The brightest and best

Having decided that Oxbridge might appeal to your teenager, the next stage is to work out whether the girl or boy might appeal to one of the two most picky universities in Britain. You cannot apply for both places, but their tastes are so similar that you do not, at this stage, need to make a choice.

So, what kind of students does Oxbridge want? The simple answer is in all their publicity bumph: they want "the brightest and the best". This is excellent news for today's generation, because things were rather different in the past. In his autobiography, *All Souls in My Time*, the historian A.L. Rowse recalls that when he applied for his first lecturing job at Christ Church College, Oxford, in the 1920s, the question put to him by the appointment panel was: "Would you be more interested in teaching the more intelligent pupils, or the less intelligent?" Rowse replied "the more intelligent" - and was promptly rejected.

© ALL SOULS IN MY TIME (Duckworth, 1993)
Reprinted by permission from Johnson & Alcock Ltd.

When an Oxbridge working party in the late 1950s proposed to restrict entry to academic students in response to Government pressure, the master of Pembroke College, Cambridge, R.B. McCallum, implored his fellow dons to maintain "a rational suspicion of over-intellectualisation...there are young men and woman who by their heredity and upbringing in more leisured and cultivated homes have some special contribution to make."

Even a 1965 Commission of Inquiry could not persuade all Oxbridge dons to select by brightness alone. The eminent Classics don Sir Maurice Bowra warned that "young men (and perhaps young women) who are chosen for not strictly academic reasons may not feel entirely at home in a society of which the members are for the most part chosen for their academic promise, and this may be bad for their self-respect."

This was a tragic prospect indeed, but it too could not stop the onwards march of brightness, driven by an influx of new, often state-educated dons, as well as by Government threats to cut university subsidies. In 1996, Professor John Stein, admissions tutor at Magdalen College, Oxford, declared that "all our students are admitted on their individual academic achievements alone." Stein would briefly come to national prominence four years later, when justifying the university's rejection of Laura Spence, but the principle stood. Laura's place, said Stein, had gone to "another talented candidate from a similarly modest background."

QUALITY STREET

When reminded of the old ways, today's Oxbridge dons respond with the embarrassment which a young man visiting home with his first girlfriend might feel as his mother affectionately brings out a framed picture of him on his potty. Oxbridge, like the young man, has long outgrown that childish stage. One Oxford admissions tutor I met proudly told me that he had just rejected the son of fellow professor.

"The brightest and best" is an extremely vague term. It does not tell you what qualities or personal record Oxbridge candidates need if they are going to stand a chance in the highly intensive selection process. There is no measuring rod that is marked with the words "Brightest and Best" at the top and, presumably, "Daftest and Worst" at the bottom. So, how can you possibly know whether the hunched figure gripping his mobile with one hand, a tattered copy of Beowulf in the other and a bag of crisps with his teeth fits the Oxbridge bill?

An IQ test is certainly not the answer. Oxbridge does not administer the standard test and is not interested in the results if it was taken elsewhere. The SATs tests used by American universities are seen as too easy for potential Oxbridge students.

Formal testing used to be seen as pointless, given the interviewing skills of Oxbridge dons, but views have changed. Since 2001 the two universities have used a range of standard "aptitude tests" which may even determine whether a student is called for an interview. The *Thinking Skills Assessment Test* (TSA) devised by Cambridge, was initially hailed as a brilliant success. A few years later, its dons complained that private schools were intensively coaching their pupils for it, thus distorting the outcome, though it remains in place.

A National Admissions Test for Law (LNAT) also proved unsatisfactory. By 2011, Cambridge had created a Law test of its own, but a few colleges still prefer to put Law applicants through their own exam at the interview. Only the Biomedical Admissions Test (BMAT) was strongly praised by Cambridge dons.

Somewhat surprisingly, Cambridge in 2016 nevertheless introduced standardised tests, called Assessments, to be used by all colleges and for almost all courses. They are said to focus more strongly than at Oxford on students' reasoning skills.

Oxford has taken a more optimistic view of standard tests and the number used there keeps growing: applicants for the vast majority of its courses now sit one of those. Some tests are Oxford's own, but the externally devised BMAT, LNAT, HAT, ELAT and an Oxford version of the TSA are also used university-wide.

It is not entirely clear for how much these tests count: a high score does not guarantee students an offer. Admissions tutors say that they base their decision on a range of indicators, some of which may compensate for others.

So, what does count? In search of some details about "the brightest and best" whose application Oxbridge awaits, I interviewed numerous dons involved in the admissions process and others who had spent some of their working life at Oxbridge before moving on to other top universities. Although my interviewees taught in widely different fields, from History to Physics and from Mathematics to Medicine, the lists they produced were almost identical.

There was a kitbag of very specific qualities which, all of them felt sure, marked out the potential Oxbridge student. At the top was intellectual curiosity, meaning a desire to learn more about a familiar subject and find new subjects to learn about. The right candidate was interested in exploring problems, not just in rattling off solutions. A highly motivated young person, she had a flexible, logical mind and, ideally, a creative bent. The dons also invariably mentioned more general qualities like independence, resourcefulness and determination.

These are very impressive qualities indeed, and if your teenager does not have them all, don't panic. Almost nobody else's does either, certainly not at the tender age of seventeen. Any expert on teenage development will tell you that pupils gearing up for university entrance are only at the start of their intellectual growth curve. They have not yet developed definite character traits, a permanent learning style or a clear sense of their own abilities. They will acquire these later, as a result of time, experience, trial and error.

BRIGHT SPARKS

This is not to say that brightness never manifests itself early on. The boy who gets obsessed with a different grown-up subject each month, which can be anything from architecture to zoology, and then reads every scrap of paper he can find about it, could well be Oxbridge material. So could the girl who is almost exclusively interested in IT, but does not merely use it to play: instead, she is forever trying to create new games and will also use her computer for Maths or Physics related problem solving. Talent in the humanities (or arts, as Oxbridge calls them) can take longer to show up. A future English student writes well, ploughs through the library shelves and may wonder how his favourite tales are constructed years before he starts shaving. Future philosophers and theologians, on the other hand, are more difficult to spot. Although avid readers, they can be dreamy, unfocused and helpless, rather than independent, determined or resourceful. And that little pest who keeps asking difficult questions when she should be finishing her homework may just be the candidate Oxbridge seeks. Brightness, as experts will tell you, can show up in a variety of guises and in combination with all sorts of character traits.

So, the dons' list merely describes a pretty unattainable ideal. Like the teenage girl who dreams of a relationship with Kellan Lutz but ends up dating the gawky lad next door, Oxbridge has to make do with the talent available in the real world. Still, it would be nice if at least two items on its wish list, intellectual curiosity and a real interest in exploring problems, were there, even in embryonic form.

Cynics may argue (and more than one cynical state school teacher has done) that it is the job of a university to inculcate these very qualities in their students. Many universities indeed do so every day of the week. In fact, Oxford and Cambridge can be brilliant at turning a bright and dreamy teenager into a deep and focused young thinker, but both seem strangely unconfident about this.

All this means that your teenager's Oxbridge ambitions may well be realistic and therefore worth pursuing. As long as the girl or boy is blessed with some of the above traits and perceived by most teachers as intelligent or academic - two terms which suggest a university-oriented type of brightness - the road is open.

HOW TO BE ACADEMIC

To be on the road is not the same as having reached one's destination, of course. Given that most Oxbridge applicants have at least some academically desirable traits, this leaves a student with the question of how to develop his own enough to stand out. Is there anything you can feed that teenage brain with, apart from smelly capsules of fish oil?

Fortunately, you can find suitable, brain-enhancing activities in many places, often independently of any school. A bit of online or library research, along the lines suggested below, will unearth a huge range of options. Many will be free or cheap (if threatened by expenditure cuts), and all are good at creating the academically "interesting young people" admissions tutors like. So don't worry if your son's comprehensive school has no science society, or if he is nervous about joining it, in case he is persecuted as a swot.

But how should you choose? Well, if you are a parent you can only suggest. The rest is up to your son. You want him to feel that he is an explorer, not saddled with yet more pesky chores. So, merely explain that the best activities expand academic learning, but also indicate to a university that a student is capable of both individual initiative and hard work.

Identifying activities which will perform this multiple task may take a bit of thought and forward planning by the lad, but this also quickly pays off. School subjects become more comprehensible and university choices increase. The right activities may also provide a student with interests or hobbies he will enjoy throughout life.

STARTING THEM YOUNG

Where you start on this quest depends largely on your son's age. If the boy is still young and you live in a larger town, just take him along to the odd children's event at your nearest library, museum, NAGC Explorers' Club or young people's learning centre. "Catalyst" (www.catalyst.org.uk), a new Science Discovery Centre in Merseyside, runs hands-on chemistry clubs for different age groups. Similar projects can be found in other towns. It does not matter if these offer a talk, a workshop or an exhibition. If your son shows any interest, check whether the notice board offers relevant leaflets or further events. Or is there, perhaps, a junior car-making club?

And once you've both gone to the event and it has not been a disaster (most events are amazing, but occasionally a lecture can be dull, workshops under-staffed or geared to the wrong age) let your son take charge. Ask whether he might like a book that will explain more. Accept that interests will change and suggest that understanding can be enriched by looking at quite unrelated issues. The subject of light, for instance, can be explored through the disciplines of physics or art.

An older pre-teen can probably be persuaded to attend a workshop only by explaining that it will help her with a particular school project, but it is worth suggesting. Once there, your daughter will not only pick up educational tips but meet other young people interested in a field which may have marked her out as peculiar at school. She will also get used to different styles of adult academic language, to different accents and vocabularies.

Such a visit gives the girl a chance to experience what could, if encountered for the first time, be intimidating physical environments. The premises of the Royal Geographical Society or of Somerset House in London, where many junior academic events are held, are not a bad preparation for the imposing architectural splendour of Oxbridge. (Don't point out the old building's features in awe, just move comfortably amongst them.)

Of course, outings like this will only work if your daughter cares to find out more. There has to be some flexibility on your part, too. If the girl is into art, but only wants to see contemporary installations, don't try to make her pour over Russian icons. Do encourage her to explore all aspects of her field via exhibitions, books and internet sites. Ideally, not all her pursuit of the subject should be via the net; while it can help explore things at great depth, there is no real substitute for personal contact with adult experts and other young fans when it comes to sustaining an interest. If you can get a word in edgeways, try to get across (ideally by questions, not by statements) that every subject has its rules, history and protagonists.

IN AT THE DEEP END

While starting academic life young is a good thing, the reality is that Oxbridge appears on many family horizons only once a pupil reaches her teens. This is also the stage when being among one's peers matters most, so keep an eye out for group events and workshops.

There is no need to think narrowly in terms of exam subjects here. Some theatres offer workshops in drama technique or script writing. Professional associations run free taster days introducing young people to architecture, engineering or ancient history. The Royal Society offers lectures on intriguing topics like "the detection of extra-terrestrial life". The British Science Association runs STEM clubs for pupils interested in science and technology and will even help you to set up your own club.

Oxford and Cambridge themselves list free, challenging subject events for Year 10s on their website, while several other universities now hold junior summer schools to flag up unfamiliar academic areas. The "Sound and Music" Summer School at London's famous Purcell School of Music not just enables young people to learn new instruments but also the skill of composing. The School offers some student bursaries.

Sadly, there are no longer any similar government projects. The "Gifted & Talented" scheme, which made schools identify very bright learners and fund academic extension activities, was abolished in 2010. It had not been universally loved. Quite a few teachers and parents seemed to feel that while it was right to help young people develop their sporting abilities with public funds, doing the same for those good at Science or History was somehow wrong.

CLUBS AND SOCIETIES USED BY SUCCESSFUL SCHOOLS TO DEVELOP OXBRIDGE-GEARED MINDS

- Astronomy Club
- STEM Club
- Ecology Club
- Robotics Club
- Forensics Club
- Maths Club
- Chess Club
- Book Club
- Aeronautics Club
- Medical Society
- Coding Club
- Earth Explorers Club
- Creative Writing Club
- Reporters' Club
- Language Club (for films, plays, music & quizzes)
- Amnesty Society
- Modern History Society
- Economics Society
- Politics Society
- Model United Nations

Sadly, budget cuts have meant that few universities offer more than just degree course tasters for pupils keen to learn more about a challenging subject. However, a teacher contacting her nearest university may find that it can often spare one of its academics for an afternoon's workshop or talk to the members of her afternoon club.

A younger teen eager to dip a toe into the full range of academic subjects, on the other hand, may want to stay online with the free, youth-geared Khan Academy. The lectures offered there should make sense to year 10 students, though they won't quite yet take you up to Oxbridge standards. Also useful, if more advanced, are many of the introductory subject talks found on YouTube.

If you prefer slightly more personal involvement, note that most scientific societies in England, Scotland and Wales run their own junior branches. Designed to encourage interest and spread expert knowledge, they are either free or charge as little as £10 per annum. For this money you usually get a magazine, invitations to scientific outings or field trips and a chance to meet other young members.

How though do you become a society figure? The best route is via the internet. Reptile lovers, for instance, will find that they can join a junior herpetologists club (www.thebhs.org), which offers local talks, wildlife walks and involvement in nature projects. The Royal Geographical Society offers young members fieldwork training, careers advice and a magazine. By joining the Marine Conservation Society, you could find yourself helping with sea life surveys or cleaning up beaches.

Public events can be another road in. At Birmingham's annual Big Bang Fair, 13 to 19 year olds studying science, technology, engineering or maths can take part in experiments, as well as make contact with professional groups running workshops and trips. The 2018 British Science Festival will be held in Hull, while Oxford itself each year runs the lively Oxfordshire Science Festival. Cambridge runs both an annual Science Festival and a Festival of Ideas, focused on the humanities, which may appeal to older teens.

And if your Year 11 knows what he'd like to study at Oxbridge but fears that he may have joined the wrong science society or club, tell him not to worry. Science has general principles and rules, so an interest in reptiles can prove helpful, even if you later decide to study Physics. It is certainly alright for a pupil to explore some obscure, narrow field, as long as they are thorough about it.

Maths lovers can aim for the British Mathematical Olympiad (www.bmoc.maths.org). If you sign up with BMO, its staff will provide you with a steady supply of interesting problems. Then, if you're really good, they will send you on one of its summer camps at Oxford or Cambridge for a week of maths lectures, problem-solving sessions, competitions and social events. For those who get into the finals, the next stage is a free trip to the International Mathematical Olympiad. Coming up is Romania in July 2018. Another key event, the European Girls' Mathematical Olympiad, will take place the same year in Kiev (Ukraine). Fancy some free travel?

Those vaguely considering a university course involving history, inspired by the flood of excellent TV programmes, may have to start out on their own. Once your son is clear what he wants to know more about, which can be a personage, place or a period, even a holiday with his cousins in Ireland can, with a bit of forethought, become an opportunity for research. Suggest the lad makes contact with one of the many local history societies, again via the BBC's website. Your basic family history can now be researched online, but you may want to explore the wider context. Delving into the files of the National Archives in London, which are open to all, can be the best way forward and will teach you how to do historical research.

READ ALL AROUND IT

A sixth former who already has a specific Oxbridge course in mind needs to focus more sharply. The rather vague advice you are often given at this point is to "read all around it". Just in case you are wondering, this does not mean that you are expected to slowly girdle the nearest tree while holding open a copy of *Plant Pathology*.

Instead, what to do depends on the subject you have picked. An aspiring biologist simply needs to add to his stack of knowledge. A specialist magazine will tell him about new discoveries in the field and the problems raised by older ones. If he is lucky, he will find it in the library. If not, an online subscription to *Geography Review, Nature, New Scientist, Scientific American, The Psychologist, Biological Sciences Review* or *Student BMJ* can makes a wise Christmas gift.

A good science book, aimed at adult readers, will help the student see the point behind his own experiments. Instead of just getting the powder in his lab dish to turn green, as predicted in his school text book, an A-level chemistry student will learn to perceive what the scientist Richard Feynman has called "the beauty of the inner structure". He'll discover how scientists think and how they arrive at their understanding of the natural world.

For a pupil hoping to study something not taught at school, "read all around it" means grasping her way towards a quite mysterious subject. A budding architecture student, for instance, may dream about the cool new buildings she will design, but first she needs to look at (and perhaps sketch) some existing ones. This might be followed by a book on architectural history or styles. Next, she'll want to explore the physics of engineering, which prevent that brick ceiling above from falling on your head. Specialist magazines, although they exist, may not make sense until the university stage.

Equally, "reading around" a subject can mean exploring it through university-type sources. The largest, of them, JSTOR (http://www.jstor.org/), which you can access for free from any library, contains outstanding features on areas of academic interest. The BBC offers great radio programmes on science (mostly on Radio 4) and great TV ones on art, history and architecture. Many of the more intellectual BBC series are now archived or available as a Podcast, so you can explore them whenever and wherever you like. The BBC's site also contains lively, detailed fact sheets on lots of subjects.

WHAT ABOUT ENGLISH?

It is now time to qualify the above advice. To a potential English Lit. student "Reading around it" means keeping your eyes largely on the printed page. As a sixth form mentor, I did not know whether to laugh or cry after hearing from one bright boy planning to read English Lit. I had recommended a favourite novel to him and when he did not contact me after the summer holidays, I sent a slightly worried email. The answer was clearly meant to reassure me: "Haven't had a chance to look at *Brighton Rock*, but I did some internet research on it."

That student, sadly, had lost the plot altogether. No amount of research would make any sense to him unless he read the novel first. (See also the "English" chapter on p. 187)

CAUGHT IN THE WEB

Quite a few other websites can be a boon to the aspiring Oxbridge student. What matters, though, is finding a reliable source. Those run by universities, academic societies, specialist magazines and quality newspapers offer full-length, expert-written features on almost anything you might like to research.

Just reading what comes up first on Google, as a staggering number of sixth formers still do, can mean that you end up being not just under-informed but wrong. Anyone can set up a website and, if carefully linked to others, it might come up on page one. Corporations are highly skilled at promoting their goods online in this way.

Even well-respected sites may not be problem-free. Wikipedia recently had to admit that a 24-year-old Kansas student, pretending to be a professor, had altered over 20,000 of its entries as a joke. The contents of some popular pages is also frequently changed by vested interest groups. Another problem for younger searchers can be the huge length and detail of many Wikipedia entries, which makes it difficult to memorise key points. If you need a quick, reliable digital reference work, use the Encyclopaedia Britannica.

For prospective Oxbridge applicants, on the other hand, the BBC's excellent, compact fact pages are almost too tempting. Skimming a couple of reports, summaries or extracts, picked by key words, can make you feel smart within minutes. Unfortunately, this may be an illusion. More suitable at this stage may be the subject-specific features put online by Oxbridge itself and listed at the end.

Ultimately, though, if you plan to impress a major university, you need to draw at least some extra knowledge from a primary source, which usually means a book. Only this will provide you with the necessary context and sufficient details. A course-related feature written by an academic expert and published on her university's website will aid understanding or introduce new ideas, but even this alone may not be quite enough.

There is only one exception to this rule: even the most ambitious maths A-level student can probably get by without ever moving from the screen. Thanks to good, specialised maths sites like *Meikleriggs, Plus Magazine* (http://plus.maths.org/content/) or *NRich Mathematics* (http://nrich.maths.org/public/) it is the net, rather than the library, which can offer her the endless supply of problems, debates and explanations on which born mathematicians thrive.

OXBRIDGE CANDIDATES

Having a sound knowledge base is essential for Oxbridge success, but many pupils who worked hard to build it still won't apply because they're unsure what kind of person it seeks. To help you decide, here are some brief profiles of four imaginary Oxbridge candidates, based on the dozens of young people I interviewed for this book.

Kate goes to a comprehensive which used to be a grammar school in an industrial Midlands town. She is extremely hard-working and when she gained eleven top GCSE's the headmaster suggested she should try for Oxbridge. Although the idea had not occurred to anyone in her family, they were delighted. Her father is a van driver and her mother looks after three younger children. The family is evangelical and Kate is active in Church work: she helps to run a youth club for girls, plays netball and sings in the choir. An avid follower of events in Africa, she is also the head girl of her school.

Arun attends a large, regional Sixth Form college. He has long been interested in engineering, has read up about it online and built his mother an electric mangle once. With only a one-room, part-time library in his small town, he is unsure what else to do. Arun's father is a tiler and his mother used to be a cook. When he gained outstanding GCSE results for his college, this meant little to them. Arun's maths teacher had planned to put him on the college's "gifted and talented" scheme, which funded enrichment trips, but that year the scheme was abolished. Busy with integrating students of very different attainment levels, he could do little else. The teacher did, however, advise Arun to buy an engineering book and encouraged him to apply to Oxbridge. Arun spends his free evenings either with his girlfriend, playing strategy games or listening to Techno. He also has a weekend job delivering pizzas.

Jill attends a selective state grammar school in an affluent southern suburb. The smallish school regularly sends around four pupils a year to Oxbridge and when Jill proved to be an excellent language student, she was put into its Oxbridge group for more reading and extra lessons. Jill's parents run a thriving specialist shop and encouraged her to follow a range of interests. She cycles, plays the viola to concert level, won a prize for her sculpting and is active in the School Assembly, which led to her being sent as its delegate to a national schools conference. During her language exchange, she ran a musical movement class.

John goes to a small rural public school near his father's farm, which takes pupils of all abilities and sends about eight students a year to Oxbridge. John gained twelve, mainly good GCSEs, taken over two years. He is not a great reader, but is the chairman of the school's Physics Society, has been to university science talks and acts as treasurer of a recycling scheme for the local village. He also plays squash and is on the school's rowing team. John commands his school's cadet force, has completed the *Duke of Edinburgh Award Scheme* and plays the tuba in his spare time.

Well, who got in? If you instantly blurt out "only John!" you are still living in the 1960s. If you think everyone of these remarkable people did, you are an incurable optimist. The real answer is everybody but Arun.

But why is that? To the careful reader, it will be obvious that every student except Arun could point not just to academic ability but also to appropriate extension activities and wider interests. These created the kind of personal profile which, according to experienced headmasters, Oxbridge dons liked. Brains mattered most, but there had to be evidence of independent use, usually provided by an academic interest beyond the school syllabus. In addition, "good candidates" had often done a spot of voluntary work, practiced some sport or were involved with music. Many had also held a leadership position, however minor. Students who fitted the bill were most likely to get in.

Most of the candidates admitted certainly were busy young

people. As one Physics student put it to me, "You want to come across as quite driven." The Cambridge educated author Philip Hensher, writing in *The Independent* of 15th April 2002 under the title "Sorry, but Oxbridge graduates are the best", took this point rather further by claiming, "The sort of people who at 18 have the drive to get into these universities are the sort of people who are going to rise to eminence in later life."

Although he has what psychologists might regard as the clearest indicators of academic ability, Arun, unfortunately, did not fit that bill. This is not his fault. He did not know about suitable external sources and, while he likes to read, he has few opportunities to discuss his interests. His college, which serves a huge area, has no sporting or research facilities. Having to integrate students who arrive with vastly differing standards, his busy teachers cannot give him much personal attention. Arun also lives in an area with little public transport and his parents do not have a car. Nor do they have the money to fund extracurricular activities.

. The Oxbridge way of picking pupils has traditionally worked against state school and especially poorer applicants. They could seem dull and unmotivated in comparison with young people from private schools. There, teachers run regular school competitions whose prizes can add distinction to a pupil's record. Many provide their teenagers with carefully manufactured adult CVs: cultural, scientific and sporting activities are laid on and can even be mandatory. Besides, pupils are quite often boarders and cannot choose to go to the movies instead.

As a result, teenagers leading sheltered and tightly structured lives would sometimes come across as more determined, resourceful and academically curious than bright young people who were handling the complexities of inner city life. Proving that you have "the drive", which Philip Hensher identified as a key feature of the best, can be harder if you are poor.

CHANGING TIMES

Perhaps not being poor yourself, you may wonder why you should care. The answer is because of one vitally important thing about Arun: he is a thoroughly modern teenager and so is most likely to resemble your son. Listening to CDs or playing computer games (or going to gigs, or shopping) are favourite leisure pursuits among the brightest of today's teenagers. With every generation physically maturing a little earlier, today's Oxbridge candidates often have an active sex life, or at least actively seek to acquire one by clubbing.

Fortunately a new generation of dons blessed with CD racks, store cards and torrid love lives of their own feel that modern lifestyles are compatible with academic thought. They have no trouble grasping the abilities of non-traditional Oxbridge candidates or doubts about admitting them. More than one told me with feeling that he never wanted to hear about the Duke of Edinburgh Award again. Unfortunately, it was not safe until recently for candidates to generalize from this.

In his review of this book's first edition (2003), Geoff Parks, the Cambridge Director of Admissions, described it as "doing an excellent job of identifying and describing what is good and distinctive about the two universities and why it is worth going to them", before dismissing the importance of extra-curricular activities. "Selection", he pointed out, "is based overwhelmingly on academic potential". This is undoubtedly true, but given the presence of so many students with a broad range of cultural achievements, it was hard to believe that extra-curricular activities were, as he claimed, "entirely incidental."

Nevertheless, a couple of Oxbridge dons promptly went on student websites to indignantly declare that they, personally, had never asked candidates about sport or music. Consequently, academic ability was all that counted at their university. Students, they said, would be wise to disregard any references to extra-curricular activities.

This was not always good advice, as other dons, sometimes working from the college rooms next door, merrily went on grilling students at length about these same incidental activities at the Oxbridge interview. Questions like "What could you contribute to college life?" or "If you could only pursue three extra-curricular activities here, which ones would you pick?" remained fairly common. More importantly, when faced with two applicants thought to be of equally high ability by their school, dons tended to choose the one with extra-curricular activities.

So, has there been any change? Colin Hall, head of Holland Park School, one of London's inner city comprehensives, does not think so. In an interview with the *Financial Times* published on April 19th 2008, he claimed that his students were culturally discriminated against when applying to Oxbridge. "I imagine it must be very difficult to chose between someone who's outstanding at Maths and someone who's outstanding at Maths and can also quote TS Eliot and play the violin," he quipped.

This leaves us with two questions: are extra-curricular activities still important or not, and what was their original point?

After all, doing very well in your school subjects is a pretty good indication of academic interest and ability. Must you also de facto study elsewhere? Also, why should future historians hit the race track or concert hall? Which benefit, exactly, do future scientists gain from rattling a collection box? And what is the point of a post that a teenager can hold?

No convincing answer was ever forthcoming, but it is clear that entrance criteria often just reflected individual preference. A friend teaching at a private school during the late 1990s recalls the guidance offered to him by a visiting Oxbridge don, who was also one of the school's governors (a not uncommon situation). "Not much point sending us a linguist this year," proclaimed the distinguished figure. "Too many good ones coming up already. But let's think: there's a new college fellow. What he might go for is an interest in microscopic sea urchins and a taste for Chopin."

Other dons' explanations were far from revealing. During my book research, one leftish, public-school educated admissions tutor described extra-curricular activities as merely something you could dip into in order to break the ice at the interview. A very conservative one, educated at a state grammar school, suggested they proved that the candidate was good at time management. A young female don from a top comprehensive argued that such activities "show that you've got a bit of a life."

When it came to sport, there was more of a consensus. The ancient Greek belief that there is "a healthy mind in a healthy body", today associated with totalitarian rulers who like to see their name spelt out by the bodies of massed gymnasts, featured in several replies.

VICTORIAN VALUES

In fairness, the emphasis on music and sport has its roots in something slightly more spiritual, the ideal of Muscular Christianity embraced by the Victorians. Originally coined by the author E. Cobham Brewer to describe the qualities of the perfect Christian knight, the concept was developed by Charles Kingsley, a professor of Modern History at Cambridge and in later life the author of *The Water Babies*. In the 1860s Kingsley, who supported universal voting rights, put forward the argument that physical prowess could and should co-exist with moral and mental activity. This meant that there was nobility also in the working man.

The idea of a Christian manliness that combined aggressive action with mental pursuits was next taken up by Matthew Arnold, a professor of Poetry at Oxford. Arnold, though, had a different agenda.

To him, the male student's sporting values could prevent the same working man from taking over. Strength and piety were the qualities needed by a Victorian gentleman, in addition to learning. They were also handy for defending British civilisation in its Imperial outposts. Arnold advised educators to strive for "harmonious perfection, only to be won by unreservedly cultivating many sides in us."

It is this salad of somewhat contradictory Greco-Victorian values that for generations helped to determine who would be a successful Oxbridge applicant. Academic ability was a must, but when it came to choosing between different candidates, "the best" were often those who spent their leisure time like a Muscular Christian.

While girls of a similar background were sometimes willing to play along, even the brightest, most ambitious modern working class boy was likely to reject the Victorian ideal with horror. This worked in favour of wealthier pupils from traditional schools.

A mix of generation shift, government concerns and Oxbridge soul searching has gradually altered the picture. Also, the changes have become explicit and thus binding on all dons. For a start, they can no longer grill students about their sporting prowess. Such questions, Geoff Parks told the public in 2006, "are now in the past". By 2007, Oxford was stating that there were no credits for extra-curricular activities and Cambridge that "all admissions decisions are based on academic criteria, and excellence in an extra-curricular activity will never 'compensate' for lower academic potential".

Oxbridge, this suggests, does now accept that widening participation is incompatible with vague, old-fashioned entrance criteria, a fact first pointed out by this book in 2003. Students, teachers and parents should rejoice at the news.

SHOULD YOU SHAKE A LEG ANYWAY?

If you are a potential Oxbridge candidate happily hunched in front of your screen, the announcement that you don't need to ever think about Scottish country dancing or cricket may go down rather well. This does not necessarily mean that you should load up the next computer game.

Why? Primarily because reading, writing and researching beyond curriculum requirements do not come under extra-curricular activities but under academic interests. Also, many of the qualities and skills Oxbridge does seek are most easily acquired in this way.

Drama is a case in point. While directly relevant only to an English Literature or Modern Languages course, learning how to hold the stage can benefit students targeting other subjects. An Oxbridge interviewee who thinks before she speaks and clearly articulates her words may be judged more intelligent than one mumbling rush answers. Students who have been involved in dance often come across as thoughtful and calm.

Or take politics, as leadership is now known. Campaigning for change teaches you to argue your points clearly and convincingly, as well as to counter other people's. By becoming a member or chair of an organisation, however small, you'll develop self-discipline and teamwork skills. Don't worry that strong views might alienate Oxbridge. Whatever their own convictions, dons tend to look equally kindly upon a candidate writing for the Conservative Party's *Heartland* magazine and for *Socialist Worker*, upon a canvasser for the Green Party and a contributor to *Young Labour eZine*. What matters is that a student can rationally defend her views, but also grasps that these are not immutable facts. The two universities have been in the business of producing leaders, as well as thinkers, for hundreds of years and are not easily shocked.

An applicant keen to hone his arguing skills without going out into the world might want to join a debating society. Once common, such societies are now quite rare in state schools, but there is little to stop you from starting up your own. There is almost invariably one teacher keen on verbal battles who will help you find topics, time-table space and unbroken chairs.

While the concept of a debating society may be too far removed from some pupils' lives, concerns about human rights are not. Groups like Amnesty International, which has branches in many schools, offer members a chance to talk. So do school conferences, set up to discuss burning issues from the European Union to Climate Change. Students will research and prepare the event, organise and publicise it and often invite outside speakers. It's a great way of learning how to clarify your ideas, phone up total strangers and cope with last minute disasters.

Alternatively, a student-run Astronomy, Creative Writing or Ecology Club may deepen existing skills. Volunteering for a local charity has benefits too. Unlike those charity sponsorship projects which charge you a fortune to do unskilled work in a far-away, sunny country full of poor people who'd love to be paid, local ones really help local people. Placements can be hard to find because under-18s need to legally be chaperoned, but keep looking. One project, *Inspired*, set up by the Department of Education, offers 16 to 24 year olds a chance to pass on their own skills, from sports coaching to creating websites.

Students aged eighteen plus have a broader range of volunteering options. You are now old enough to help the homeless or distressed, or to hit the campaign trail. Jobs in which you get initial training tend to have the greatest Oxbridge appeal. At the very least, your voluntary work should bring you together with people from whom you can learn; you don't just want to input data all day.

Although Oxbridge now plays down the role of extra-curricular activities, a challenging or unusual volunteer job may still make you stand out. This can happen even if that job, mentioned in a student's statement, is not referred to at the interview A *Guardian* reporter observing Cambridge admissions tutors pick medical students in 2011 found that what swung it for one young man with care home experience was that he had also trained as a special constable.

Do especially consider volunteering, at least for a brief period, if you are planning to take a year off after your place is confirmed. Teachers often encourage the idea. It may seem especially harsh to suggest disadvantaged young people should play Lady Bountiful, but charities claim that volunteering benefits both sides: it fosters maturity, increases confidence, develops skills and helps you to meet fascinating people at both ends of the social spectrum.

Taking your gap year before actually applying can be slightly more problematic: post-gap applicants for Mathematics and courses with a strong mathematical element such as Physics, Computer Sciences or Economics often discover to their shock that by the time of their interview/test they have forgotten much of their maths.

You don't, of course, need to go away to engage in good works. Even the mere fact that you've been appointed your school's head girl or break-time librarian tells others something positive about you. Oxford's former head of admissions, Mike Nicholson, has praised candidates for "exhibiting significant responsibility in roles that they have within their school, colleges and/or local community."

Playing an instrument has lots of potential spin-offs, apart from conceivably getting you into one of the prestigious Oxbridge Music courses. Being in an orchestra or a band teaches you to cooperate, playing on your own encourages you to focus or, if it is a leisure activity, to relax. Singing can even benefit you financially. Colleges at both Oxford and Cambridge offer choral scholarships worth several hundred pounds a year.

But what about sport? If you love it, the answer is obvious. Even if you remember those ghastly, sweat-soaked gym shorts with dread, try to admit that physical exercise has its uses. Running or aerobics will stop you from getting fat while you comfort-eat before exams. Winning a kick-boxing match will make you feel great and just kicking a ball at the dog can unstress you after a bad day's revision.

It's even worth checking what will be on offer at the Oxbridge college you are aiming for and limbering up for it. Sport has come a long way since an Oxbridge candidate was asked to make clear whether he was "a dry bod or a wet bod", which meant whether he played the "dry" university sports of cricket or rugby, or preferred "wet" rowing. Now badminton, mountain biking, water polo, netball, snooker and table tennis all have their fans. Football, played by both sexes, is today more popular than rugby at both universities. It's also great for meeting new people.

Other activities can improve personal confidence. Writing poetry, setting it to music and producing your own CD helps you see yourself as literate, creative and organised. Teaching drawing skills to disadvantaged kids can make you feel worthy, grown-up and responsible.

Such activities can even give you something to talk about in the first, awkward seconds of the interview, although the response will depend on your degree subject. The fact that you directed your school's drama society production of "Blasted" will impress an English don far more than an Engineering one. Your membership in a junior mountaineering club could thrill a Geography don, but not a Philosophy one. Be prepared to say what specialist knowledge you have gained and what uses it might have.

And don't automatically assume that, however useful, such an involvement will take much of your precious time. We are only talking about a couple of hours per week at the most, and not always spent away from home. The road from first year A-level work to Oxbridge interview is quite a long one.

In the meantime, don't be overawed by the potentially scary words "brightest and best". Just like in a washing power ad, this is a promotional term, rather than a fair description of the product at hand. Oxbridge has a high proportion of very smart young people, but when your son goes on his taster visit, he is sure to discover that most are pretty normal, nevertheless. There are not enough genuinely driven, charitable, opera-singing, cricket-playing, leadership-oriented, microscope-fixated geniuses in this world to fill a university, never mind two.

3
GCSEs, AS and A-levels

Beyond brightness, interests and certain character traits, applicants also need some official bits of paper such as exam results. Taking note of school exams is not, contrary to popular belief, an ancient Oxbridge tradition. Until 1939, Oxford and Cambridge admitted students without any formal entrance qualifications. Any young gentleman with enough schooling to read a few Greek and Latin texts was welcome -- assuming he could pay.

Until the middle of the 19th century, most students didn't sit any finals either. They simply claimed their degree upon an attendance certificate from their college. If you could afford Oxbridge you were entitled to all the blessings it could bestow.

Less well off young men with a grammar school education could apply, once an academic had recommended them, but acceptance often depended on them also gaining a small grant from a church, charity or Oxbridge itself. Most grants went to prospective clergymen. Competitive tests were only for the handful of very poor candidates admitted each year. A.L. Rowse, the son of a clay miner, started his career as a historian by winning the sole Oxford scholarship place available for the whole of Cornwall.

The result was that Oxbridge fell behind continental universities like Paris and Marburg once those had started to prefer qualified students. A steady flow of reforms, fiercely resisted by public school heads and many university dons, was gradually pushed through so it could regain its intellectual lead. From 1940, grammar school pupils willing to stay an extra term could get in by passing the new Oxbridge entrance exam. Well off candidates, however, were still accepted on the nod of a college head.

The Oxbridge entrance exam was resented by many applicants, mainly because it was conditional on them staying on at an often fee-charging grammar school, and because it did not apply to everyone. In 1987, a new system was introduced, covering all applicants, although colleges retained some discretion to offer places to exceptional applicants.

As a result, the academic school exams, GCSEs, AS and A-levels became the standard qualification required by UK students applying to Oxford or Cambridge. This seemingly puts Oxbridge on a par with all other British universities, which have been using these qualifications since they were introduced. Still, great differences in what is acceptable remain and pupils need to be clued up about them very early on. So, below is a guide to Oxbridge thinking on exams, based not just on official publications but also on dozens of private conversations with college dons.

HOW MANY AND HOW GOOD?

Today's UK pupils take an infinity of exams, but what really matters to Oxbridge are GCSEs and A-levels (for the changing status of AS-levels see p. 41). Scottish Highers have long been accepted and are evaluated in line with the above. So is the Welsh, European and International Baccalaureate. Candidates studying for the challenging Cambridge Pre-U Diploma are now welcome too.

Cambridge also accepts Advanced Diplomas for Geography, Natural Sciences and Engineering, but only in certain combinations with other qualifications. Oxford currently accepts only the Advanced Diploma in Engineering.

What exam record, though, does your son or daughter need to stand a real chance of success? And how much allowance is there for the different types of schooling?

The answer, in terms of GCSEs, is simple enough. Oxbridge candidates are expected to have the normal number of GCSEs taken by students at their education establishment. In practice, this can mean eight at a comprehensive or 12 plus at a public school.

When it comes to GCSE grades, allowances are again made for the type of school: over half of a state school candidate's grades have traditionally been As or A*s, the rest Bs, with perhaps the odd C in a practical subject. Those sitting the exam in the private sector should aim for at least As. What will be the exact equivalents of these in the new, numerical GCSE grades yet remains to be seen.

Oxbridge is willing to concede that, at the GCSE stage at least, someone in a class of thirty-five pupils cannot be judged exactly like someone in a class of fifteen. As we reach A-levels, though, this awareness disappears. The rules become more complex and are shrouded in mist.

One of the worst bits of misinformation I encountered came from the education department of my local council. I had phoned them on behalf of a new neighbour. The woman, who speaks little English, had wanted to know whether there were any extra classes her teenage son, described by his teacher as gifted, could take in preparation for Oxbridge. A female voice of authority replied crossly: "There are other universities, you know. All the Oxbridge applicants there have five A-levels at A*. They are all gifted."

Almost everything in the council dragon's statement, except for the first sentence, is factually wrong. To start at the end: the National Association for Gifted Children (now *POTENTIAL PLUS*) estimates that 2 per cent of the population are of exceptional ability, meaning "gifted." The total number of "gifted" entrants among the 300,000 new students accepted by British universities each year is likely to be 6,000. Not all of these wish to go anywhere near Oxbridge. Even if all of them did, there would still be places left for other, fairly bright kids. Oxford and Cambridge, between them, admit some 7,000 new undergraduates each year.

Another thing parents and students need to be clear about is that AS levels have now been decoupled from A2s in terms of academic standards. As a result, Oxbridge is officially no longer interested in a student's precise performance at the AS stage.

Having said this, the situation is somewhat more complex. Dons say that outstanding AS results should still be flagged up by teachers. They also admit that students aiming for certain courses may still benefit from an AS in a specific subject if the school offers it. Examples include a foreign language for Cambridge applicants to Modern Languages and Classics courses. AS Maths will also benefit students not taking the subject at A2 but applying for Cambridge Natural Sciences. At Oxford, the same goes for some science courses and PPE. An AS level in Further Maths is helpful for Economics & Management and almost essential for Cambridge Economics applicants without a full A-level in Further Maths.

Now let's deal with A-levels. On these, too, myths abound. The official requirement for Oxbridge entry are three A-levels, as for most other universities, and dons insist that is all they demand.

However, candidates from the private sector, where an entire Year 12 may apply for Oxbridge after being taught for years in small, single ability groups, are often advised to sit four A-levels. So are students at the remaining state grammar schools.

Having said this, taking a fourth A-level often does make sense, whatever your school. Adding A-level Maths or Further Maths to a clutch of science A-levels can make you a considerably more appealing science candidate, able to cope with the complex calculations now required in this field. With a foreign language A-level as number four, you might seem better prepared for History, as well as for Asian and Middle Eastern or Oriental Studies. Five A-level subjects, though, are pretty rare and not demanded anywhere.

MAKING THE GRADE

But what about grades? Well, Cambridge applicants need A-level grades of between AAA and A*A*A* to gain a place, depending on the course and college. Oxford still accepts some applicants with AAA, but A*AA offers are becoming more common. Courses such as Law (at some Cambridge colleges) and Mathematics (at Oxford) are already asking for A*A*A. Grades below AAA will rarely do: in 2009, when Oxford only ever asked for AAA grades, a total of 37 candidates were admitted with AAB, and this so far still holds. With predictions of ABB you probably should not be applying.

Raising entry grade requirements had initially been described by Oxbridge as making the admissions process fairer. Geoff Parks, the Head of Admissions at Cambridge, argued that "more independent school offer holders would have been screened out by A*AA offers than students from any other group."

The August 2010 A-level results proved Parks wrong. They revealed that students from private schools were over three times more likely to get A*s than students at comprehensives. Even state grammars could not quite compete because of class size. Perhaps in response, 2011 admissions tutors quietly let it be known that there was still some flexibility, especially for candidates with high GCSE grades. Research has shown that students who get top GCSE module marks often do best in their university finals, so dons now take a keen interest in those.

Moreover, teachers' grade predictions have so far not been found to be very accurate when it comes to A-level grades of A*. This means a bright student should probably still apply if just predicted As.

So, while A-level grade predictions need to be high, teachers and parents should be aware that a place offer made after a smooth interview and a very good test result can be slightly lower. Individual Oxbridge colleges (a subject we shall get to) have always been entitled to admit the odd candidate with modest grades, if they so wished. How else would Prince Charles have spent his undergraduate years at Cambridge?

What certainly remains true is that no amount of talent will get a student into Oxbridge unless the school can provide her with decent exam results. This rule sets it apart from other Russell Group universities. One inner city teacher I interviewed proudly told me that one of his brightest but poorest students had just received an offer of CCC to read Medicine at Queen Mary College, London. Such unconditional offers, made to express a university's trust in an applicant's outstanding potential, don't really exist at Oxbridge.

HOW TO GET AN A*

The simple answer is: by knowing more than just facts. Academics have long complained that too many university applicants can only parrot the information fed to them at school. So, in 2009 government educationalists responded by redesigning many of the key A2 questions. What these now seek and reward through a new mark scheme are problem-solving skills and a broader understanding. Students will be faced with unfamiliar contexts, encouraged to think for themselves and expected to give longer, more detailed answers than in the past. These should draw on the concepts, theories or techniques relevant to their subject.

In a biology exam, for instance, you may not just be asked to name the cardiac blood vessels shown in a drawing of the human heart, but also be told to "describe *and explain* the events that occur during ventricular systole in the cardiac cycle". Confronted with an unfamiliar graph, a student must certainly be able to tell the examiner what it means in numerical terms, but may also be expected also say whether it does or does not support a specific hypothesis.

In arts subjects, it is confidence, assurance, strong arguments, fluency and good construction that will get you a top mark. What this means is that you should trust your judgement, know your text, be decisive in your views, keep an eye on your writing style and construct your piece carefully. Do, however, also keep in mind the marking points.

While much of this assumes that good answers will simply arise from students' brain cells working extra hard on the day, the "holistic understanding" sought can, in fact, be developed. Schools ambitious for their students have always encouraged classroom debates on problems and their causes. If you're trying to teach yourself, help is available in the section called "Read all around it".

Asked for a comment a year after A*s were introduced, Andy Gardner at the Institute of Education felt that people were still learning about this on both sides of the classroom desk. However, there was progress: "Teachers are now identifying extension work at A2 which will help you get an A*, so it's really important that students listen to the teacher's advice."

What this means is that although the new grade still has to bed in, you must now stop texting during lessons. No less important is writing practice, best gained by undertaking writing projects during your A2 course. If your sixth form head does not set you any, you could always write something for one of those competitions set by Oxbridge colleges for this year group. Using effective revision skills matters too. *YouTube* has a very helpful talk by a student explaining how he got three A*s by breaking up this task into small bits, found on https://www.youtube.com/watch?v=gOtH8vtX4Yc. Lastly, students who are able to express themselves well and at length generally have strong grammatical skills. You can acquire those painlessly from a book called *My Grammar and I (or should that be 'Me')* by Caroline Taggart and J.A. Wines.

MATHS PROBLEMS

It is also worth knowing about the obstacles encountered by some students aiming for the Oxford or Cambridge Maths course. While the ability to think mathematically is innate, it needs lots of nurturing to reach Oxbridge entrance standards. These are quite a long way from the requirements of the Maths A-level syllabus and it takes Further Maths to bring you closer. Unfortunately, many comprehensives do not offer this A-level course. Their students can, at best, take an AS level in the subject. While this qualification is acceptable to some colleges, it does not really prepare you for the standardized Maths tests now set by both Oxford and Cambridge to applicants for both Mathematics and Computer Science.

As a result, state school candidates struggle to gain a place: in 2012, their success rate when applying for the Cambridge Maths course was a mere 16 per cent, compared to 36 per cent for private school students. At Oxford, the gap was smaller but there, too, has remained almost static. As there is no research showing that the IQ scores of students from private schools are more than twice as high as those of state schoolers, deeper subject knowledge is clearly behind the divide. But how do you ensure success for a student with great, inborn mathematical ability if her school cannot help?

Faced with this problem, Conservative Universities Minister David Willetts had suggested already in August 2010 that perhaps universities ought to look beyond exam results and consider a candidate's potential. Willet's successors have echoed this.

The ministerial suggestions were coolly received at Oxbridge, but at least students who just need a good A-level grade in maths for other courses should be able to achieve it. Assuming they have a strong GCSE base, they just need to grasp that A-level Maths is about practice. It is not about understanding some great principle and then being able to relax. The more problems you solve, the better you get.

Moreover, the same six topics are covered in Maths A-level papers each time. So, if students were asked to engage with division by polynomial last year, they will be asked to do so again. All the past papers are available online from the exam board website. Only if you really cannot work out an answer by yourself should you try to corner your teacher. Still feeling stumped or need more sample problems? If so, your next port of call should definitely be AskNRICH (http://.nrich.maths.org), and, after that, PLUS Magazine (http://pass.maths.org.uk). Both sites were set up by mathematicians at the University of Cambridge. What can also move you on is www.meikleriggs.org.uk, as will "Advanced Problems in Core Mathematics" and "Advanced Problems in Mathematics", two now online booklets by Stephen Siklos.

These sources also help with the STEP test sat by Cambridge Maths candidates and by students applying for Computer Science or Engineering at some of its colleges. Worried by the poor Maths skills of especially comprehensive school applicants, the university now offers all prospective maths applicants a free online support programme at www.maths.org/STEP, designed to help them develop their advanced problem-solving skills and prepare for STEP exams. Oxford uses its own Maths entrance test and will recommend preparatory summer reading to the few successful candidates who have just an AS Level in Further Maths.

Students who prepare for the admissions process by themselves with the help of the books and sites recommended by the universities, are not necessarily disadvantaged. What they need to know is that successful candidates tend to have a strong, active interest and a firm but not always very broad knowledge base. One Oxford admissions tutor stated that pupils who did well in his Maths interview had a grasp of calculus, a method of writing a good proof, and a more abstract notion of what ''a function'' was.

The Mechanics option in the Math A-level course can also help, so dons say, as will A-level Physics. Unfortunately, since 30 per cent of those teaching Physics in state secondary schools do not have a degree in the subject, it may not help much. This takes us further along the admissions route, into A-level subjects.

PICKING THE RIGHT SUBJECTS

Once upon a time, this was a simple matter. Candidates needed only Latin and Classical Greek. By sheer coincidence, these languages were the sum of every young gentleman's education. They were not studied by anyone else. By keeping them compulsory, Oxbridge excluded both women and working men for 700 years.

Almost all of today's candidates have studied more modern

subjects. A-level choice, though, can be horribly confusing for those without Oxbridge links. After all, comprehensives and sixth form colleges offer up to forty A-level subjects. How can your stressed daughter, faced with all those exciting options in her school's brightly illustrated course brochure, possibly decide which ones to take? Well, the choice is far smaller than both of you might think.

What you need to know is that both Oxford and Cambridge prefer applicants to take three A-levels in academically demanding "hard" subjects like English, Maths, Chemistry or History, which they have studied at school in considerable depth and over many years. This is why even the most expensive public school will offer no more than twenty A-level subjects, including a range of languages.

This rule applies even if the "soft" A-level subject is also the one your daughter is planning to do at university. For instance, a student dreaming of a future in computers might think that A-levels in Computing, Electronics and ICT would be ideal. She would be wrong. It is Math, Further Maths and Physics or another "hard" science which are the gateway to Oxbridge Computer Sciences.

The same applies to Law. A-level Law is rated as not intellectually demanding enough at Oxbridge, so applicants for any Law degree course offered there should go for more traditional subjects. English is almost a must, plus perhaps History and some "hard" science subject. A-level Maths is welcome here too, as it can be helpful with business-related cases. Oxbridge Medicine too will normally consider only candidates with at least two science A-levels and almost all have three (see p. 165).

Oxford's degree in Politics, Philosophy and Economics (PPE), which has become a ticket into Parliament and is the only media studies course as far as broadsheet editors are concerned, cares less about A-level subjects. It is keen on History and likes Maths (which helps with statistics), but will consider any "hard" A-level or even a "soft" but smart third. The choice is a just little wider for two new Cambridge courses, Social and Political Sciences and Psychological and Behavioural Studies, which in 2012 replaced Politics, Psychology and Sociology (PPS). Like PPS, the new courses officially require no specific A-levels, but this does not mean that three soft ones will do.

Take on board, too, that even a subject merely described in the prospectus as "recommended" or "useful preparation" may improve your success chances considerably.

Except when it comes to the two above courses, Cambridge is somewhat more particular than Oxford here and specifies not just the

A-levels it will accept but also the combinations it seeks. While this is very useful to know, the list may shock some teachers. Only fourteen subjects are recommended, with another ten as occasional possibles. Critical Thinking never counts as part of your three because dons feel "it lacks academic contents." It is, nevertheless, often worth doing as an extra because it develops students' reasoning skills.

General Studies, which does not count either, is said to foster a better grasp of contemporary issues in disadvantaged students.

None of the above are iron rules. Faced with a child genius who has taught himself nuclear physics while caring for his dying grandmother on a condemned housing estate, a college may choose to accept him, whatever his A-levels or grades. A politician's son from a distant British interest zone much in the news could find himself invited in with any odd qualifications.

However, if your son or daughter does not fit this bill, but is just the clever child of non-university parents, they will need to play it safe. Students should certainly check the entry requirements for attractive courses very early on, or should pick A-level subjects that are widely acceptable and may give them an edge.

ARTISTS AND SCIENTISTS

Oxbridge sciences, as already said, include Psychology; Oxbridge arts are everything from languages to History and Philosophy. While the arts/science divide continues to exist, it is not as rigid as it once was. Successful science applicants almost never have a mix of A-levels, as most admissions tutors at both Oxford and Cambridge far prefer three science ones. Having less may be read as a lack of scientific commitment. If your daughter has built her own mini computer lab, but is also interested in baroque paintings, Fine Art might therefore have to be A-level number four.

The arts are more flexible. A set of A-levels consisting of History, English and something clever like Maths is a highly acceptable qualification for almost any non-science course. Very rarely, a student sitting History, Maths and Physics might be considered for a History course, but she would need to convince the interviewer that her interests really have shifted and have very impressive grades.

Students wishing to study Archaeology and Anthropology or Geography have perhaps the widest range of options when it comes to A-levels. Here, one "soft" A-level alongside two "hard" ones is most often acceptable.

When it comes to languages, the rules are different yet again.

Those wishing to do a modern language course, such as German, need a top grade A-level in the subject. However, candidates wishing to do an Oriental language, such as Chinese or Thai, do not need to have studied it at all. Their four-year course will include intensive language training and a year abroad.

Latin and Classical Greek are today essential for only one subject: Classics (know at Oxford as "Greats"). Both Oxford and Cambridge, however, have turned this into a four year BA course, which allows applicants from comprehensives to pick up those dead languages as they study for their degree. This is quite a tough option, even for able linguists, but students usually find it worthwhile.

HARD CHOICES

So, what should you advise your wavering son? The admissions tutors I interviewed had no doubt: go for almost any "hard" A-level mix in either science or arts, though maths enhances almost anything. Once an applicant has proved that he can think via his A-level subjects and grades, Oxford especially can be flexible about precise course requirements. Tutors in the arts, though not the sciences, tend to perceive A-levels largely as proof of an applicant's capacity to learn. They do not expect fully fledged experts. Only students planning to take a degree in one of their A-level subjects need to show detailed prior knowledge.

Certain combinations, though, maximise a student's options. Science fans with A-levels in Physics and Chemistry and Maths can apply to a huge range of courses from Engineering to Medicine. A-level English, History and a language (or Maths) are a sound basis for most arts courses, in the way Latin and Greek were once.

Remember too that three top A-level grades are easier to obtain than four and will make a state school candidate attractive to all colleges, including the most famous ones.

What if your daughter has independently made up her mind? Going through the school's large range of A-level subjects on offer, the smart and curious girl has picked the ones that seem most exciting and fit her wide interests. Unfortunately, all three are "soft" A-levels, chosen not because they are easier but because she has done enough English, Maths or Biology, she feels, and does not plan to do these subjects at university.

This, of course, is her choice. She is almost an adult now, as she will no doubt remind you. There is no point in trying to impose your will. Getting any A-levels is a long, hard slog, and I was warned by several sixth form heads that unless a student selects their A-levels on the basis of at least some real interest, they could well drop out. Many top universities acknowledge this fact.

If your daughter really wants to go to Oxbridge, she will have to compromise. Don't browbeat her into changing her A-levels, just get her to accept that candidates who get in with more than one three "soft" A-level are as common as hen's teeth.

Then check which of her "soft" subjects might still be worth doing. Media Studies and Textiles are definitely out. Oxbridge defines them as non-academic. An A-level in General Studies or Critical Thinking, as said, doesn't count either, but it can broaden an applicant's understanding of the world and so helps with some entrance tests. Other subjects, especially Politics, Economics, Sociology, Religious Studies and Drama, are fine in the context of a relevant degree.

Now do the sums. If your daughter's state school has links with a specific college, she may indeed get into of its degree courses with one "soft" A-level. A well-disposed admissions tutor might even, on a whim, consider her for one of its less prestigious courses with two, as long as those are vaguely relevant and she has top grades. However, in a competitive environment these are not really very good odds. Colleges have been known to suddenly drop "their" comprehensive in favour of some other worthy cause. Candidates need to be acceptable to more than one place, in case their chosen one has more talented applicants that year than it can take.

Your daughter might also have a horizon so broad that three "hard" A-levels cannot possibly satisfy her. If the girl really wants to write English well, learn about society in some depth, live in Spain and and follow a well trodden path into politics (via PPE or HSPS) she might indeed want to take four A-levels.

There is another good reason for taking four A-levels. This is if your hard-working son is willing to give up midweek nights out (though not, of course, football practice) for good grades, but unsure if the degree course he has picked will suit him. Oxbridge is fairly easy-going about students changing subjects in their first weeks, but if he wants to make a bigger switch than, let's say, from Ancient History to Modern History, he will still need relevant A-levels. A set of four broadens his choice, at least among arts subjects.

However, do keep the grade issue in mind. It would be a shame if your teenager ended up with AAAB, if he could narrow his aim and gain A*AA, the actual grades required. And be aware that while Oxford will only insist on three specific grades, however many A-levels you take, Cambridge has been known to specify the grades it wants in all four.

FOUR LEGS GOOD

Let's say your ambitious daughter has come round to the idea of four A-levels (as long as one of them is Spanish). Unfortunately, her problems are far from over. Many comprehensives cannot deliver them. This is not because they don't want to, but because of under-funding. A shortage of qualified teachers and pressure from other duties result in many students finding that a chosen A-level option is only offered when they are not actually free. Those wanting to combine science with arts subjects such as languages frequently discover that their timetables clash.

This is another, quite important reason why the vast majority of applicants doing four A-levels come from generously-staffed private schools.

Now the truth is that missing out on a language A-level is far from fatal for adult life: students who have a grounding in French will have no difficulty becoming fluent in the language later on by means of evening classes or videos. Others acquire fluent Portuguese by working in Brazil or fluent Urdu by marrying someone whose family speaks nothing else. Human brains do not actually suffer meltdown at the average graduation age of twenty-two.

When it comes to other subjects, though, being unable to take a fourth A-level can close your options. This is because the Oxbridge attitude remains highly ambiguous.

One the one hand, all the dons I spoke to insisted that it is not necessary to have four A-levels, never mind five, in order to follow even the most demanding course. After all, almost everyone managed fine with three until a decade ago. On the other hand, many of the same dons declared themselves impressed that nearly half of recent candidates "were bright and hard-working enough" to get four A-levels. This does imply that four A-levels count as an achievement.

THE A-LEVEL MARKET

A-levels are not simply the reflection of a teenager's talent and hard work. They are also consumer goods. It is more difficult to buy a top grade vintage car in the UK than a top grade A-level. Some education experts fear that even the new A* grade, designed to reward innate intelligence and now sought by both Oxford and Cambridge, can be attained by financial means.

The market supplies what the consumer wants and can pay for: so, if Oxbridge wants its applicants to have at least As, whether they studied for them in a rural crammer with five pupils to a class or in a comprehensive in which the Maths teacher has a Geography degree, half the pupils have English as a second language and the crumbling science lab predates Apollo 11, then those parents who can afford it will reach for their cheque book.

Almost any public school, especially if it has boarding facilities, will today steer your reasonably bright child towards a clutch of good A-levels. It has the language and science labs, the qualified teachers, the single ability groups and the one-to-one tuition that can do the job. There will be lots of support and few distractions. A-levels will be carefully matched to a pupil's ability to ensure top grades. Pupils' own interests often count for rather less, but the end result is in the bag - if you are willing to pay £10,000 upwards per child per year, that is. Got two children? Tough luck. Advantage, as far as Oxbridge goes, is a term used in tennis.

But is there any other way of looking at A-levels? Steve Allen (not his real name) the head of science at a sixth form college whose pupils come from poverty line homes and include many refugees, has no doubt. "Oxbridge," he argues, "is not contextualising our pupils' achievement. To them an A is all that counts, and four A-levels are better than three. They don't understand that the young people we send have made enormous gains. We have students who live in a bedsit with their whole family, yet get very good grades, despite their insecure existence and family problems."

Would students with less than three top A-levels be able to keep up? Steve suggests that his do even better than that. "Once accepted into a good university, our students often become top of their year and the university is pleased it took them. They are hard-working and resilient. Oxbridge should take more of a chance on kids like ours, they overshoot once they are accepted." As an example, Steve cites one of his students, the son of a packer, who went from a C in A-level Physics to a first in his finals at King's College, London. A-levels, Steve argues, tell you about a disadvantaged applicant's past, not their future.

Every year, Steve and his colleagues encourage a dozen of their best students to apply for Oxbridge; they are determined to maximise these young people's potential. And their students do get Oxbridge offers some years, but these are still based on A*AA or AAA. Such offers, the staff feel, are so unrealistic they might as well be rejections. Oxford is not comparing like with like, they complain.

It is a view echoed by others, invariably off the record. Teachers who have no qualms about shouting at their school's 6'6" Karate champion for running on the stairs will drop their voices to a whisper and glance nervously over their shoulder when criticising

Oxbridge. They are desperate not to offend the universities that can do most for their pupils. Each of them, though, knows of a gifted mathematician or other scientist interviewed at Oxbridge who then failed to get the required AAA. Maths, Chemistry and Physics require intensive, daily, small group teaching for top A-level results. Research methods have to be explained, findings interpreted. These aren't teach-yourself subjects.

In public schools, it is almost unknown for a student not to get the required grades. This is not because state school pupils are lazier. Those who do get in tend to have educated parents who can help or at least don't work after school. They also often attend selective grammars or successful comprehensives in comfy neighbourhoods.

Some of those working with very able children are also unhappy with A-levels being given so much weight. One of these is Deborah Eyre, who founded the now abolished National Academy for Gifted and Talented Youth (NAGTY) at the University of Warwick. Professor Eyre shares the view that A-levels are an unreliable predictor of university success. A scheme adopted some years ago at Warwick led to the acceptance of students from the most poorly equipped and funded institutions, further education colleges, on lower grades. The result confounded its critics: the FE group actually got more Firsts in their finals than the best A-level students.

A study by the Government's Higher Education Funding Council (HEFC), released in July 2003, lends further weight to such views. Having tracked the progress of all 18-year-old A-level students who entered degree courses in 1998 and graduated in 2001-2, its researchers found that, on average, a state school pupil performed as well as a private school one who had up to four A-level points fewer, the equivalent of comparing AAA with ABB.

The fact that A-level success must be seen in a socio-economic context is gradually dawning on some Russell Group universities and has already led to more realistic offers, even from departments academically rated just as highly as Oxbridge. Some actively seek out new types of candidates.

At a seminar about medical school entrance organised by London universities, which was attended by the careers teacher of a "tough" London comprehensive, an admissions tutor recited the usual mantra about medical schools wishing to attract the very best students. "Just tell us what you want, we'll send you candidates with six A-levels, if that's what it takes!" was the instant response of a private school head.

"It is not your students we're interested in here at this point," replied the tutor with obvious irritation, "we're trying to achieve a more representative intake here, doctors who can empathise with more of their patients."

The careers teacher left in good spirits, but also aware that no such views have yet been expressed by Oxbridge.

Even worse, when Bristol, another university with a high public school intake, in 2003 announced slight A-level level allowances for disadvantaged pupils, there were howls of protest in the media.

For weeks, frantic voices warned that letting in some state school students on lower grades was not only discrimination but a form of "pernicious social engineering" or "inclusion by the back door" and, as Simon Heffer put it in the *Daily Mail* of March 5th 2003, "an assault on the most hard-working people in Britain". In London's *Evening Standard*, Stephen Pollard from the Centre for the New Europe warned that "in America such thinking has come close to destroying the very basis of academic standards".

One education expert wheeled out by the Headmasters' and Headmistresses' Conference, which represents the heads of private schools, actually claimed that "to go for such crude rebalancing at this level will create more unfairness than already exists".

Beneath the hysterics, you could just detect the gloom of a father who had been paying thousands (frequently £100,000 over a school career) to ensure that his son got into one of Britain's top universities, only to find that "his" place had gone to another kid.

EXTENDING YOUR MIND

But how do you prove that you're really the smarter applicant? A student keen to show that he had more to offer than just (!) top A-levels could from 2002 also take an Advanced Extension Award (AEA). However, there was very poor uptake and the awards were abolished in 2010. Its place has been taken by the Extended Project Qualification, which allows students to pick their own topic and research methods. A number of dons have praised it as a genuinely useful innovation, but a problem is that it can take up rather a lot of student time.

So, what can you do out of school to give your academic mind that Oxbridge-sought depth? When it comes to foreign languages or cultures, this is easy enough. The cultural centres run by the French, German, Spanish, Italian, Russian and Chinese embassies in several British cities will welcome you with open arms. Most offer not just language classes, but also books, talks and a great choice of foreign films. Some have websites which let you access their country's TV shows and press. All this comes in handy at a Modern Languages interview.

Honing the skills you already have can be just as important. One way to do so is by taking part in an essay competition. Oxbridge colleges, financial institutions and the Archbishop of Canterbury annually run one of these for sixth formers. Researching a set topic and condensing your insights into just 2,000 words will move you on, especially in History. The effort also shows Oxbridge that you are willing to engage academically. Even better, there is often an impressive cash prize.

You may also want to learn how to create or interpret boxes of graphs or columns of figures. With the exception of Music, Languages and English Lit., almost all Oxbridge courses these days have at least a small mathematical element. This means you could find yourself asked to interpret some numerical data already at your test or interview. Students doing Maths A-levels would certainly be wise to add a statistics module, relevant for a wide range of courses. A basic book like *Statistics for Dummies* will help. Get to know the difference between mean, median and average and know what variables are. Medical candidates can go a step further and leaf through *Medical Statistics Made Easy*. Don't panic if most examples go over your head: the first section is for you and will prove invaluable.

If you want to not just be able to read statistics but to know when you are being bamboozled by them, dip into *Bad Science* by Ben Goldacre.

In the case of English, a regular burst of creativity develops literary skills. Writing for (a however modest) publication also teaches you not to miss deadlines and check every word. If your daughter's school won't publish her stories, reports or poems, of if there is no school magazine at all, she could always try to get them into one of an infinity of online magazines. Some of these offer prizes for the best work (for more about English, see p. 191).

When it comes to formal learning, a great option remains the Open University, which offers online modules in interesting topics like robotics or planetary science. Although not free, OU courses are a good preparation for degree subjects not taught at school.

Students fancying a short but completely free, top-range university course should go to www.openculture.com/freeonline. Most of the four-lecture courses offered there are taught by academics from Yale, Berkeley or MIT. Topics range from American Literature to Ethics, and from calculus (crucial for Economics!) to String Theory.

One-off lectures by Oxford and Cambridge dons can be found on *iTunesU* and *YouTube*. Some but not all are designed to engage non-experts, so don't panic if a don's critique of, say, post-structuralism goes over your head. Once you are at university and have done some reading, all will make sense. For now, try another lecturer or topic.

Great thinkers may even come to see you. A charity called *Speakers for Schools* sends inspiring experts into state schools anywhere. Talks cover technological, scientific, political, economic, historical, cultural, artistic, ecological and ethical subjects. You will come away knowing which key questions these people are trying to resolve (do take notes!) and how to explore further. There is no cost to the school: all your teacher has to do is apply.

WHAT DOES IT ALL ADD UP TO?

The answer, despite all these grim tales, is that success is possible for state-educated students from even the poorest backgrounds. A further reason for optimism is that both Oxford and Cambridge are now officially committed to widening the range of their students' backgrounds, undoubtedly out of idealism but also because future government grants to Oxbridge may depend on it. Even more importantly, every year nearly four thousand state school students, including several hundred from working class backgrounds, already enter these universities.

Almost all of these students managed to get top grades, so it is worth helping your child to do the same, perhaps in between lobbying for government action on a more representative Oxbridge intake.

But how is it done? You can find the answer in every basic study guide. To get top A-levels, a sixth form student should pick A-levels for which he has at least some aptitude, pay attention in class, establish a home study routine and plan out his work carefully, so all of it will be completed. He should also seek help from teachers, textbooks or websites such as www.s-cool.co.uk, rather than hope that what is still unclear to him will not come up.

There are also things that mothers and fathers need to know. Below is the best A-level advice from the parents of highly successful students and education professionals. What will be relevant depends on your circumstances and on the time left.

WHAT NOT TO DO (AND HOW NOT TO PANIC)

Don't go on at your son about how he really must get top grades for his A-levels. Grading is what other people, namely the examiners, do. He does not really have the power to determine their decision, which will depend not just on the quality of his work, but also on the standard set by other students. Instead, calmly encourage him to cover all the ground - a realistic and far less scary target. It simply means working through the books, chapters, problems, hand-outs, sample papers and/or revision notes he was given.

Don't be swept along by his inevitable moments of despair. If he is about to chuck all his books into the fire, don't just agree that perhaps Oxbridge is not for the likes of you. Instead, suggest a break and gently remind him that young people from his background do get through this frustrating work load every year. Also, the work he is doing now is not just a shot at that blurry goal, Oxbridge: it will raise his chances of getting into any good university.

If he's still stressed, take him out for some fun, shopping or to a sporting event. Then, find a moment to ask whether you can help. Are there any books he needs? Would he like you to video a relevant programme for him?

Another crucial thing is not to over-do things. A student who wants to stay the course must pace himself. Revision is about working hard, but also about taking regular breaks long enough to stretch a few times and polish off two cream eggs.

Keep reminding the lad that there is help in class too. Seeing himself as an independent young adult may have prevented him from requesting it. If a teacher's explanation still leaves him confused, it may help to consult shop-bought revision guides or a Maths website like http://meikleriggs.org.uk/.

Real exam panic calls for more active steps. An A-level student who has not uttered a word for days or bursts into tears as soon as he takes out his course-work will not simply snap out of this. So, don't keep this problem in the family: ask his teacher whether she's aware of it. Can she think of any specific reason? Are there any short-term tasks she can set him to move him on? Sometimes one seemingly impossible task paralyses an able but insecure student.

If the panic does not subside, you might want to address it more directly. Suggest that the lad takes a day off for an intensive dose of football or swimming. Physical exercise helps to re-programme the mind towards a more focused state.

Then, if necessary, get professional help. A session with the school counsellor may reassure your son that his goals are realistic.

Alternatively, he could try listening to a relaxation tape, or watch one of those "achieve your aims" type self-help DVDs which use mild hypnosis. Their soothing background tracks can be remarkably effective. Drawing on psychological support does not mean that your son is going mad.

While trying to help, make sure you're not impersonating a bulldozer but the AA, an emergency service for car break-downs. Move the lad along, then let go. Accept that some mornings he will spend an hour staring at the wall, or kicking a ball into it. It's all part of the study process.

Lastly, don't encourage your son to see his A-level work as a competition with his class mates. True, some kids thrive on rivalry, but for others exams are the time when they need peer support most. His sixth form will be going through this mix of slave labour and adrenalin rush together and, rather than worry whether his best friend is getting on any better, he might want to team up with him. The two might waste some time discussing chart hits rather than studying Chemistry charts, but having company takes the panic out of revision. This often enables a student to arrive at previously missed solutions himself.

A-LEVEL TIPS

1. It helps to grasp the real A-level time scale. With GCSE grades, rather than AS results, now being closely examined by Oxbridge, it can seem that Year 12 work has become less important. However, most of what is learnt then still forms the bedrock of a student's A2s. So, try not to schedule a big family trip abroad, the renovation of your home or your messy divorce for that year. Also avoid moving home during the sixth form years, if that involves a change of schools. Adjusting to new class mates, a new syllabus and exams set by different boards can be tough.

2. Studying is work and saps your energy: that teenager lying on a book-strewn floor with his eyes half closed and listening to what cannot possibly be music is (hopefully) memorising the church structure of Old England, in between worrying about whether his girlfriend will like his radical new haircut. He might be too exhausted to look for food, so coach him gently towards it. There'll be protests that he is not a kid anymore, but he probably appreciates the effort.

3. Make sure that your daughter doesn't use up too much of her precious energy now on paid work. If she currently has an after-school and weekend job to fund her clothing habit, this may have to go. Otherwise, she will be far too tired to concentrate properly, either at school or at home. She should be able to earn a little money: a Saturday morning at the supermarket till or a Saturday night sitting an exceptionally calm baby are fine, but anything more is likely to affect her results.

The poor girl will probably be distraught at the idea that her new spring wardrobe might have to wait until July, but you should stand your ground. People are not actually being evicted from clubs for wearing a six months old crop top. Could you offer something like a small Hennes voucher in the meantime? If nothing else, this will prove to her that studying can pay off.

4. If your son is working not for extras but in order to keep your family afloat, the answer is not quite so simple. First make sure all of you receive the benefits you are entitled to. The EMA, which used to pay all pupils on free school meals £30 a week, has now sadly been abolished.

A-LEVEL TIPS cont.

Instead, there is a new, modest   government "bursary" for the very poorest, and head teachers can disburse small sums to penniless students. You can also claim child benefit until your son leaves school.

Then there is Child Tax Credit, paid directly into your bank account if you are responsible for the children, at least while the new Universal Credit system is still being rolled out. You don't need to be employed to qualify. If you work sixteen hours per week or more you may also be entitled to another benefit, Working Tax Credit. To find out how to apply, phone the Tax Credits Helpline on 0345 300 3900. You can also go to www.gov.uk/child-tax-credit, or visit your nearest HMRC Revenue & Customs office.

You must also discuss your financial situation openly with your son. Make it clear that you thoroughly approve of his university plans and that you don't resent the cost of keeping him: you'd be surprised how many kids think that their parents do. Try to also get across that the drop in his own after-school income is only a temporary blip. Good grades will get him into a good university, which in turn should lead to a good job and an income which, if you are currently hard-up, may be almost beyond his imagination.

Make sure, though, that the lad does not try to bridge the gap with credit. Some card issuers will happily sign up 18-year-old, non-earning pupils. The result can be massive debts, a bad start for his university life.

However, if your family finances really would collapse without your son's contribution, don't give up on the idea of Oxbridge. Just make sure that his school knows of your circumstances and mentions them in its reference.

Alternatively, he himself might want to talk in some detail about his paid work and the reasons for having to do it in his UCAS statement. Family poverty is not a character flaw he needs to be ashamed of. Allowances are made these days for seriously disadvantaged students, and an admissions tutor genuinely committed to "Widening Access" (there are quite a few) might well be impressed with the young man's persistence.

4
Getting the exam experts in

Having said all this, I must point out that none of the above steps will get your son into Oxbridge if the school's teaching is poor. If his school's results are consistently below the national average because its teachers do not have degrees in their A-level subjects or because of severe discipline problems then no amount of hard work by your talented lad can tip the balance. He'll need external help.

What help you'll be able to get depends largely on the time your teenager has left. Nobody will have any magic solution to offer if you find out a fortnight before the crucial exam that large chunks of the syllabus have remained utterly incomprehensible to him. As the drunk, sitting in a puddle, told the lady asking him the way to the local savings bank: "Madam, you don't want to start from here."

On the other hand, if school reports or test grades indicate that the boy is not achieving his potential, despite having been defined as very able by his teachers, then a revision course can be one way forward. It is best not to wait for the results of his springtime mocks; by then most courses will be booked up.

REVISION COURSES

Easter revision courses are run by some state schools, local education authorities, groups of teachers in serious need of cash and lots of private institutions. None of these courses are a substitute for a student's very own hard work. Nor can such a brief experience provide her with comprehensive understanding of her A-level subject. Some subject mysteries, though, will be resolved in class and study priorities established.

Mainly, revision courses teach students to provide what the examiners really want. Teachers explain what they need to write, then make them practice writing under exam conditions. At the end of what is usually a week's intensive work, participants should have picked up enough study skills and exam techniques to show themselves in the best light.

What lies behind this is the assumption that exams are not just about knowing your subject, but also about preparing and packaging what you know. Some pupils can do this unaided, but most need to learn. This tends to result in better and, in the case of able, hard-working students, in excellent grades.

SCHOOL-RUN COURSES

An increasing number of state schools and sixth form colleges now run their own revision courses. These are free, voluntary and aimed at encouraging students who the staff feel might benefit most. Teachers seek to ensure that students have worked through the relevant course material, rather than blindly thrashing their way through everything they were ever taught. There may also be another mock exam at the end. Often, though, there is only limited emphasis on exam technique.

Still, your teenager should at least be given a copy of the examiners' mark scheme, which tells her what exactly the crucial extra marks that will take a student up to an A-grade are awarded for; in English, for instance, this will include putting a literary work into its historical context; in History, examiners reward students, amongst other things, for providing a "web of causation", rather than just a sequence of historical events. Students aiming for A*s need to seek detailed advice from their teachers, as mentioned before. The mark scheme itself can, however, also be downloaded from the website of your examination board.

How much time there is to resolve individual student's queries depends on the structure of the revision course. Some individual concerns can certainly now be addressed, since classes will be smaller than in the school's term time A-level group. The classes might, though, still be mixed ability and run by the students' regular teachers.

A few state sixth form colleges also run vacation courses and some of those are open to outside students. If your daughter has been unhappy with the quality of her teaching, then a highly rated sixth form college (its Ofsted report will be on the college website) could be a better bet, assuming that its pupils are studying for the same board.

PRIVATE COURSES

Private revision courses, once the preserve of the rich but dim, are a growth industry. Some are run on a Saturday basis all year long, but most are holiday ones. Such courses, advertised in the press around three months in advance, offer intense revision work in very small groups, albeit at pretty large fees -- anything between £200 and £700 for a week. The cost depends partly on the number of subjects to be revised and partly on whether it includes accommodation. Day school courses are just as good as boarding ones, though you may not have a choice if you live far away. Courses are often run on the premises of private schools and might employ some of their teachers. Students here will usually be guided towards a deeper understanding of their subject. They will also be reminded of fundamental principles and teachers will try to sharpen key skills, for instance grammar in the case of languages.

Nevertheless, in most short courses the emphasis will be on what one revision college principal described as "technique, technique and more technique." Some revision courses are actually held inside colleges in Oxford and Cambridge. These are based on boarding and explicitly aim to make your son or daughter at ease there, as part of their preparation for the Oxbridge entrance process.

Before you part with such serious money, though, ask a few questions and don't be swayed by the freshly painted buildings and lush green lawns. It will take more than a generous application of Growmore to turn your teenager into an AAA plus student. As a start, you need to know the qualifications of the course teachers. Reputable revision colleges will list those on the publicity material: John Smith, B.Sc. Biology (Cantab.) tells you that Mr. Smith has a Bachelor of Science degree in Biology from Cambridge. If it was a degree from Oxford in an arts subject, such as English, the qualification would be BA English (Oxon.). The letters M.Sc. or MA after a name indicate a higher qualification in most cases, but former students of Oxford and Cambridge can claim this title automatically a year after graduation. Some revision courses are taught by university lecturers or teachers who also moonlight as examiners.

You also need to know whether you are booking your son into a new or established revision college. New tends to be bad until proven otherwise. How big are their classes? Will they prepare your daughter for her specific subject exam and examining board? Do they specialise in helping their students to pass or to get top grades? And how many hours a day does the teaching actually take? The answers, you will discover, can vary greatly.

What you would, ideally, want to hear is that they teach a single subject in groups of at most six, for at least two hours a day, with extra time set aside for exam practice, feed-back and advice on further work to do at home. It would also be nice if the college took lots of bright students aiming for Russell Group universities and perhaps Oxbridge. Generally, smaller groups are better value than longer hours. By this stage, your daughter needs personal attention. In this spirit, a good revision college will want to know which GCSE and A2 exams she has taken, plus her current grade predictions. These details enable them to fit her into the right course. If the principal is trying to make you sign a cheque without showing any interest in the girl's record - don't. You are probably being sold a pup.

I am less sure about the apparently rather well taught A-level courses at Oxford and Cambridge. Tempting as these may sound if your daughter clams up when confronted with quaint old university towns and the clipped vowels of their teaching staff, such a course does imply that Oxbridge is her sole possible destination. If she then fails to get in despite her very best efforts, the disappointment can be harder to bear.

HOME TUTORS

Getting one-to-one attention, even for a fairly short period, can dramatically raise a pupil's attainment. A good tutor will explain previously incomprehensible bits of the syllabus, focus on those aspects of a subject which are likely to come up in tests and, in an ideal world, suggest wider reading. He can also make even the driest subject sound exciting, thereby coaching your son towards doing more work.

To get the best results you must spell out the basics. Is the tutor there to help improve your kid's general grasp of a school subject or just to prepare him for an imminent exam? If exam performance is all you are after, the tutor will have to be familiar with the type of questions likely to come up. If he is not currently a teacher, this means that he needs to be given copies of previous years' papers, available from your son's school. The tutor may or may not cover exam skills such as timing, ordering material and clarity of expression. Unless you make clear what you want, no tutor can provide it.

(A word of warning: tutors can make a difference, but cannot magically transform a middling pupil into a top student. If that is what you hope, I'd drop the idea of Oxbridge. For the sake of family peace and your teenager's self-esteem, it would be better to focus on another university. Having two fairly strong subjects is the minimum requirement not just for getting into Oxford or Cambridge, but also for surviving there.)

So, where do you find a tutor? Well, Prime Minister Tony Blair found his state-educated sons' tutor at the nearest private day school, and there is no reason why you should not copy him. It is quite OK to ring up yours, picked from the Good Schools Guide, and tell the school secretary that you are looking for someone to do a few weeks' private tutoring. If their own staff are too grand to take the extra job (in the era of huge mortgages, few are) they might well have a friend or a former pupil just down from Oxbridge who is keen.

Don't be put off by a potential tutor's youth. When it comes to exam coaching, someone who left school only a few years earlier and so may have worked through the same syllabus as your son towards very similar exams could well come up trumps. And don't be ashamed to ask the young postgraduate student earning his rent in your sitting room what grades he got and how he got into Oxbridge himself. Is he keeping in touch with staff there? It's a good sign if he is. He might have picked up gossip about new priorities and admissions policy or might even be able to put in a good word.

Alternatively, A-level tutors seeking work advertise on www.gumtree.com and in local papers. They are often retired teachers and some have worked in both the public and the private sector. Ask how long they have been retired (because A-levels have changed much in the last decade) and if they give the school as a reference, follow it up by phone. You never know whether you'll hear songs of praise or some tense, embarrassed waffle. The latter can mean he left under a bit of a cloud -- drink or perhaps a taste for under-age boys. Schools rarely prosecute.

There are also lots of tutorial agencies offering their services in the papers. Told what kind of help your teenager needs, they'll try to come up with someone suitable. It's best to insist that this means a tutor who has graduated in the subject he will teach. The kind of person registered with the agency is often an Oxbridge graduate still looking for the perfect city job or for enough bookings as a comedian. A few are young academics trying to pay their mortgage. Some agencies check tutors' references, others are just groups of university friends sharing out the work.

As for the financial side, this is pretty straight forward. Expect to pay between £20 and £50 per lesson (which means tutoring is, alas, only a solution for better-off state school parents) and settle for between one and two lessons a week, depending on the amount of time left. A good tutor can massively improve a willing student's understanding of a subject and his exam skills in two or three months. The emphasis is on "willing": if you have scheduled the tutorials in place of your son's weekly football practice the tutor will be as popular as Bayern Munich.

Before finally striking the deal, clarify with the tutor how long a lesson will be and if you have to pay his fare on top of the fee. Then, fix a time and place and don't allow circumstances to alter them. The time should be after one of your daughter's easier school days or a quiet weekend afternoon. The place, ideally, around your bare kitchen table or your daughter's tidied up room. Being able to spread out reams of paper is what matters here. This is not the moment to show off your new, extra-soft three piece leather suite.

In some cases, the tutor may suggest to hold lessons on the school premises or elsewhere. This may be tempting, especially if you feel embarrassed about your home, but it is worth keeping in mind that the tutor himself was probably not raised at Buckingham Palace. I'd certainly agree to this only if you can be sure that other, trustworthy people will be present. If the person who will be spending private time with your child was not vetted by anyone, you might even want to remain at home (but not in the same room, of course) during lessons. I'd also make clear to the girl that the tutor, however nice, is technically a stranger, which means not a trusted family friend whose invitations she can accept.

Lastly, it may be wise to review progress after two or three lessons. Ask your daughter how she feels about the tutor. Is he good at explaining a problem? Approachable? Responds to questions? Does she feel that she is learning anything or is she just watching a dopey stranger scoffing the chocolate biscuits you thoughtfully put out?

If things go wrong, don't be shy about starting again. Tell the tutor you are moving away (or whatever), then quickly look for another one by the same route. Tutors are just human beings and vary tremendously. The next one might be a teaching genius.

MOVING SCHOOLS

If you conclude that your son's school is not good enough already at the GCSE stage, you have different options. He might agree - or even badly want - to move to another, more successful institution for his sixth form years. What you need to work out is when and where.

The answer to the first question is simple: no later than the start of year 11. The best comprehensives want all applications in by January or February of the previous school year, which means eight to nine months ahead of entry. The same is true for technology colleges, but entry rules for academies and free schools vary.

As for where to move your teenager, the choice is, on first sight, considerable. Legally, you no longer need to live near a school to apply for a place there, and your son is now old enough to travel considerable distances. However, some popular sixth forms are selective and have entrance tests.

Picking a good school seems simple enough. Its website should answer your general questions. Both you and your son, though, must also attend its open day for sixth formers, which will be in November of the year before or in January thereafter. This is the time to check out the basics. Does it have the facilities and/or labs he might need? Are you struck by the positive attitude of the pupils who are showing you around? Do the teachers impress you as qualified, likeable and ambitious for their pupils? Are they sending pupils on enrichment schemes or Access events to broaden their horizons? Do they prepare some for the Oxbridge entrance process, and does anyone ever get in?

A good school will tell you the rest, such as which subjects it offers at AS and A2 and where they might lead. The information given should include the previous year's exam results and which universities, if any, their students went on to. There will be some mention of class size, which in the A-level group should ideally be twenty or less. If there are entrance tests, there will be a form and a registration deadline.

The school may also display extracts from its Ofsted report, although I'd treat those with caution. It's is nice to know that "students work cooperatively in the classroom," but you should probably read the full school report on www.ofsted.gov.uk/ for more. It also helps to know that Ofsted's grading of schools has been clarified. It now ranges from 1 (outstanding), 2 (good), 3 (requires improvement) and 4 (inadequate). So, anything below "good" is not what you're looking for.

Similar rules apply to Academies although, being quite new, some have not even been inspected yet. Others may have received poor Ofsted reports because they recently replaced a failing school. To know if an Academy does what it says on the box you sometimes have to wait a few years. Success rates vary greatly. Free Schools, too, will take time to prove their worth. They can legally use their freedom to be selective, either socially or through tests. Ask who their founders and what their values are.

Then, if you're happy with your findings, go ahead and fill in the application form, remembering to emphasize your teenager's academic abilities. You have done what you could and must now hope for the best.

Unfortunately, such steps have a really good chance of success only outside the big cities. In London, certainly, top rated comprehensives are hopelessly oversubscribed. When it comes to the sixth form, many admit only a small proportion of outside pupils. While it is worth trying hard, which includes making sure that the school is aware of all your son's strengths and potential contribution to the school's academic glory, he may have to consider other options. The most obvious one, and increasingly popular, is a sixth form college.

SIXTH FORM COLLEGES

State run colleges of this kind used to have a poor reputation, mainly because they largely catered for a very mixed intake of young people. Some would come from failing schools, others from disadvantaged homes. This means that their overall exam results could not equal those of a school in some executive suburb. However, such colleges can still be great at developing a pupil's individual potential. Also, these days quite a few of them specialise in taking students doing well already. And don't be automatically put off by the presence of refugees: some of their parents may well have been teachers or civil servants before they had to escape and will encourage their children to study hard.

Most importantly, huge amounts of government money have gone into this sector in recent years, which have paid for into state-of-the art facilities from language labs to IT equipment. The funding has also attracted more and more highly qualified teachers. As a result, your local sixth form college could be far more geared towards Oxbridge than the struggling comprehensive down the road.

Having said that, the above rules still apply: read the Ofsted report, attend the open day and go through the college bumph with a tooth comb. Exam results in this sector are often good, but the range of subjects taught varies a lot, so you must check if your son will be able to study (or combine) those required for his chosen Oxbridge course.

FURTHER EDUCATION COLLEGES

Although these institutions do not focus mainly on school qualification and are not inspected by Ofsted, they run A-level classes in lots of subjects. The number of students continuing from there to higher education has gradually increased as a result.

Top universities used to be sniffy about FE applicants, but this is beginning to change. Oxbridge now encourages the very best to apply and runs special Open Days for them. FE students have a fairly low success rate (14 per cent at Cambridge in 2017), but that year sixty-one of them still got in.

IF YOU CAN'T BEAT THEM...

Having explored these options, you may still dream of sending your son to one of those schools which, in exchange for annual school fees well above the annual minimum wage, smooth their pupils' path to Oxbridge. As it happens, some private sixth form education is available at little or no cost, at least if your child is really talented and you play your cards right.

What you need to know is that almost all private schools have scholarship schemes. Most of these cover a proportion of a child's fee, usually 20 per cent. The traditional function of this is to enable those of their old boys who have fallen on hard times to send their kids there.

Quite a few schools, though, also have 100 per cent scholarship schemes. These have quite a different purpose. They enable a private establishment with a mixed ability intake, which is what most public schools really are (except for a tiny group of highly selective ones) to strengthen its academic base. The top A-levels won by its hand-picked scholars will ensure that the school retains its high ranking in private schools' league tables. Once this has been achieved, it can hike up its fees as much as it likes. In other words, scholarships are not a form of charity and you need not be embarrassed about accepting one.

There is only one problem. While these schemes might even get your son into some of the grandest boys' schools, including Eton and Harrow, full scholarships to girls' schools are like gold dust. The trick here is to think outside the box, at least with an older teenager. You need to know that many top boys' school now have mixed sixth forms. Ambitious headmasters at such schools are forever in search of brilliant girls.

While most existing schemes are aimed at pupils entering at 13, big schools often set aside half a dozen full scholarships per year for sixth form entry. Both are usually means-tested, i.e. aimed at parents who are on the dole or earning £20,000 a year at best. If you are slightly better off, the school might drop part of the fees.

The scholarships usually cover all costs, including tuition and, if applicable, boarding. If asked, most schools will also find a way to fund the scholar's absurdly overpriced uniform and other kit. And when your son has lost his flannel blazer and cap for the third exasperating time, a kindly teacher will reveal to you that the annual school fete always includes a "good as new" second-hand uniform stall. Then watch the most genteel of middle class mothers get into a scrum so the money saved can go to Harvey Nichols.

When do you throw your child's name into this particular hat? The answer is very early. While state sixth forms do not usually decide on admissions until February of the year in which the sixth form course is to start, private schools think fourteen months ahead. This means you probably should first contact their admissions officer in July or August of the year before your teenager will be starting her sixth form.

Below is a sample letter I suggest you send in order to set

the process in motion, but you may want to tailor it slightly to fit an individual school. As you will discover by looking at a school's website, expectations from scholars can vary; some schools like to find the perfect all-rounder, the boy who performs equally well in all subjects without obvious preferences; others look for exceptional ability in one academic field. Most schools like a pupil who can offer extras like sporting ability or a great musical gift.

LETTER TO A SCHOOL (SAMPLE)

Dear... (check the website for the name of the head*),*

I am the parent of a child currently attending Year 10 of his comprehensive school. My son has been assessed as a very able pupil by his school (or an educational psychologist, or some other expert), especially as far as the sciences are concerned. He works hard and has consistently high exam results. He is also a keen athlete and plays basketball for his school.

His gifts, I feel, would be best developed at a school such as yours. I would therefore be grateful if you could advise me about your admissions procedures. Unfortunately, I am a low earner and unable to afford current school fees. Perhaps you could let me know whether there are any scholarships or bursaries available for boys in my son's position.

Yours sincerely,

If the school is interested, an application form will be in the post. The school may also ask for documentation such as school reports or teachers' comments. All being well, the boy will then be invited to an interview and exam session lasting anything from a few hours to two whole days the following November.

This is a promising result, but don't count your chickens yet: a large private school may be offering 20 sixth form places to non-pupils, but interview up to five times that number. If possible, your son should therefore sit exams for more than one such school.

The private school entry process has several parts, which vary with your child's age but cover "Maths, English, verbal reasoning and non verbal reasoning". With young children, teachers may primarily use conversation and mental problem-solving to assess ability. Teenager are put through written tests to determine how much they know about the subjects they have been taught, especially maths. They might also be asked to write a one page piece on a set topic, using correct tenses and punctuation. At some schools, teachers start with a brief lecture, then quiz listeners about its contents.

Some schools also interview parents, but don't be nervous about this either. They are not looking for airs and graces, but for a commitment to your son's academic goals. This means that you will encourage him to work hard at home if an exam is looming, that you won't disappear abroad just before he is due to come home at half term or keep him away on holiday long after term started. They get quite enough of this sort of behaviour from the fee-paying parents, thank you.

They will also expect you to back the strict school rules. You'll have to make your son understand that there will be little tolerance of misbehaviour. Private schools maintain discipline and try to prevent breaches of the law, such as drug-taking, by mercilessly expelling culprits. Parents of rebellious pupils, however bright, have reasons to fear the headmaster's dreaded phrase: "He would be happier elsewhere."

Can you prepare for this entrance exam? The honest answer is, most applicants do. You can start by asking the school for more details. Many some information on exam contents, or even previous papers. Obviously, your son should be having another look at his GCSE notes in the subjects he means to continue with. It may also be a good idea to do some newspaper reading. After a few weekends with *The Observer* or *Sunday Times*, he should be able to express a personal opinion on a few issues of the day: war, climate change or plastic surgery are some examples. Remember, there are no "correct" views on such things, only arguments backed by a few facts.

Your son also will probably be asked to talk a little about his interests. It would be nice if those included a few scientific or cultural ones , but sporting ones may also appeal to the school. Make sure he can rattle off a short list!

When it comes to the written work, it is obviously important not to overlook any of the mandatory questions. Most crucially perhaps, an applicant needs to be able to complete an essay within a set time, often 45 minutes. This means acquiring the skills of timing, structuring and summarising. Check he's got a working watch!

If you're uncertain whether your son is properly prepared, consult the Independent Schools Information Service (ISIS), which might be able to tell you which sample papers your son wants to look at before sitting for a particular school.

WILL HE BE HAPPY THERE?

The answer is, it depends. I've rarely heard of a day school pupil on a scholarship regretting the choice they made. Sleeping in a different world can be more stressful. An outgoing teenager who likes group activities and understands that he is contributing to the school's fortunes will probably settle in fast. Large boarding schools tend to have separate scholars' houses and your bright son might really enjoy living with lots of other fast learners.

On the other hand, most private schools are single sex, and living an hour's train ride from the nearest place selling hair gel does not suit everyone. Having less freedom than at a comprehensive can be a pain, although boarding schools are no longer the prisons which earlier inmates remember them as. Physical punishment and fagging, the public school version of bullying, were abolished nearly a generation ago. There is some privacy and a universal youth culture has reduced the once enormous gap in pupils' lives. One Eton teacher, quoted in the *Daily Telegraph*, insisted that it can now be hard to tell who comes from where: "By the time you've opened a few doors, you see that everyone has the same rickety CD system and the same posters."

The range of well-resourced leisure activities can thrill a newcomer. Still, a very shy teenager may be thrown by the unfamiliar environment, and not everyone fancies the wide open spaces, which may include dormitories, as well as playing fields.

There can be other problems: a small school's intake may be too white to make an ethnic minority child feel at ease, or too intellectually average to stretch a fast learner. A few schools get so obsessed with A-levels that they (metaphorically) stamp on the more original pupil who is doing work outside the curriculum. To invent a game, design a machine or write a poem in school time can be seen as betraying the struggle for top marks.

In short, private education, even if you can get it, does not meet every gifted child's needs. There has to be a fairly precise match between abilities and facilities. Anecdotal evidence suggests that mixed boarding schools work best for working class pupils (think Atlantic College or Bedales) but a current A-level student should not get too excited about these options. While Winchester has launched a £70m. bursary appeal to eventually o fund sixty-seven boys and St. Paul's seeks to raise £250m. so that it can go "needs-blind" within twenty-five years, the number of free six form places currently available is tiny. There are only a few hundred a year, which does not quite make them a superhighway to Oxbridge.

5
Which degree course?

Picking an Oxbridge degree course is something many pupils do in the first, exciting weeks of their A2 year, almost as an afterthought. The forms arrive in September, and finishing a class essay in time can, at this point, seem far more important to your son. So might finding out whether leggy Jessie from Maths has really broken up with her naff boyfriend in the holidays. Other pupils are probably not even discussing courses yet. After all, entrance applications to most universities need to be submitted over two months later. So, why worry? If you fuss now, you might well get your head bitten off. ''Filling in the form just means applying for a course in what you're best at, right?'' Wrong, actually.

Course choice is fairly crucial for enjoying university life, as well as for getting in. The problem is that by the time they fill in their Oxbridge application form, most pupils are perfectly clear about theirs. They want to study the subject in which they got the highest marks at school. Teachers may strengthen this idea by telling the proud dad on parents' day that ''she is a natural mathematician'' or assure a mother that ''he has a real gift for English.''

For a pupil harbouring some doubts, the school's careers adviser may be the next port of call. Some are wonderful at making even a timid but clever science pupil see herself as a future Professor of Physics. Others can be overwhelmed by the requirements of so many new pupils, universities and courses. In a school which does not normally sends students to Oxbridge the focus might be on making disadvantaged pupils consider any university at all.

So, while all careers advisers have a shelf full of dog-eared books and booklets to lend or may suggest a few links, only a few will explain to an Oxbridge applicant while she, especially, should take time over them.

Nor is there much emphasis on the link between careers and courses. While it is pretty obvious what you can become with a degree in Law, the same is not true of, for instance, Linguistics. Its name alone sounds like a sexual practice. To a pupil nervous about striking out into the alien adult world in general and Oxbridge in particular, sticking with a familiar school subject also provides some reassurance. So, Maths or English (or History or French) goes on the application form.

WHAT'S ON OFFER?

This is a great pity, as a start because your son will never know what he could be missing without a leisurely study of the Oxford or Cambridge undergraduate prospectus, available online some six months in advance. Not only has this once dreary document now caught up with the lively and colourful material issued by the former polytechnics, it also no longer assumes that every reader knows what Economics is or what jobs it can lead to. Every year too it contains more non-school subject courses, a few of them entirely new, others newly combined or newly opened to candidates without Latin.

Admittedly, the number of courses offered by Oxford and Cambridge is not huge. After all, for most of the two universities' long history, only three subjects, Classics, Divinity and Law, were taught there. Even the introduction of English Literature was fiercely resisted for decades but, once its academic supporters had won the day, the subject was, in true Oxbridge style, elevated to a national mission. Speaking after his election as Oxford English Professor, George Stuart Gordon announced in his 1922 inaugural lecture: "England is sick, and... English Literature must save it. The Churches (as I understand) having failed, and social remedies being slow, English Literature now has a triple function: still I suppose, to delight and instruct us, but also, and above all, to save our souls and heal the State."

Academics elsewhere tend to see their role in slightly more modest terms and so managed to create a wider choice earlier on. The new universities, in particular, try to cover every possible student taste, with some offering up to a hundred degree options, from Accounting to Culinary Arts (Pastry), both taught at Thames Valley University. Cambridge, in comparison, tends to list only around thirty degree courses in its prospectus. Oxford lists just over fifty.

Oxford and Cambridge have also taken seemingly different paths. While Oxford has gradually added an interesting set of combined courses, such as Physics and Philosophy, Modern History and Economics, and Religion and Oriental Studies, Cambridge offers rather less of this, or so a quick skim though its prospectus suggests. Here the early 20th century range of academic disciplines, topped up by one newcomer, Computer Science, survives almost intact.

This impression is misleading. Once a Cambridge student has done her initial year, working hard to absorb a single subject at great depth, she has an amazing range of study options. Thanks to the many experts and expert libraries on tap, a History undergraduate interested in, for example, North African History, will be able to explore even its most obscure angle with a world-renowned expert.

And if she wants to combine this with another discipline, say Cultural Studies, this is not just fine but actually encouraged.

In other words, although History and Culture is not a Cambridge degree course, you can actually do it, and probably to a higher level than elsewhere. This so-called "Tripos" course structure means then a student is sometimes even able to move from his official course subject to a fairly unrelated one. If your son has started off in Asian and Middle Eastern Studies, but wants to broaden his outlook (or is struggling with Persian grammar) by year two, he might be able to move to Social Anthropology, Law or Management Studies and continue with this into year three. This means he will end up, in practice, with a combined course.

In science too progress options are huge, though only once you have completed the first year of what in Cambridge is called Natural Sciences, but in Oxford comes under either Biology, Biochemistry, Biomedical Sciences, Earth Sciences, Chemistry, Biochemistry, Materials Science or Physics. Other science courses, tend to offer the student either a wide module choice or at least some subject combinations. Teaching methods can vary too and you need to remember that, unlike in many other universities, the science approach here will be theoretical rather than applied. If Robert Stephenson had gone to Oxbridge, he might have been encouraged to explore the scientific principles making a steam engine possible, before building one.

It is also worth knowing that some subjects are absent only in name: "The word sociology, being a Latin-Greek hybrid, was not used in polite academic society," recalled Cambridge don Thomas Howarth. So, must you go elsewhere for this popular hybrid? Actually, no. Nowadays all Oxbridge Anthropology courses, as well as the new Cambridge HPSP course and Oxford PPE (see below) put their students through the Sociology reading list, albeit in between lots of other books.

No subject is today out of bounds to state school pupils. As mentioned before, this includes Classics, which now accommodates the study, from scratch, of Latin or Greek, or both. The Oxford Classics course, a tour de force through Greek and Roman literature, history, languages, thought, art and culture, is not even terribly hard to get into. The only problem is that applicants from comprehensives need to do more independent reading than others to prove their interest. Private and grammar school pupils plough through loads of Classics-related stuff at school.

THINK BEFORE YOU JUMP

As a result of there being so much on offer, working out your course options from the prospectus alone can be hideously confusing. Don't even think of signing on the dotted line before you have read the clearer but also much more detailed information on the course website. Keep in mind too that two courses of the same name may be quite different at Oxford and Cambridge. Oriental Studies at Oxford, for instance, is largely language-oriented. At Cambridge, the same course (now renamed Asian and Middle Eastern Studies) has a substantial history and culture element.

All admissions tutors I spoke to emphasized that it is absolutely fine for students to email their department or college with specific questions. For more general queries, you can phone the university's admissions department. All the email addresses, phone numbers and websites you might need are listed in the back. The best person to ask for is often the undergraduate studies secretary, a goldmine of information on exciting but unfamiliar courses.

On the other hand, simply sticking to the school subject he knows may well disappoint your son intellectually. For instance, doing school Maths eight hours a week is not at all the same thing as doing the more abstract Oxbridge version for thirty hours a week. Reading fiction for pleasure and writing essays about the narrative of your book is very different from concentrating on literary theory, as you would with Oxford English Lit., or on literary structure, as you would at Cambridge. Of course, some bright students absolutely thrive on this approach and will spend endless blissful university hours discussing iambic pentameters in English or Fermat's Last Theorem in Maths. Others, though, will love the inspiration found very much further afield.

So, don't rush your choice. It's best to think of your degree course not as the automatic continuation of your school career, but as a new and carefully considered beginning.

PICKING TO GET IN

Course choice at Oxbridge also matters hugely (and far more than at many other universities) in terms of acceptance chances. Not knowing this trips up especially ambitious students from non-university families. So, what is it that you should both know? Well, let's say that your daughter has returned from an Access trip to Oxford or Cambridge determined to live for three years under the ramparts of a medieval nunnery, but also to study her favourite school subject. Unless she is a really outstanding pupil, this can be a problem. Each year, there are vastly more Oxbridge candidates than places for English, Maths, History and courses involving French; poor teaching often handicaps candidates for school subjects more than others.

If your daughter is determined to go to Oxbridge, but also to do French, the only foreign language taught in all English schools, she might have to choose between these two perfectly reasonable ambitions. Suggesting this to her could trigger a tantrum bigger than the one she threw, aged three, when she couldn't take home the hole she had dug in the playground sand pit. And, if she has read her way through the French novels shelf in your local library or is beginning to take an interest in Parisian existentialism she is quite right to ignore you.

Clinging to French just because it comes easy to her and she is curious about the world, though, might be the wrong decision. Oxbridge offers lots of alternatives -- and we are talking mind stretchers, not cheap substitutes here. A pupil who fearlessly walked the horrifying tightrope of French grammar may actually find it more rewarding to tackle a non-European language with a whole alphabet of its own. Future explorers can, at the same time, learn about the history or culture of a new, unfamiliar country through courses like Oriental Studies, Asian and Middle Eastern Studies or Archaeology. Or, if the girl has a more theoretical bent, she might want to explore the science of languages, Linguistics, together with a new modern language of her choice.

All these are stimulating, often extremely well taught courses and they have another very attractive feature: they admit around a third of all those who apply. State school candidates are especially good at getting into the Cambridge Archaeology course: in 2017, nearly half of them were successful. Graduates in what used to be known as "Arch & Ant" also do well in life: the former Governor of the Bank of England, Mervyn King, is one of them.

For students keen on both languages and early English literature, the Anglo-Saxon, Norse and Celtic course at Cambridge is another option: each year almost exactly half of its applicants are successful.

Some of these courses don't even require prior knowledge of another language, certainly not a non-European one. Others have admissions tutors who will be delighted to hear that your daughter speaks Polish to her grandmother or learnt Arabic in the mosque. She will still have to prove her interest in the course by reading around it, but her multi-lingual background can give her that slight edge.

And if the girl does get in, she might get a very good degree. Many a language student finds herself alongside some of the classic Oxbridge ''coasters'', rich but less academic students who have picked their mother tongue as a course subject and coast along on the strength of that. But to do well takes more than basic language skills, and if she works hard on all aspects of the course, your bright daughter might well overtake the coasters and get a First. On the other hand, if the girl insists on clinging to her school subject, she might not even get into Oxbridge.

TARGET PRACTICE

One of the open secrets of Oxbridge entrance has always been that you can get in by targeting a course which offers a high chance of success. Rates vary greatly: Oxford Economics Computer Science, Medicine and Law accept roughly one in eleven applicants, while History, English, Earth Sciences and Chemistry accept roughly one in four. At Cambridge, around half of Classics applicants gain a place, but only one in nine of those applying for Architecture.

For unusual language combinations, success rates can be even higher: only Oxford and Cambridge can afford to run courses which, during certain periods of history at least, hardly anyone wants to attend. Some of these courses are relics of the British Empire, which exported thousands of young men with a grounding in the various "native languages" to the Colonies. Elderly Oxbridge dons still recall the frantic War Office search in 1941 for graduates in Serbo--Croat who could be dropped behind enemy lines in German-occupied Yugoslavia. Younger dons will talk of a similar search in 1999, when the British Government prepared to enter Kosovo.

Until recently, few people would have thought that Sumerian, the ancient language of what was Mesopotamia and is now Iraq, had any public use. However, the looting of Iraq's museums in 2003 deprived the world of valuable ancient documents and made the study of the remaining ones crucial.

As a result, courses which combine a language with historic or cultural studies are kept going even if there are very few applicants for them. After all, the dons teaching the course are around anyway, engaged in their own specialist and highly reputable research. What this means is that while it can be murder to get into Law, there are few barriers before the student wanting to do Sanskrit, or a language mix including Czech (with Slovak). Here, a bright applicant willing to broaden his horizons might greeted with open arms.

Why don't more state school students go for courses like these? The answer lies in the information available. Neither Oxford nor Cambridge will tell you, for instance, what the acceptance chances of a candidate applying to do a particular language course are. Instead, the success rates listed are overall ones, based on all the degree courses run by an individual faculty. This was fine when a candidate could always call on a cousin or family friend who had been to Oxbridge and knew what was on offer there. Alas, times have changed and, without such key data, how can a student from a non-academic background possibly decide?

Families also like to know about the practical value of courses. Without this information, many parents understandably fear that they might not be spending their hard-earned cash on something worthwhile. Actually, when it comes to languages, this is a case of no worries: they are amongst the most popular degree subjects in the eyes of both British and foreign employers. However, while French remains useful to diplomats, business now loves Spanish, Chinese and Russian.

All these facts, of course, are exactly what public school teachers, who are most often Oxbridge educated, have at their finger tips. They are aware that relatively few people apply to do a combination of German and Turkish, or Arabic and Portuguese, even though these courses require only a prior knowledge of the European language. They know the success rates for Egyptology at Cambridge, and the chances offered to their particular students by the existence of so many Oxford courses involving Classics.

These teachers will also tailor their suggestions to the individual student by explaining that Materials Science (once called Metallurgy) at Oxford is not as academically demanding as Engineering and Materials, or that Land Economy at Cambridge is less of a tough intellectual slog than Economics. They are aware that Cambridge Theology turns out graduates interested in comparative religion, while Oxford Theology suits potential vicars, and that few eighteen-year-olds aspire to become either of these things.

One of the main reasons such a disproportionate number of Oxbridge students come from their kind of schools is that they apply to a far wider range of courses than state school students do. Public school teachers also realise that being flexible about your degree subject does not make for a disappointing outcome. Many of their students return to recommend their course to others, not only for intellectual satisfaction, but also on career grounds.

This does not, of course, mean that a student should completely disregard her own instincts in order to get in. If you hate languages, don't apply for a course requiring full-body-immersion in two of them. If you hate scientific research, looking at flow charts all day could make you feel sick. Most students, though, do not have preferences quite as strong as this and a little open-mindedness can be very rewarding indeed.

If you are wondering whether you should consider a course which is in no great public demand, the answer is probably yes. Do look at previously unconsidered options like the mysteries of Assyriology and, if they even vaguely spark your interest, skim through one of the relevant course textbooks listed on the faculty website. The excellence of Oxbridge teaching often makes a not (as yet) loved subject a highly stimulating experience.

Equally importantly, the student will still have access to the lively intellectual scene which characterises Oxbridge. Not only do students mix socially by college rather than by course, but the brightest often attend lectures in a subject other than their own. There is also nothing to prevent an interested science undergraduate from joining many of the Oxbridge arts societies and vice versa. More than one lost Engineering student has found his spiritual home on the university's drama stage.

So, you should certainly take a close look at non-school subjects. If a course description baffles you even after you explored the relevant faculty website, try to discuss it with a teacher or find some introductory book.

The key here is to be flexible. Don't assume that your talents or ambitions can only lead towards one Oxbridge course. Even more importantly, beware misconceptions about the world of work. Disadvantaged students, especially, often see Economics as their sole road to riches, unaware that careers in the business world can just as well be built on studying Chinese. The vastly over-subscribed Economics course is certainly a high-risk option. Unless a candidate has the right A-levels, interests and grades, plus a real aptitude for this very demanding choice, she is likely to end up without a place.

PICKING FOR A CAREER

The psychologist and ability expert Joan Freeman discovered that very bright children can find it especially hard to make career choices. To a quick, thorough mind, Latin and Persian, or Maths and Medicine, can seem equally manageable and attractive. Even ambition is not necessarily a good guide. Your son may want to become a successful, well paid young professional, but teenagers outside the educated middle classes often know far too little about white-collar jobs to link university learning with the work people do. The gifted sixteen year olds interviewed by Professor Freeman thought that bankers handle money, or that chemists hand out medicines at Boots.

Knowing more about the reality of work helps pupils to make better choices. It is useful to realise that a banker, for instance, benefits from knowing about politics. He might have to decide where money should be kept, and a bank's investment decisions will have to take into account political developments. City institutions also need science graduates to evaluate business plans and mathematicians to devise financial products (the state of our economy suggests most are pretty terrible at it, but they do get well paid).

Then there is the historic precedent. Britain was, for hundreds of years, ruled by white men with an Oxbridge degree often known as "Greats". The idea behind this was that a politician needed a good grasp of the moral principles taught in Classics courses - if only to disregard them. Today's politicians are more likely to have done Politics, Philosophy and Economics (PPE), which elderly dons still call "Modern Greats". It's a course only available at Oxford.

If you are after an academic reputation, it helps to know that this does not depend on the subject an Oxbridge don has specialised in. Cambridge Celtic is taught by people who are no less world renowned than those teaching French or, say, History at the same university. By choosing a less popular course, your son is likely to get personal, undiluted attention from some of the best minds in the field.

Parents doubting that their son has the potential to become a don may not be convinced of such a course choice. Aren't Norse, Oriental Studies or Medieval Languages odd interests which lead nowhere? Surely, a solid, familiar subject like Maths or English is a far safer bet? You want your son to have a career, after all, not to be on the dole.

Luckily for the lovers of deeply obscure Oxbridge courses, this is not so. For instance, Oriental Studies degrees built around complex, demanding subjects like Japanese, Chinese or Egyptology, appeal to top employers in finance or law and supply Britain with a steady trickle of ambassadors. So do Classics, perhaps because they really involve moral judgements, or perhaps because so many people in a position to offer highly-paid jobs got a First in them and still feel deep loyalty to the subject. Classics graduates make the Mafia look like a loose-knit group.

In short, by choosing his degree subject, your son is not automatically embarking on a "till death do us part" relationship with Norse or Chemistry. He might remain faithful if he becomes a teacher or lecturer. Otherwise, his degree course will have served as a kind of mental fitness gym in which he can practise unloading cartloads of jumbled facts, writing reports that need to be ready by dawn and having polite, informative chats with people he never met before, even over the most disgusting sherry.

What about the business world, though? Cambridge Economics may well sound less useful to a budding tycoon than Business Economics, a subject widely offered elsewhere. The world-famous Cambridge course will, in fact, cover this aspect alongside others, but will stress the subject's theoretical base and its historic and political context. The university is proud of the fact that the groundwork for the British welfare state was laid in Cambridge by the economist John Maynard Keynes. Once a student is able to produce sound essays on all these topics to sharp weekly deadlines, many employers will assume that he can learn how to actually trade in bonds or beer cans at work.

Oxford's Economics & Management course is not all about making money either. While its Management element does appeal to corporate employers, exploring the causes of poverty is at least as much of interest to some of its quite famous academics as the route towards wealth.

Lastly, we must tackle many an English student's secret dream, that of becoming a writer. Don't you need an English degree for that? Actually, no. Some experts even argue that you might be better off finding something to write about instead.

Dreamers of literary stardom should certainly be aware that neither Jane Austen nor Charles Dickens, George Orwell, Virginia Woolf or Doris Lessing had any university education.

Of famous Oxford writers, Evelyn Waugh, who celebrated its upper-class students in Brideshead Revisited, did History at Hertford. Shiva Naipaul did Chinese at University College, John Le Carré did German at Lincoln, Julian Barnes did French at Magdalen, Marina Warner did Italian at LMH and Monica Ali did PPE at Wadham. Salman Rushdie read History at King's, Cambridge, and J. G. Ballard read Medicine there.

Other famous and prize-winning literary authors are non-Oxbridge: Pat Barker read International History at the LSE, London, Anita Brookner did her degree at the Courtauld Institute of Art and Hanif Kureshi did Philosophy at London's own King's College. The poet Linton Kwesi Johnson has a Sociology degree from Goldsmiths' College, London.

So, don't be too narrow in your choice. All Oxbridge degrees, especially if they are "good", which means a First or Upper Second, will open up a wide range of interesting careers.

WHAT NOT DO (ABOUT COURSE CHOICE)

Quite a few parents, delighted at the thought that their son or daughter might indeed stand a chance of getting into Oxbridge, will now be tempted to impose their own dream. More often than not, this is for their daughter to become a medical consultant or for their son the family's first-ever lawyer. There is no denying that these are indeed satisfying and financially rewarding careers. They might even happen if your teenager is very smart and hardworking and actually fancies one of them.

If he'd rather do History or English, though, forget the idea. Telling the boy about the sacrifices you have made by keeping him at school and saving for his tuition fees is unlikely to make him change his mind. Nor will constant hints about the pleasure it would give his dear old gran to see him in a doctor's scarlet graduation gown. Today's young men pick their own colour schemes and careers.

But let's say your more soft-hearted daughter obeys your command, drops her plan to do Oxbridge Philosophy and applies for the "sensible" subject. All well? Unfortunately, not. Medicine and Law are highly competitive fields. Admissions tutors look not just for innate ability, but for genuine, bubbling, information-packed enthusiasm. Faced with a sullen, wistful teenager secretly pining for her abandoned pet subject, they'll rapidly move on to the next candidate. So, there goes the poor girl's Oxbridge dream - and yours.

This is not to say that, in the case of Law, you need to totally give up hope. Many lawyers reach the profession by following up a first degree in another subject by a conversion course leading to a qualification called CPE (Common Professional Examination).

This less known option involves an extra year or two of paid study, but is an entirely respectable route in: not only are there always too few good Law graduates for the legal profession to choose from, but solicitors' firms and barristers' chambers do welcome the variety of intellectual approaches graduates in other degree subjects bring along. These need not even be related ones. Science and engineering graduates, in particular, have a type of expertise which is very often useful in court.

You might also find it reassuring to know that even if your girl scoffs at this option, your dream of having a lawyer in the family need not go into the dustbin yet. The Open University offers an excellent Law course, open to applicants of all ages. All it takes are a few undisturbed hours a week, perfect for a parent whose children have flown the nest...

WHAT IS BEST WHERE?

What subject, though, is best studied where? Well, as a start the old saying that Oxford is best for arts and Cambridge for sciences is hopelessly out of date. Oxford regards itself as tops in Medicine, while Cambridge points to its excellence in Maths. Both have world-famous English departments. In real terms, there is little to choose between them. The Government assesses the quality of teaching and research at British universities and regularly lists Oxford and Cambridge among the top three in these fields, which means both have extremely high general academic standards.

What about the best colleges, though? Well, since each of these famous universities is made up of colleges, it is fair to assume that no individual college will be completely useless (we'll deal with the Oxbridge college, a mysterious beast with some very odd feeding habits, in the next chapter). Not every college will take students doing every single subject and you must therefore work out which one offers what from the university prospectus. A college not offering your degree course subject may still accept you, which is nice if you have picked it for its great church organ or badminton court. However, you will then be taught by academics who are fellows of other colleges, while the staff of your own college will take little interest in you.

Experts will tell you that some colleges are the best in the world for some subjects, for instance Trinity, Cambridge, for Maths and Magdalen, Oxford, for Classics. While this may be true, it is most important for an ambitious postgraduate seeking to become an expert. An undergraduate need not worry about this or might have other priorities: different colleges may specialise in very different subject areas. What this means is that a student interested in Human Geography will get the best tuition at one college, but someone more interested in Physical Geography could well be better off at another.

How do you find out where to best study your preferred subject area? The answer to this question was once jealously guarded by private school heads who dined in their old Oxbridge colleges several times a year and kept up with developments. Nowadays, all you need to do is go into the Cambridge Geography course website. This will tell you that many of the fellows (lecturers) who specialise in Physical Geography are at Sidney Sussex, while others specialising in Human Geography are at Emmanuel (www.geog.cam.ac.uk/people/academic.html). That's college choice sorted.

On the other hand, if your teenager is open-minded and likes to explore new directions within a subject, any college that enjoys a good academic reputation will do him fine. Many students I met had picked a college without worrying too much about its course specialisation and none regretted the result. It can be thrilling to discover aspects of a subject you never knew existed at school.

In other words, the option is either to look thoroughly into the subject angle taken by specific colleges or to be fairly relaxed once you've made a general subject choice and go with the flow. In either case, you will end up in a place that has a library, a lawn, a supervisor with a doctorate and a wardrobe without any decent coat hangers.

This, however, takes us to the subject of Oxbridge colleges, which is dealt with in the next chapter.

6
College daze

One of the decisions Oxbridge candidates are asked to make as part of their application is which college they would like to attend. Once upon a time, this was a simple matter. Writing in the "National Review" of October 1906, an anonymous public school head offered this advice:

> A parent who asks "which is the best college at Oxford" means "where would my son fall in with the most desirable companions." If your son is a clever boy, send him to Balliol. Even if he does not appear clever, still send him to Balliol, as that is where any latent abilities which he may possess will be drawn out. But if you cannot, will not or do not send him to Balliol, why then send him to New College, Christ Church, Magdalen, Trinity or University (College), and he will have every chance of spending two or three, or even four, completely happy years.

Over a hundred years later, the bit about sending a clever boy to Balliol remains pretty valid. But there are lots of other places at Oxford and Cambridge which that boy (or girl) might like to consider for happiness and intellectual stimulation, as well as to improve their entrance prospects.

How do you, though, choose between fifty-nine different Oxbridge colleges? As the college system hardly exists outside Oxbridge, this question can flummox even university educated parents. To make matters worse, there are quite different places called Trinity, St. John's, Pembroke, Magdalen(e), Jesus, Corpus Christi and St. Catherine's at both Oxford and Cambridge. The really famous ones have vastly more applicants than others for the same course. At Merton, Oxford, up to ten students may be competing for each of the college's six History places, while elsewhere you might be competing with only four.

As a result, some candidates would rather not pick at all. Both the Oxford and the Cambridge prospectus make clear that this is perfectly OK. All students need to do instead is to submit an "open" application. This will leave the decision as to which college his application will be sent to the university itself. But is that wise?

It can certainly be tempting. As some dons will point out,

almost every college now contains some undergraduates who had ticked this option. However, you need to know that open applications have traditionally been far less successful than targeted ones. The reason for this is unclear. Perhaps colleges do like to be chosen or perhaps candidates who shrink from such a choice come from schools academically less geared than others towards Oxbridge.

Certainly, putting in an "open" Oxbridge application rather than picking a specific college should not be taken as an obvious way out. It does work, but mainly "for excellent candidates with exam scores in the top percentile marks", as one admissions tutor put it. In other words, if what you have to offer is more mixed, pick your own college.

One way to do this, of course, is by putting down a name at random. Another, traditionally suggested in the Oxford prospectus (and echoed in the Cambridge one), is "not to worry too much about choosing a college," as this is mainly about "your living environment". To the uninitiated, this could suggest that the size of the snooker table in the student common room is all you should really care about.

Candidates might want to take this advice with a large pinch of salt. It is not just that the most academically renowned ones have vastly more applicants but not necessary more places. It's also that not all colleges take students for all courses. Most importantly, interview questions at top colleges can be considerably harder than elsewhere. And while a growing number of candidates invited up by Oxford are now seen by two colleges, Cambridge candidates are usually not. A Cambridge college faced with a good candidate it nevertheless does not wish to admit will merely put her on a university-wide shortlist (the so-called Pool). Around a fifth of Pool candidates in the end get a place elsewhere.

Most importantly, each college has its own ethos, preferences and, to some extent, admissions policy. Such details are never spelt out, but a college which describes itself as "exceptionally informal" or stresses its students' varied social and educational background is really saying that it would love to find yet more smart applicants from modest homes. This information can narrow your choice, while still leaving you with a decent shortlist.

LOOK AT THE FOUNDATIONS

One way to understand your real options is through a potted history. Oxbridge colleges started off as separate monastic foundations in the 13th century. Religious scholars gathered there to study philosophy and theology, as well as to train clergymen. To fund themselves, they also trained pious students in law and, later still, less pious ones to become gentlemen. Great minds slaved away at great works alongside this job for several hundred years, but college scholarship gradually declined. Some colleges became little more than finishing schools for any 14 to 18-year-old boy whose father could pay. By the early 19th century, standards within the two college clusters which made up the universities of Oxford and Cambridge varied shockingly. Often, the better academics did no teaching. In some colleges bored students fought or vandalized halls to pass the time. Lord Byron arrived at Trinity Cambridge with a live bear and complained: "College improves in everything but learning, nobody here seems to look into an author, ancient or modern, if they can avoid it."

When it became clear that the more academic universities in Germany, Belgium and France had overtaken Oxbridge in reputation, there were calls in Parliament for British standards to be raised. A raft of changes duly followed, but as they were up to individual colleges, they did not produce identical results. Instead, colleges evolved into three distinct types.

At Oxford, Benjamin Jowett created a "nursery of public men" as Master of Balliol. The college picked the most intellectually hardworking students and turned them into civil servants, diplomats, politicians, colonial governors, judges and law lords. Trinity College, Cambridge, a centre of mathematical learning which had produced Isaac Newton, was bitten by the science bug and began funding research and laboratories.

Other college masters emphasized character development through sport. Identifying with the Athenian philosophers, they saw college as a place to watch "our young barbarians at play", which meant having lots of jolly sporty chaps and the odd classics scholar. Training clergymen was now a minority pursuit.

Colleges did not have to account for their choice to the university, because they lived on their own endowments and the fees they charged. Like local councils within a town, they cooperated at times, but more often defended their independence tooth and claw. The subjects a college taught, how it taught them and whom it chose to teach were its own business, and each had its own Royal Charter to prove this. Some Oxbridge colleges taught no-one at all.

An endless series of reforms, sometimes imposed by the Government but more often by the colleges themselves in order to pre-empt greater Government regulation, have narrowed college options. The reward has been Government funding. Public money allows Oxbridge to spend about twice as much per student as other universities because it tops up the funds most colleges have accumulated over the centuries from benefactors and property investments. The result is that Oxbridge students, as well as dons, enjoy a stunning environment. Most study and dine in priceless antique surroundings and relax in beautifully kept gardens closed to the general public. Even first years get their rooms daily cleaned by college servants. One Midlands student told me he felt like a lord at his Cambridge college when told he wasn't even expected to lick his own stamps (porters there frank all students' mail), but this shows a slightly warped view of peers' privileges.

The price of reform has been a degree of standardisation. Today, all colleges must comply with Government teaching standards, equality laws, health and safety rules, etc. Out went poorly qualified, non-publishing academics and in came lots of women students. Ethnic minorities, taken as one group, must also be represented, at least if enough of them can be persuaded to apply. Accommodation too has improved. The damp, medieval student rooms, so cold that older graduates recall sleeping in their coats, have been replaced by spacious, electronically equipped bedsits.

Oxbridge colleges, though, remain a mixed bag when it comes to levels of academic success, atmosphere and social mix. Pupils asked to list their preferred college on the application form therefore need to find out as much as they can before clicking it. They should certainly disregard the advice given by both Oxford and Cambridge that these places are all alike and so students might as well leave the section blank if they're unsure. This hands the choice to the university administration, which may push such applicants towards a less renowned college. Measures are being taken to counter this trend, but a 2004 Oxford study revealed that nearly all self-selected ''open'' applicants were allocated to four of its colleges. The practice has since become less common, though not quite disappeared.

But what can your poor confused daughter, stuck with two parents who stubbornly insisted on earning their living from an early age, do instead? Take her time is the most immediate answer, but below are some methods people use to arrive at the right choice.

ASKING FORMER STUDENTS' ADVICE

If you are considering a college, it is tempting to ask the opinion of someone who went there. For people who don't move in Oxbridge circles, this is often a teacher, the family doctor or a clergyman. Elderly chaps with fond memories of Oxbridge tend to wax lyrically about the special character of their college and its unique features, telling you categorically: "Sidney Sussex is the only place to be. Nowhere else has such a jolly crowd, once threw a chap into the Cam for wearing the wrong bow-tie."

On the other hand, quite a few who went there from disadvantaged backgrounds have very bitter memories of their college as a place of loneliness, braying public school boys and no respect for hard work. I was struck to discover that several of the working class students I interviewed turned out to have a father or uncle who was accepted by Oxbridge, but dropped out because he absolutely hated the place. Forget the fun of the Footlights: there were no Swinging Sixties at Oxbridge and, a generation ago. Some college boys still wore plus fours. The younger students I met almost didn't go because they were put off by such accounts.

In the end, all were extremely glad they had gone. The Oxbridge of the 21st century, a place where women and state school pupils make up over half the undergraduate intake, works even for students who don't know what plus fours are (for those who care: they are knee-length sporting trousers).

Some quaint college customs, like holding the annual May Ball in June, remain unchanged. Some dons still like to say grace in Latin. Some students are still very much richer than others and strangle their vowels. A surprising number know how to jet-sky. All Oxbridge students, though, now wear jeans and communicate by that unique social leveller, the text message.

This is not to say that college life is a vision of perfect harmony. You can still become a hate object, only it will not be for your strong Yorkshire drawl but for pinching other people's chocolate mousse from the fridge. Old men's tales are not a reliable guide to the Oxbridge of today. Its colleges have strong, not always lovable individual traits, but none remains the idle public schooler's haven or the working class student's nightmare of yore. So, you might as well choose your new abode by whichever positive features are most relevant to you.

PICKING BY ACADEMIC REPUTATION

The general fame of a college, often based on the writers, scientists, TV historians or Kremlin spies it has produced, is no reliable guide to what it can offer the undergraduate.

Brilliant minds regularly pack their bags for the stratospheric salaries of Princeton or Yale. Dons become bestseller writers and decamp to the Georgian mansions of Hampstead. And even if they keep living opposite your side of the quad, they will probably be far too eminent to teach greenhorns like you.

Academic reputations certainly need to be date-checked. Trinity College, Cambridge, used to proudly state on its website that it had won more Nobel prizes than France, and a little research will reassuringly tell you that the last time it garnered one of those prizes was in 2017. On the other hand, some colleges still base their reputation on educating a famous philosopher, poet or scientist who has been dead and buried for well over a hundred years.

However, there is a league table of colleges, which tells you at which Oxford or Cambridge college students get the best degrees. The better the degrees, so the theory goes, the better the teaching offered there. Traditionally, the top half makes up a kind of academic college elite, so the respective lists for 2017 are overleaf.

There are problems with relying on these data alone. For a start, the Norrington table, thought up by a 1940s don while in the bath, is largely based on the Firsts which students at an Oxford college obtained, with little weight given to Upper Seconds. The same is true of the Cambridge version, the Tompkins table.

The difference between the top and the 30th ranked colleges can be a mere handful of Firsts here and there, which can radically change the table from year to year. New College, Oxford, for example, shot up straight from 18th place in 2016 to first place in 2017. At Cambridge, King's College, which has one of the highest proportions of state school student at the university, jumped from 14th place to 8th in the same period.

Another problem is that Firsts can also by multiplied by careful student selection. A college which picks nearly all its candidates on the basis of hyper-intensive schooling and obvious intellectual promise, ignoring singing skills and rowing stamina, may find itself higher up on the table, whether or not its teaching is brilliant. Degree subjects can affect the outcome as well. In colleges offering mainly Engineering, a subject that can attract less academic candidates, 35 per cent of graduates may get Lower Seconds or Thirds. Few Oxbridge English or History graduates do.

Still, this gives you some idea. If a college is somewhere in the top half, it will be harder to get in. On the other hand, once admitted, a really bright student should be in her element. So, if you are dreaming of an academic career or want to spend three years in the presence of truly brilliant and influential minds, this is what you should go for - at least in the humanities. Aiming low can feel less risky, especially when you're young. However, you should know that this does not always make it wise.

COLLEGE TABLES

Cambridge 2017   _Oxford 2017_

Cambridge 2017	Oxford 2017
1. Trinity	1. New
2. Christ's	2. Merton
3. St. John's	3. Pembroke
4. Pembroke	4. Worcester
5. Churchill	5. Queen's
6. Emmanuel	6. St. John's
7. Queens'	7. Brasenose
8. King's	8. University
9. Selwyn	9. Trinity
10. Peterhouse	10. Balliol
11. Gonville & Caius	11. Magdalen
12. Corpus Christ	12. Keble
13. Clare	13. Wadham
14. Jesus	14. Mansfield
15. Trinity Hall	15. Corpus Christi
16. Magdalene	16. Lady Margaret Hall
17. Sidney Sussex	17. Christ Church
18. Lucy Cavendish	18. Jesus
19. St. Catherine's	19. St. Anne's
20. Downing	20. St. Hugh's
21. Fitzwilliam	21. Oriel
22. St. Edmund's	22. Somerville
23. Newnham	23. St. Edmund Hall
24. Girton	24. Hertford
25. Robinson	25. Exeter
26. Hughes Hall	26. St. Catherine's
27. Wolfson	27. Harris Manchester
28. Homerton	28. St. Peter's
29. Murray Edwards	29. St. Hilda's
	30. Lincoln

Changes have also been made. In 2009, Oxford introduced a new admissions scheme designed to make applicants' success less dependent on college choice. Promising candidates may be interviewed at two colleges, or re-directed to a more suitable college. Most Cambridge applicants are still only seen at the college of their choice but might attend several interviews there, conducted by different dons. However, these somewhat complex arrangements have not visibly improved the odds, so students (or teachers) should try and pin-point the most suitable college.

College choice is slightly less crucial in the sciences. The 20th century growth in scientific knowledge forced Oxbridge to centralise. Many science students now treat their college as what one professor I spoke to called "a bed and breakfast establishment." Rather than sitting all day hunched over a little Bunsen burner in their college, they will work in one of the new physics or chemistry laboratories built with millions of pounds of taxpayers' money. These faculty labs are shared by students from the entire university. Much of the students' progress is assessed by staff working there, although tutorials will still be held in their own college.

So, if your chemistry-mad son ends up at Cambridge, but not at Trinity, his college of choice, do tell him to cheer up: it does not mean he won't make professor, invent a new wonder drug and/or win the Nobel Prize.

PICKING BY STUDENT TYPE

Pupils unsure whether Oxbridge can really want someone like them often try their luck at the colleges with the highest state school intake. These can be easily pinpointed by looking at the university website's statistics page and are, consequently, engulfed by such applicants. As a result, many have to be turned away.

If your articulate, well qualified daughter really wants to get into Oxford or Cambridge, she might, in the current political climate, be wiser to look elsewhere. It is the colleges with the more conservative entrance policies which are being leaned on to change, so let her target them. One of those castigated for always picking candidates who happen to be fourth generation Oxbridge might love to snap her up. The college will, of course, be doing so because it values her intellectual gifts, but accepting her will also save it from having its knuckles rapped by a nervous university administration.

But how do you find out which college is on the prowl for students like your girl? The answer is that there are two ways. One is by sussing out who might be particularly keen to change their intake. Every so often, a news story appears about a college criticized for having too few ordinary state school pupils and this sometimes is followed by a wider recruitment drive. This does not mean that you need to scan the education press for Oxbridge stories each day. Colleges keen to change their intake proportions tend to be extremely pro-active. If a college keeps adding to the Access initiatives listed on its website, bombards your daughter's inner city school with emails and welcomes the girl on her Access visit like a long lost friend, it is what dating agencies call "ready to commit."

In practice, this means it intends to take perhaps half a dozen pupils like her, so it might be worth getting an application in, even if the bright girl is not quite sure yet of getting the expected A*AA.

Another way to check for promising colleges is the traditional "minor public school house master's route" to Oxbridge: if a college is small, poorish, far from the town centre and low down on the relevant league table, tell your ambitious boy to make a beeline for it.

The natural prey of such a college is the rural private school chap who rows, has been in the cadet corps and plays the bagpipes. As a result, it will have far fewer really bright candidates than the rest. Relegation to the bottom of the league constantly threatens this college, and in these days of "Widening Access" even applicants from bog-standard comprehensives are welcome if their presence can avert this fate. They no longer need to be male or middle class, but it helps if they are smart all-rounders with a good singing voice.

Another default choice are the four original women's colleges. Low down in the academic league tables because they are relatively poor and few of their dons are quite eminent enough to set university exams, they don't lightly turn away a good applicant.

While Newnham and Murray Edwards (a college previously called New Hall) remain single sex, Somerville and St. Hilda's in Oxford would welcome more really bright males. Before you opt for such a college, though, read the chapter on Oxbridge women.

A final option that should not be dismissed out of hand are Oxford's Permanent Private Halls, originally established and run by religious groups.

Housed in attractive buildings, some of these de facto colleges teach only Theology, but Regent's Park, which is mixed, also offers a number of well-taught secular courses, including PPE. So does St. Benet's Hall, which was all male for its first hundred years, but started to admit women in 2015. Their students need not share the college faith and some dons take a special interest in disadvantaged students. Regent's Park, which was founded by Baptists, works closely with black pupils attending inner city schools, so as to increase their Oxbridge presence.

Applying to such a place also gives you a unique advantage: while students may generally pick only one college, a PPH may be listed as a second choice, thereby doubling your admission prospects.

BUT WILL SHE BE HAPPY THERE?

Some colleges can be hell for some students. Many a young Oxbridge feminist has been furious to discover that her lovely college gardens are infested by rugby players barking sexist ditties and trying to bear hug every passing girl. A quiet, non-drinking male student will loathe to share his JCR with teams of drunken rowers listening to what one such wretch described to me as horrible Welsh Indie Rock. If you want to avoid these experiences, don't pick Oriel College, Oxford or Peterhouse, Cambridge. These are the favourite haunts of sporty boys from small public schools.

If, on the other hand, you combine academic interests with a real talent for a major college sport, you'll find a warm welcome in such a place. Don't worry about your background; a winning rugby team knows no class distinction.

This is not to say that you will feel the same way. Your rugby mates may, after all, be far from bookish and only got in because their school coached them to the hilt. Even in this day and age, a well taught "young barbarian" can still melt the heart of a sporty admissions tutor. So, while your college mates will be half-heartedly aiming for a third in some undemanding subject, you might be trying to pick up top professional skills and a good degree in between games. This kind of mismatch has spoilt the university experience of quite a few male working class students. Female ones tend to cope. Perhaps girls just get on with life.

Some colleges look scarily grand, but don't assume that you'll feel lost there. Wadham, whose classically decorated Oxford buildings date from the early 17th century, today has a student body which is very largely state school. It also each year admits a substantial number of foreign students. Blissfully ignorant of the British class system and its linguistic quirks, this group neatly bridges the social gap. Queen's College, Oxford, a soaring 18th century structure, is known as a very friendly place. It has close ties with northern schools. Students often come from Cumberland, Westmorland or Yorkshire – great if you are still unsure about Southerners.

At Cambridge, Fitzwilliam has both a considerable student intake from the North East and a large international student community. Downing has links with state schools in Cornwall, Devon and Dorset and a well above average intake of state school students.

What is most striking, though, is that most Oxbridge students, whatever their background, display a remarkable affection for their own college. As long as the place actually has a strong state school presence, even people from non-university backgrounds tend to cosily settle in. Fears about being among all those terribly posh kids often fade as soon as students meet. Very few privately educated students have parents who are aristocrats or millionaires.

So, don't be automatically put off by a college's reputation as popular with public school cricketers or piano-playing southern girls. There will probably be some such students about, but chances are they will be perfectly nice, and outnumbered too.

Having said this, a good social life in your college is undoubtedly harder to build if you are black or from a solidly working class background. Breaking into a group of students who may have known one another from age six (which can be true of comprehensive school girls from smart urban areas, as well as for public school boys) sometimes does feel like mission impossible. And you'll be more tempted to give up, convinced you are being snubbed, if you're the only girl from Moss Side or an Afro-Caribbean boy from Liverpool.

More often than not, such fears are unjustified. These people are just used to hanging out together. They also tend to study different subjects and so will gradually grow apart. By the end of the first year, students have far more in common with those struggling through the same enormous reading lists than with their bosom pal from nursery. Their best friend now will be the person they share their tutorials, seminars or college microwave with. Others bond over drama, student politics, football or darts - though if you're really shy, getting past the bonding process can feel like a long wait.

HOW TO BE HAPPY

Happiness at Oxbridge is often a function of understanding what you are meant to be doing there. The answer is certainly not just "get a degree". Instead, dons vaguely mumble about wishing you to explore both different ideas and activities in the company of your peers.

Foreigners are sometimes best at translating such waffle. In his wonderful account of how he made his way from a Burmese guerilla camp to to the calm world of Trinity College, Cambridge, Pascal Khoo Thwe says that being there was not simply about competing; nor was it just a means to an end:

> "It was a place where you were given the gift of an "interval", a time of leisure, where you did not have to make up your minds about your beliefs, and learned as much from conversation as from lectures and books.
> Reprinted by permission of HarperCollins Publishers Ltd. from *The Land of Green Ghosts* by Pascal Khoo Thwe (© 2003)

Annie, a giggly Danish friend who came to stay with me after a placement year at a terribly famous Oxford college, put the same thing more simply: "They have all these funny clubs and societies where students meet. At first I couldn't understand why, but then I thought it's a bit like Legoland: you're meant to play with all the little houses, not just to swot. The university put them there as a kind of practice for grown life, I think."

So, try and persevere in finding new playmates. Beth, a nurse's daughter from Northern Ireland, recalls that she walked into Fresher's Week at Hertford College, Oxford, shaking with nerves, but forced herself to think: "Excellent, here's 115 potential new friends."

It worked for her, but if your college is really useless at supplying friends, remember that there is always the university. Just treat the college like a plush but rather boring hotel and join the university's Student Union, Mountaineering Club or Manga Society. Take up kick-boxing, jazz-dancing or skydiving. Talk to people in your faculty lab, offer to write for a university mag, volunteer for charity work or political campaigns. There are over 10,000 people roughly your age and ability in the place. Surely, you are not so unique that you have nothing in common with any of them?

This is not to deny that college life does stink for some. I have spent many hours over the years listening to former students who have been utterly miserable. Until the mid 1980s, this was almost entirely a matter of class: the tone at Oxbridge was set by a wealthy, privately educated majority of students and those without their kind of manners or money had to be quite assertive to survive. Also, quite a few of the older college dons were horrible snobs or misogynists.

But we're talking about your parents' or even grandparents' generation. If an Oxbridge student is constantly unhappy now, there may be other factors. Often, these are personal, and it is worth knowing that student counselling and health care are pretty good. Both Oxford and Cambridge have come to accept that students can be badly thrown by events happening elsewhere: it is hard to settle into college life when you've learnt that your best friend is now sharing a hammock with your former lover in Goa, the family dog has fallen ill or your father has left home to have the op and become a lap dancer.

Alternatively, a student may just be doing the wrong thing. One exceptionally bright working class student tracked by Professor Freeman in a study of gifted children had been used to being always top of her class. Finding herself surrounded by people who were at least equally smart, her response was to rush back to her books. Rather than enjoy the company of her intellectual peers, she tried to out-work them until she collapsed with exhaustion.

Depression can also be the result of a student not acknowledging that she really needs more cash. Which brings us to yet another way of choosing a college.

PICKING FOR FINANCIAL SURVIVAL

As said before, no student has to leave Oxbridge due to poverty, but survival may now require a more complex strategy. Since the replacement of the Government annual maintenance grants by maintenance loans, designed to help students pay for food, rent and library fines, some financial planning is essential. This primarily means having a monthly budget and regularly checking your bank statements to see how close you are to exceeding it. The university's student union will have lots of helpful saving advice. What's most crucial is to engage with money issues well before you run out.

This is not to say that if you worry about future debt, you must live on discarded bread crusts. A student who has been smart enough to learn how to cook as advised, can now put his skills to good use. College food is not wildly expensive but costs do mount up, so pick a college with a proper student kitchen.

College rents vary considerably, as said before, and do need checking out. Many colleges are now charging £600 upwards a month, depending on the facilities. This is much the same you would be paying at any top urban university, but Oxbridge terms are considerably shorter, which does save you money. In any case, your Government maintenance loan will cover your rent.

You could also get more money coming in by taking a college job. There are quite rare and so you should find out whether a college which appeals to you currently offers them or if the university does. Oxbridge used to ban students from taking jobs in town, but has rather backed down on this now the fees are so high.

Above all, keep a beady eye on your financial affairs, as not only have Oxbridge fees gone up, but so has the interest charged by the now privatised Student Loan Company. And while some banks offer students large, interest-free overdrafts, remember these will have to be repaid after graduation. So, check your bank balance regularly. While Oxford and Cambridge grants remain high, they may also be outpaced by rising prices.

What may save your bacon (or veggie stew) is a college grant, bursary or scholarship. Traditionally, small sums of money (between

£50 and £500) are available to students for books, essay projects, travel or financial emergencies. Aware that the new Oxbridge fees make the universities seem scarily expensive, many colleges are busily fund-raising, so they can to dole out much larger sums. Meanwhile, though, they will be dispensing funds at the old rate, which varies from college to college. Richer, older colleges can be far more generous, and this may affect how well you do academically.

A student needing to improve her French language skills because she is studying the subject, but has never been abroad, will have no trouble securing a travel grant from one of the older colleges. These may also offer substantial bursaries for book purchases. Rents at such a college may be kept low by subsidies and students will usually be able to live in for three years, rather than move into more expensive private housing for part of their course.

In addition, there are many other types of bursaries, often funded by grateful former students. Some are essentially a cash prize for a good essay on a specific topic dear to the donor's heart. Others are designed to fund small-scale research projects.

When it comes to helping needy students, both universities have some central funds, but undergraduates are expected to seek help from their college first. What you should know here is that the older the college, the wealthier it is likely to be and the more generous its help. In 2014 Oxford's student paper, *The Cherwell*, reported that the average hardship grant for students in financial straits was now between £250 and £500 at Jesus, but £1,697 at St. John's. If many students at a college are well off, moreover, there is little competition for such grants.

College wealth is usually derived from outside property: according to Oxford lore, St. John's used to own so much land in the 1930s that people claimed you could walk from Oxford to Cambridge without ever leaving college property. It's almost equally generous neighbour, Christ Church, earns a whopping £4.5m. a year from investments alone. (In case you are interested, the Cambridge equivalents of these two rich colleges are Gonville & Caius and Corpus Christi.)

There is, of course, another and even more crucial consequence of a college's wealth: it will be able to attract the best, and therefore most highly paid academics - albeit sometimes in exchange for a promise that they won't have to teach beginners. Its libraries too will be better stocked and they may have a smaller students per tutor ratio. Wealth and academic glory quite often go hand in hand, at least within Oxbridge.

PICKING BY SYMPATHY

Are you a thoughtful, confident talker from an academically oriented, high achieving, well resourced school? Did you gain top marks in all your exams so far, and are your teachers predicting the same for your A2s? Have you won the Maths Olympiad or recently published a book? If even one of the above student profiles fits you like a glove, you stand an equally good chance at any Oxbridge college.

Most Oxbridge candidates, of course, have more modest achievements and many get in nevertheless. The trick is to target the right kind of college.

Students from ordinary comprehensives, especially, may want to do a bit of research first. What you need to know is that dons at some of the most ancient, academically highly ranked and visually stunning colleges (think Trinity, Cambridge, or Magdalen, Oxford) ask the most difficult interview questions.

This is because a college that combines all three of these qualities can hand-pick its students from an infinite supply of applicants. It will still have a state school intake of fifty-something per cent, but a high proportion will come from Britain's very few grammar schools. Others will be the offspring of thinkers or academics, educated at a tiny clutch of top comprehensives. College dons can be quite a cohesive group, seeking similar academic standards and traits.

Certainly, some "three star" colleges prefer candidates already used to verbally juggling a large and varied body of knowledge. Even if their interviewers "move students out of their comfort zone" by asking questions outside their field, years of intellectual juggling do confer some advantage. Let's say you are a brilliant but less intensively taught candidate from an inner city school: being asked to discuss a totally unfamiliar subject may feel pretty scary. You've left your comfort zone by merely walk through a late medieval gate.

Fortunately, attitudes vary even among the most seductive colleges. According to *The Cambridge Reporter* of April 2009, comprehensive school applicants to Cambridge made up 76 per cent of UK students admitted at King's and 73 per cent at Sidney Sussex. Both of these are very old, brainy and fancy places. Meanwhile, down the road, the proportion of UK state school applicants admitted was just 45 per cent at St. John's and of 48 per cent at Clare.

While the average state school intake across Oxbridge colleges has now risen above 60 per cent, similar gaps continue to exist: state school applicants to Cambridge made up 77 per cent of the 2017 college intake at Churchill and Trinity Hall and 72 per cent at St.

Catharine's. St. John's and Robinson had the university's lowest proportion, 49 per cent. Gonville and Caius had 52 per cent.

At Oxford, state school applicants in 2017 made up the highest proportion of UK students at Mansfield, a massive 89 per cent. The next highest, 68 per cent, was found at Wadham and Hertford. The Oxford college with the lowest state school proportion was Trinity (not to be confused with the more famous one at Cambridge) with 41 per cent. Next up was Magdalen with 47 per cent, followed by Exeter, Keble and St. Peter's with 49 per cent.

It would be nice, of course, if Oxbridge found a good way of evening out these numbers, so college choice was less of a factor in student success, but the above list will help you decide. What you must not do, if you are determined to get in, is to instead just pick a college from the bottom of the academic league tables. Pupils from state schools often underestimate their abilities, and there are comprehensive-friendly dons even at the grandest colleges.

However, if you'd like to improve your odds, it may be best to focus on a college that is not super-famous or one that has already shown its sympathy for people like you by its intake proportions.

PICKING FOR POWER

While Oxford and Cambridge like to present themselves, at least to the general public, as purely scholastic institutions, they are also something quite different. Politicians, industrialists and journalists will regularly make the weekend pilgrimage to their old college, rather like a medieval lord would visit his fiefdom's learned abbot or a 19th century Jewish industrialist his wise old rabbi.

This is not merely a sentimental journey. While sipping port from cut-glass goblets in a college's panelled dining room, the Oxbridge men - and a few women - who run the country will discuss public affairs, form alliances and take crucial decisions. They will also graciously mix with a few promising undergraduates brought by their tutors. This (to the justified fury of non-Oxbridge graduates) is where to pick up news of top jobs coming up, of Government reshuffles and of business plans that may shake the finances of ordinary people.

But which colleges hold the power key? The answer used to be that there were two: Peterhouse, Cambridge, which produced much of Margaret Thatcher's various Cabinets, plus Magdalen, Oxford, the intellectual cradle of most Prime Ministers. To this had to be added All Souls, a postgraduate college which raised editors for *The Times*.

Times aren't vastly changing. Prime Minister Theresa May was educated at St. Hugh's, Oxford and her first (2018) Cabinet, is 48 per cent Oxbridge. Of its Oxford graduates, Boris Johnson went to Balliol, Jeremy Hunt to Magdalen, Philip Hammond to University, Michael Gove to Lady Margaret Hall, David Gauke to St. Edmund Hall, Damian Hinds to Trinity, Matt Hancock to Exeter and Claire Perry to Brasenose. Of Cambridge-educated Ministers, Baroness Evans went to New Hall, Chris Grayling and David Lidington to Sidney Sussex and Greg Clark to Magdalene.

Labour's current Shadow Cabinet, meanwhile, is relatively low on Oxbridge graduates, even in terms of the party's own history, Party leader Jeremy Corbyn attended Middlesex Polytechnic (now Middlesex University), but of Cambridge-educated Ministers, Home Secretary Diane Abbott went to Newnham, Richard Burgon to St. John's and John Healey to Christ's. Nia Griffith went to Somerville, Oxford.

PICKING FOR BEAUTY

Budding aesthetes in flowing silk scarves will have no problem picking their perfect college: it has to be St. John's, Cambridge, with its Bridge of Sighs spanning the river Cam, or Christ Church, Oxford, with its Tom Tower, Christopher Wren's masterpiece. While other colleges spoilt their appearance by adding nasty modern fripperies such as labs and snack bars, both remain pure examples of Britain's Classical architecture. There can be no more perfect backdrop for the photo the aesthetes plan to email to their world-wide chat-group on English life.

On the other hand, one young fashonista I know confidently opted for Churchill, Cambridge, with its streamlined 1960s architecture. Setting it apart from the rest of the university, its style underlines the fact that the college is also innovative in other ways. For a start, its Senior Tutor, Richard Partington, was educated at a comprehensive. The college buildings are defiantly modernist, with clear, broad windows that let in the sunshine. Even better, these windows close rather more snugly that the small medieval ones nearby, thus keeping you warm in the long Cambridge winter.

7

Accessing Oxbridge

What can make a student decide against applying to Oxford or Cambridge at the last moment, sometimes even after he has found a course he really likes, is not what he knows about these places, but what he thinks he does.

One survey found that many comprehensive school pupils put the proportion of Oxbridge undergraduates from state schools at below 10 per cent. Actually, it has been above 50 per cent for over a decade and is slowly rising further. In 2017, state schoolers, for the first time ever, made up 64 per cent of UK students admitted at both Cambridge and Oxford.

Others have heard strange and deeply off-putting rumours. One boy proudly told his father's boss of his university plans, only to be told "Cambridge? Well, it wouldn't have been my thing. Do they make you wear them jackets with the long tails only in class or do you have to wear them to the shops as well?" (For the record, Oxbridge students wear jeans during the day, and dark suits or two-piece outfits to formal occasions. It is Eton pupils who pre-pay for a lifetime of privilege by wearing the naff tailcoats at school.)

Schools deal with Oxbridge during careers advice, but this can mean anything. The sixth form head may well give your son a detailed pep talk, based on his own Oxbridge years or on a teacher Oxbridge workshop he attended. Such a talk will help a pupil understand what is special about studying there, as well as cover entry requirements, courses and the tutorial system. At best, it will also address the most common fears: "Can I afford it?" and "Is it for people like me?"

More likely, though, your son will have the following experience:

Teacher (slightly rushed as she has to explain university choice to ninety first-generation higher education applicants before tea):

"Hi John, I see you've had excellent GCSEs and your A-level prediction are impressively high too. Have you considered Oxbridge?"

Pupil: "No, not really."

Teacher (brightly): "Well, you might want to. Anyway, let me know what you decide. You might also find a leaflet on the sixth form notice board, unless someone has taken it down. I'll check the deadline for Oxbridge applications on the website, if you're keen."

Pupil: (keen to end this obvious waste of time): "Sure."

The above conversation, reported to me by quite a few people, is the end of many a promising Oxbridge career. How, though, can your son, who has never given a moment's thought to Oxbridge or, worse, tried to find it on the map, work out whether he wants to spend three of the most important years of his life there? One obvious answer seems to lie in a family visit.

WHAT NOT TO DO (ON A SUNDAY)

Having seen the odd colour snap of your son's potential university, you may think that it is enough to let the place speak for itself. Just set aside a Sunday afternoon, check out the train time table or pile into the car. Surely, walking through a pretty town like Cambridge or Oxford will help the boy make up his mind?

I once tried this myself, with my goddaughter. A 17-year-old with a couple of tatoos and a prediction of top A-levels, she needed only a bribe of double pocket money before agreeing to tag along. While her mother and I then gushed over every gothic building and ornate bridge before settling down to a traditional cream tea in a wood-panelled shop, she sulked on an iron bench outside one of Oxford's most famous colleges. It was raining and, as this was exam time, strangers were banned from entering colleges or libraries, even for a quick glimpse.

On the drive back, the girl summed up her views: Oxford was boring and old, as well as weird, three of the worst traits in her value chart. She put Sussex at the very top of her UCAS list as soon as she had walked through her parent's front door.

A disaster? Not quite. She had some regrets in her student days, feeling she would have been more challenged at Oxford, but ended up with a first in Physics and is now a high-flying financial journalist. Her best friend, who did choose Oxford, has yet to settle into the perfect job. Best not to get too worked up about university choice.

How else can you help your son or daughter to make up their mind? Luckily, you don't need to. There is a glut of publicly funded projects designed to do just that.

ACCESS, OUTREACH AND ALL THEIR FRIENDS AND RELATIONS

Public concern that too many students still come from the same class background has generated a veritable supermarket of Widening

Access initiatives. Most of the Oxbridge-linked ones have traditionally been funded directly by the government and England's Higher Education Funding Council (HEFCE). Between 2000 and 2003 alone they spent around £2.4 million a year on three projects called 'Widening Participation', 'Summer Schools' and 'Aspirations' (the last one killed off in 2010 by the incoming government). Oxbridge also drew applicants from projects seeking to promote higher education among inner city pupils, funded by the Department to the tune of £63 million per year. By 2013, Oxbridge spending on Access was over 8m. a year.

The result has been a myriad of university projects under ever-changing names. Most, but not all, of Cambridge Access activities are now run under the Widening Participation label. Part of Oxford Access has become Outreach. Excellence in Cities, which used to run an Oxbridge link-up, was renamed Excellence Hub by Aimhigher, a body itself wound up in 2011.

These initiatives which, for simplicity's sake, I shall call Access, are aimed at a wide range of targets, from to FE students to children in care and from mature students to ethnic minority pupils. They are also run by a variety of bodies. Admissions departments, university faculties, colleges and student unions have projects of their own, aimed at encouraging specific groups of potential students. Education trusts run separate schemes.

Some of the most imaginative Oxbridge projects are student-led, and the enthusiasm which these young men and women exhibit for their university is so great it makes you think of those bright-eyed moppets in Disneyland ads. Many talk with almost touching gratitude about the life and opportunities given to them.

So, how does your teenager find out whether she, too, might want to try for Disneyland?

The answer is that he can do so in a dozen ways and, even better, without cramping her style. Initially, the idea was that teachers would suggest Oxbridge schemes to suitable pupils. However, finding that many overstretched schools did not respond, Oxbridge has started to encourage individual pupils to book themselves in by a fairly simple process.

Some, but not all events are listed in the online prospectus. Students interested in what Cambridge university has on offer will find most details on its *Target Schools, Open Days*, *Student Conferences, Access* or *Events* web pages. Oxford's main Access projects can be tracked down in the same way. Some colleges at both places also run their own events, listed on their own websites.

University departments are another source. If you're a student interested in a particular course, say Law, going to the Cambridge Law faculty web page will lead you to discover that it holds an annual "Student Law Conference" in which sixth formers can explore the subject. Oxford may even be sending a Law lecturer to give talks to prospective students in your town. Oxford and Cambridge also run a joint " Student Medicine Conference" for prospective subject applicants. Below you'll find a selection of what else is on offer.

A TASTE OF OXFORD

Oxford has for a number of years run over 100 Open Day events, targeted at different groups and aimed at dispelling different anxieties. Many involve students chatting to visiting school kids about university life in terms of workload, social life and general atmosphere. Oxford also organises information events in towns which have traditionally sent very few students.

Students can attend Oxford Open Days on their own or as a group, and the event may include a workshop on the admissions process for teachers. There are college open days, and spring taster days introduce sixth formers to life in an academic environment. In addition, many colleges run a school visiting scheme in which Oxford students from state schools talk about their Oxford experience.

The assumption behind most of this is that state school students don't apply in large enough numbers because they feel shy. The events are designed to break down myths and stereotypes about the university being a posh place and replacing them with a vision of Oxford as a world in which students from all backgrounds enjoy life in a "work hard and play hard" sort of way.

In this spirit, questions on Open Days are often taken by a working class student. If you ever wondered what it's like for a girl from a mining town to share a tutorial with someone who misses her horse, here you will find out: apparently, it is absolutely fine, because she might well share your enthusiasm for philosophy and Garage. And if she doesn't there are, literally, thousands of other people to make friends with. Most Oxbridge students, like the horse lover and you, will have gone to state schools. (Surprised? Given the current level of school fees, few parents can afford to buy their privately-educated daughter a horse.)

Oxford staff unhappy about the weak knowledge base of many state school applicants are also coming round to the idea that some actual teaching may be needed. This has led the university to introduce subject-specific Study Days, often geared towards young people from non-university backgrounds, as well as Departmental Open Days which include a lecture. Some colleges offer e-mentoring to prospective applicants. Others post online lectures and broadcast academic debates on course subjects.

What isn't on offer is any explicit help in preparing for the Oxbridge interview but, even so, most are useful projects because they are open to all. Although its student organisers advertise events by writing to all schools and FE colleges in February, no teacher involvement is usually required. Pupils whose school has not organised a visit for them can book themselves in directly, but should check the registration deadlines on the Oxford open days website.

A GLIMPSE OF CAMBRIDGE

Cambridge admissions staff and student groups run projects similar to those at Oxford. There are college Open Days and subject-geared Open Days. "Subject matters" sessions offer guidance on A-level choice, and at Student Conferences staff dispense advice and encouragement. Some events are specifically aimed at care leavers or students attending FE colleges, rather than comprehensives, academies, grammars or private schools.

With the help of student volunteers, the university also runs initiatives that bring disadvantaged pupils to Cambridge, so as to raise aspirations. Visitors can explore unfamiliar university subjects such as Philosophy or Engineering and are offered information about the application process. There's also a special Taster Day for black, Asian and other minority ethnic applicants.

More recently, each individual Cambridge college has been linked to a specific area within the UK. College staff hold local events and invite students and teachers to visit. Pupils are still free to contact other colleges, but the idea is to create helpful contacts. To find out which college is linked to your home region, just go to http://www.cam.ac.uk/admissions/undergraduate/arealinks/index.html

Cambridge family events in inner city neighbourhoods aim to convince pupils that the university welcomes applicants of all sorts and offers them a useful education. Some information about course contents may be included and there is usually time for questions and answers.

Each spring, Cambridge also offers very helpful Master-classes in a small number of degree subjects to sixth formers. As these cover the most popular courses, you need to book well in advance.

While most events don't include a full-scale lecture, pupils are offered some academic experiences. Some build on the knowledge gained from the university's excellent learning sites, now covering, amongst others, English, Science and Classics. Others are based on a more innovative approach: some colleges now run events linked to popular books or films. One taster lecture at Magdalene College, Cambridge, was on "Angels, Demons and Ghosts in the Middle Ages".

For what's on offer each year, check out the "Open Days and Events" web page in the university's online prospectus.

SUMMER SCHOOLS

The Oxford or Cambridge summer schools are the nearest thing to doing a real Oxbridge course. You even get to stay in a real student room in a college. Most courses are designed for state school students in Year 12 with lots of top GCSE grades. However, admissions tutors have started to admit that Oxbridge preparation needs to start much earlier, which has resulted in the creation of academic summer events for Year 11s, Year 10s and even Year 9s.

Some students use the residential week to explore non-school subjects like Egyptology or Medicine, others to find out more about a field they enjoyed at school. Workshop talks are carefully tailored to this age group and interspersed with fun activities. These much praised events, based around talks by Oxbridge academics, are completely free: funding bodies cover all travel to and from the venue, food and accommodation, even trips and activities. Just note that students trying to book a summer school place must act fast: registration annually opens around January 10th and places go like hot cakes.

As the STEP entry test to the world-famous Cambridge Maths course depends on very strong subject skills, students also need to know that that while its STEP PREP Summer School has been dropped, the university is now running a free, online STEP support programme. Details can be found at https://maths.org/step/.

In addition, both Cambridge and Oxford host residential events for mature students, minority ethnic groups and young people in care. These again offer an experience of the academic world, but also include sessions about costs, degree subjects, college societies and career prospects. The scheme is restricted to specially chosen schools to ensure that mainly disadvantaged pupils benefit.

Short stays offer students valuable insights into the most avidly fought-over course subjects. Law and Medicine conferences allow sixth formers to find out not just what such a course would involve, but also what qualities and skills a department seeks.

COLLEGE INITIATIVES

A growing number of Access initiatives by Oxford and Cambridge are based on the *Target Schools* approach of sending their students into deprived areas, mainly "to bust myths" through class presentations. St. Johns' College, Cambridge, has a scheme in Lambeth and Clare College in Tower Hamlets, while Sidney Sussex and Fitzwilliam are active in Greater Manchester and the North West.

For several years, Churchill College, Cambridge, has also run engineering and maths workshops, an initiative funded by businessman Sir Peter Gershon. If some millionaire stars of the financial world wonder how to regain public sympathy, they could always follow his example.

Some college initiatives are based on a more defensive, scatter-gun approach. When Brasenose, one of the richest colleges in Oxford, was publicly criticised in 2003 because its state school intake was (just) below half, its Warden responded in *The Guardian* by revealing that it was now involved in no fewer than fifty-one individual events, all aimed at recruiting more state school pupils.

So, if your son likes the sound of an Oxbridge college, one way forward is for him to check out its website for a suitable event there. Chances are that there is more than one and that someone is actually being paid to make him feel welcome.

Both Oxford and Cambridge students also run "Shadowing Schemes" in which interested pupils can follow an undergraduate around for a couple of days. The visitors get to sit in on a lecture or tutorial, as well as visit a student pub, in order to find out how that mysterious creature really lives.

This approach can be immensely reassuring. Apart from proving to the young visitor that many of the turreted buildings contain not just libraries and labs but also state-of-the-art bars, cinemas and snooker halls, talking to a student guide can allay deeper anxieties. The guide may reveal that even Cambridge has a branch of HMV, point out those local businesses which give skint undergraduates part-time jobs and, by his very normality, suggest that most Oxbridge students are neither geniuses nor geeks. To become a Cambridge shadow, check out the contact list at the end of this book.

Teachers sometimes have to push their pupils hard before they will set foot on Oxbridge soil but it's worth doing. To be gently introduced to a new subject by a brilliant thinker in their field can be a life-changing experience, even if the student does not end up at Cambridge or Oxford.

TEACHER EVENTS

Oxbridge dons used to complain about the lack of enthusiasm some state school teachers were said to display towards both universities but, in a more positive spirit, these have now devised a number of events especially for this group. There are regional teacher conferences, teacher briefing sessions and even a teachers' summer school, run by the Sutton Trust. Participants have praised these events as highly stimulating, but add that there is a problem: while they may well be given the best of advice, they can't implement much of it, given the awful work pressure faced by staff at their kind of schools.

PROMISING NEW OXBRIDGE PROJECTS

Determined to cast its net ever wider and counter past criticism of its student choice, Oxbridge is steadily putting more new-type Access projects onstream. Bright student to whose peer group Oxbridge holds no more interest than Buckingham Palace may want to take a close look at those.

Cambridge, to give some examples, has increased its science workshops, adding several for pupils from under-represented groups, the university has also been offering prizes in the form of Amazon vouchers to high-achieving GCSE students. There are plans for 3,000 new after-school events, focused on school subjects valued by dons. The university has also just launched its first residential Science Masterclass. Hosted by Pembridge College in the Easter holidays, it is designed for girls in Year 11. Organisers hope to attract young people from low income families, living in low-participation neighbourhoods or attending weak schools.

Oxford has been trying to increase its intake of BME (black-minority-ethnic) students through the first-ever residential programme devised for this group. It includes accommodation, mock interviews and tutorials. The university has also held two Access Conferences designed to show students from Pakistani and Bangladeshi families how to prepare for an Oxbridge application. A similar annual event is now held for BME pupils and their families.

In addition, Oxford's Lady Margaret Hall (a college, not a person) had in 2016 launched the university's first-ever Foundation Year. What this involved to was admitting a dozen highly able young people from under-represented groups who had been prevented by poverty or personal misfortune from achieving their full potential for a cost-free residential study year. The idea was to turn them into strong Oxbridge candidates through an intensive study year, and it worked: nearly all subsequently won places at other Oxbridge colleges, and the rest got into top universities elsewhere. The LMH Foundation Year is now a permanent feature and may yet be copied by other colleges. Underachievement, it has shown, can be overcome with targeted help.

As the college head, former Guardian editor Alan Rusbridger, explains: "We started a foundation year at LMH because we want to attract the brightest and best students regardless of any obstacles that may have been placed in their way."

The LMH scheme has already inspired another, shorter one by New College, Oxford, called *The Opportunity Programme*. Designed to expand the number of the university's students from under-represented groups, including care leavers, it will admit ten young people coming from both a lower-performing school and an area of relative socio-economic deprivation who are also predicted to achieve the standard conditional offer (usually AAA). The one-month summer scheme is geared towards preparing them for their chosen course.

WHAT SHOULD YOU FOCUS ON?

While the visual perfection of Oxbridge puts some people off, sixth form aesthetes have been known to spend hours of their visit traipsing from college to college, comparing wisteria-clad porticoes. This is good, clean fun, but remember that you have come up for the grittier business of sorting out your course. Also, you may be allocated a college other than the one picked. So, focus on events indoors.

At any university or college event there will be someone who can add to your knowledge base. If you have settled on a course, ask about books that will move you on. A tutor may have favourites not on the reading list. Is there a journal, website or feature article on your special interest? Which museum or excavation site might be worth a holiday visit?

Scouring the course website at home may also have generated personal concerns: will the course allow you to explore subject areas which interest you but were not mentioned online? Are there related ones? If the course doesn't sound quite right for you, which course might possibly suit you better? Oxbridge students can be as informative on this as dons.

Having said this, don't be too rigid about course contents. The syllabus listed may well be more inspiring (or more appealing to employers) than what you had in mind. Moreover, you can often pursue a personal interest alongside your course. One Land Economy student fascinated by economic developments in the Arab world (a topic not covered by his course), obtained reading suggestions from a college don teaching Middle Eastern studies. He also took a course in

Arabic at the college language lab. It was not just top standard, but totally free, and he went on to a career in his chosen region.

Lastly, don't even think of asking whether you will have your own shower at a college. For the record, the worst-case-scenario is one for every three students. People cope - this really isn't what Oxbridge is about.

DOES ACCESS WORK?

The honest answer is: some of it does. Projects involving a visit to Oxford or Cambridge are definitely worth doing. This is because they enable hundreds of pupils each year to spend time in a different, rather pleasant world at someone else's expense. They also introduce many of them to brain-tingling new fields.

This does not mean that Access is the answer to every bright sixth former's prayer. A student overwhelmed by the range of events on offer needs to know that some are far more useful than others. Attending a course-related summer school or weekend conference is far more likely to get you in than just going on a "shadowing" visit.

Also, the longer you can stay, the better. This does not mean, of course, that he who sleeps on a sheet marked "college property" has got admission sorted. He may, however, return with a clearer picture of the knowledge gaps he needs to fill, pick up a clutch of useful new terms and get used to the fussy way in which academics ask the most simple questions.

Any Oxbridge visit, though, will give you some advantage should you be invited back for an interview. Walking up to those ivy-clad towers and stained glass windows next time should feel less like approaching Dracula's castle and more like returning to a place of nice memories like Blackpool or Benidorm. And a relaxed interviewee is more likely to impress the admissions tutor.

The hometown events held outside the university may be less trouble to get to, but they lack this psychological hook. Your daughter might come away eager to apply, but seeing Oxbridge for the first time at the interview could still scare her off. Still, a confident and very well taught pupil can certainly further improve her odds by attending a local Access talk.

Do Access projects ensure that "the brightest and best" succeed? This is more doubtful, despite the great effort put into them, especially by the unpaid student volunteers. One reason is the worrying lack of talent spotting at most events. You may have a young Isaac Newton in the family, but nobody at a one-day Access do is in the business of finding out. Although dons are involved in many events and spend time with pupils, they are not expected to even guess at an individual's ability. The Access brief is to encourage applications.

This means that while your son might be a deep, articulate thinker no formal note has to be taken of this during his Oxbridge day out. So, when it comes to having his application considered, he is in the potluck bowl with everyone else. Rumour has it that the odd don may quietly suggest to a particularly impressive participant that he should apply to her college, but this is hardly the rule.

The opposite approach is taken by America's top academic institutions. Their talent scouts annually visit schools and summer camps not to encourage the most doubtful kids, but to identify the most talented ones. The latter are then asked whether, subject to passing their SATs, they would honour the university by becoming one of its students. Which situation would you rather be in?

The main flaw of Oxbridge Access, though, is the underlying assumption that the problem lies with the pupils themselves. The schemes, I was repeatedly told, were necessary because state school pupils "are hesitant to apply because of low self esteem". So, the stated aim is to give them the confidence to apply - not to ensure that more state school pupils actually get in. Access does not even have a numerical target when it comes to raising the proportion of state school entrants, rather than just the number of applicants, to a more representative level.

When I asked Access officials if widening participation might not also require a change in entrance procedures, the response was embarrassment. People emphasized that they were not campaigning for any such thing, heaven forbid. Both paid Access staff and student volunteers insisted that entry remains a matter entirely for the university's admissions department. They had no views on whether the system was fair or could be improved. Pupils' university choice was all that mattered - and was clearly the only thing they could influence.

So, Access concentrates on broadening the field of applicants. Colleges keen to admit more state school pupils, and especially more working class ones, now have a much bigger pool to draw from. Many take advantage of it.

Access cannot, however, force a specific college to abandon the idea that Winchester public school is the main source of intelligent human beings, or curb its enthusiasm for fresh-faced kids from genteel country towns. Colleges are independent bodies or, to put it disrespectfully, college admissions tutors are a bit like horses: you can take them to the water, but you cannot make them drink.

Government expenditure of some £10 million on Access in the four years leading up to 2003 had little impact. In fact, the proportion of state school students entering Oxford actually dropped by two per cent that year, only to very gradually rise again: admission rates were a stop -start-reverse business. Having eventually reached 58 per cent at Oxford and 63 per cent at Cambridge in 2012, it then got stuck at 57 per cent for Oxford and 62 per cent for Cambridge until 2015, then crawled back up to the barely higher 2012 figure.

Moreover, while this suggested that Cambridge has made greater strides than Oxford, this is not quite so, as revealed by the actual student numbers: Cambridge had admitted 1,609 state schoolers in 2011 and a gently falling number in the next few years. By 2015, this was down to 1,566.

Where, then, did the opposite impression come from? Well, the reason the percentage of UK state schoolers at Cambridge had risen was that some 300 places a year which had previously gone to British private sector students, now went to overseas ones (who pay much higher fees). So, the state/private balance was pretty much unchanged, although each university had spent millions on Access.

Having said this, the public outcry about such figures has since ushered in further progress. In May 2018 Oxford revealed that its 2017 UK state school intake had been an unprecedented 64 per of its UK total. So, magically, was that of Cambridge. Conversations with headteachers suggest that this had been aided by improved Oxbridge Access projects, but also by more state schools using charitable or commercial Oxbridge preparation schemes.

While this makes for very good news, it's worth recalling that some 86 per cent of British pupils attend state sixth forms. As the benchmark figure which the government had set for Oxbridge ten years ago is 75 per cent, there is quite some way to go. In fact, by 2017 six Oxford colleges (but only a single Cambridge one) still had a less than 50 per cent state school intake.

It is not even clear whether the positive change we have witnessed has anything to do with Access or was decreed by nervous universities heads. Certainly, state school applicants had not just suddenly became much smarter.

WHY ACCESS IS WORTH DOING

While far from perfect, Access projects, which vary greatly in focus and scale, benefit some teens. Merely attending a day event will gain your son some brownie points if he decides to apply, and he might well do so because Oxford or Cambridge now seem less alien. It will also give him some idea of what is expected by Oxbridge, though not all the means to meet those expectations. The rest depends on a mix of things: good brains, skilled teaching, careful subject choice, avid reading, smart interview preparation and a bit of luck.

Moreover, the new Access projects launched by both Oxford and Cambridge in 2015-2018 suggest a growing acknowledgement that what is needed is not yet more friendly encouragement but far greater academic support. Given the gap between the school curriculum and Oxbridge expectations, this may even be required both at the application state and in the first university year.

Meanwhile, applicants just have to do their very best. Reassured that Oxbridge is the place for them, boys and girls from urban comprehensives and rural council estates handle the entrance process right and get in.

But how many do? Neither university, it turns out, had initially kept a record of the admissions resulting from their schemes. The explanation given was that this was too complicated (!), as not all pupils attending later apply there. However, lots do and admissions tutors privately admitted that most Access schemes were just one day events for "raising aspirations" and did not get students in.

When two studies of Access initiatives were finally undertaken, they brought great news. According to a 2011 report in *The Cambridge Student*, 76 per cent of sixth formers who went to a Sutton Trust summer school in 2008 or 2009 had gained places at top Russell Group universities, including Cambridge. Oxford then revealed that 40 per cent of those who had attended its academic summer school, *Uniq,* the previous year had received offers. Success rates in this group have fallen since due to other initiatives, but they do show a way forward.

In response, Oxford in May 2018 increased the number of *Uniq* places from 850 to 1,350. So, if you are a bright state school student with high grades, try to book yourself in, then click Oxford or Cambridge on that UCAS form.

Still, while the above figures give applicants hope, they don't yet amount to a cast-iron guarantee of success. If you are a parent, don't, therefore, let your teenage whizz kid get too fixated on the idea of spending the next three years doing PPE in a manor with its own tennis court. He needs an attractive insurance choice, just in case. Greater certainty would be nice, but it may have to wait until Oxbridge yet again alters it entrance quotas or adopts an entrance process that works equally well for all.

8

The paper trail

The most crucial thing to do, if you'd like to study at Oxbridge, is to actually apply. This means providing various bits of information, most but not all of it online, in your UCAS application. Don't even dream of leaving the job to the night before the application deadline of October 15th. If necessary, write draft versions first and note which documents or details you still need to ferret out. Then scan in, paste up or photocopy everything before you click "send".

If you're applying to Cambridge, it will next send you its **Supplementary Application Questionnaire** (SAQ), which you must return by October 22nd. If your schooling has been significantly disrupted or you are disadvantaged in some other way, your school referee should also fill in and send off the Cambridge **Extenuating Circumstances Form** by the 15th of October

Oxford does not ask for this kind of extra forms. It used to send students an equivalent, the **Oxford Application Support Form**, but this has now been abolished and teachers are asked to provide all information in their **Open Reference**.

As most students now sit formal, subject-related tests, they may also have to register for those, directly or through their school, well before the UCAS deadline. In 2018, Cambridge candidates for undergraduate Medicine, for instance, will sit the BMAT on September 1st of 2018, but must register for it no later than August 12th. Oxford medical applicants sit the BMAT on October 31st of that year, but must normally register by October 1st. Only applicants for some Oxbridge courses sit their test (referred to as an "Admission Assessment" by Cambridge) as part of a college interview.

What this means is that you must read the relevant course pages of the Oxbridge prospectus very carefully and keep a record of both the test application deadline and the date of the actual test. Do also note that you may be asked for more paperwork as your UCAS application winds its way through the admissions maze.

Daunting as all this may sound, most of the information sought is fairly straightforward. The crucial thing, as already said, is to leave yourself enough time to assemble it.

Candidates still at school don't usually battle alone with their forms either. Once you had a look at yours, make a list of any factual data required and ask your teacher to help if you lack some of it (this is not a job for parents). External candidates will have to assemble exam information from the records they have kept.

Still, there is quite a lot else to do, and doing it sloppily will make you look less bright. So, let's go through it bit by bit.

1. UCAS Information

The first thing to fill in is the main body of the UCAS form, in which you give your personal details and list all your chosen university courses. You can list up to five courses, but if you are applying for Medicine, Dentistry, Veterinary Medicine or Veterinary Science, this drops to only four. Advice on how to fill in the form is on the UCAS site.

2. The UCAS Personal Statement

This is not a school essay but your very own promo: you are trying to sell yourself as the kind of student any course leader might like. Are you hard-working, imaginative, a born linguist or a lover of abstract thought? The resulting document, which should be upbeat, persuasive and perfectly spelled, must also strictly adhere to the word limit.

If you are unsure how to start, try not to draw on internet examples. It's OK to read a couple for reassurance, but then try to forget them again. Unless you do, you will be irresistibly tempted to copy. This is a very bad idea. For a start, even the eyes of the most benevolent admissions tutor do glaze over after reading through piles of samey statements. Worse, if you parrot claims like "My interest in Medicine started at the age of five, when I accidentally set fire to my pyjamas" (as hundreds of course applicants did!) you will wreck your chances by being blatantly dishonest.

Instead, start with the bare bones. One teacher I know always tells his student to copy down his own personal statement, composed at seventeen: "I really enjoy some of my subjects at school and recently got interested in the arts. Also, I like to read books. In my spare time, I follow several hobbies."

Fortunately, his headmaster sent him straight back to his desk. Still, the teacher's younger self was basically right: to have a good statement, all you need to do is to put some flesh on the bones of the skeleton outline above. You don't even have to start at the beginning. "I've always dreamed of understanding the physics of stars and of flying my own plane" is fine.

The next stage, commonly, is to describe how you approached a curriculum-based project, but note that top universities look for independent academic activity beyond school requirements. Being able to list a degree-related intellectual interest you have pursued on your own makes you look even smarter. This could be a branch of physics, a style of poetry or medieval warfare.

Now tell the reader what inspired this interest. How are you pursuing it? What are you hoping to understand and what have you already learned? Are there social issues, paintings or science problems that intrigue you? Which books, websites or archive did you consult? Did you perhaps attend a university workshop? Admissions tutors like to feel that you have "engaged" with academe by drawing on external and not just school sources.

Hobbies should probably be next, but think ahead. If you're into scuba diving, a science interviewer may well ask you to explain the physical laws making the sport possible. Voluntary work, leadership posts and honours gained also belong here, so for heaven's sake don't forget that you are involved in the Maths Olympiad. Say which skills you have developed as a result and don't be too modest: describing your academic side does not count as showing off.

Your personal statement is, above all, a chance to create a positive (but not arrogant) academic profile of yourself. This can be made up of quite diverse elements, though every university loves a reader. When mentioning a book, make sure to give the correct author's name and title. Then spell out what inspired, thrilled or shocked you about it. If you must cut your book list to go into detail here, do so.

Should you also mention your home circumstances? If these will contextualise your achievements, the answer is yes. Parental unemployment or a carer's duties may affect your grades. Just try to avoid vague phrases. Writing that you spend time helping your parents tells the interviewer nothing. Stating instead that you help out each afternoon in the family's Chinese takeaway suggests that you are conscientious and have gained A*s against considerable odds.

Sometimes, a single, honest line can hint at the odds you had to overcome. One very shy but high achieving South London science student ended his statement by saying "What made me work hardest was finding out that even someone from a really ordinary family like ours might get to study such a great subject at a great university." A well-read girl applying from a FE college explained that she came to enjoy studying quite late, after her comprehensive was closed down as a failing school. Such information does not demean you in the eyes of the university. Both students got in.

In fact, anything you spend lots of time on might be worth adding, especially if it is slightly unusual. If you breed rare lamas or argue online with racist bloggers, try to mention it. Is there anything specific it has taught you? Don't give more than a third of your statement over to extracurriculars, but don't worry about the UCAS word limit at first. You can always cut later. Just make sure everything flows together into one story, ideally one in which most of your interests and abilities lead towards the course you picked.

Style matters too. Try to write crisply, without labouring your points, and to back up your claims with examples. You don't have to use old-fashioned language in order to communicate with an old university, as long as your grammar is correct. It's best to describe yourself in your own voice.

Don't be swayed in your efforts by confusing rumours. When the Head of Admissions at Cambridge, Geoff Parks, announced in 2009 that the personal statement would no longer count towards a student's academic assessment, he was much misunderstood. Cambridge (and Oxford) later confirmed that dons still read all statements and often base interview questions on them.

Do, however, beware of exaggeration. Having seen a TV doc about George Stephenson does not yet prove that you are passionate about engineering. Above all, don't mention that impressive-sounding book you were planning to order ages ago. You won't get round to reading it in time for your interview and fibbing will do you no good. Oxbridge dons have had centuries of practice in teasing out the truth.

3. The UCAS Open Reference

This piece of writing by a teacher or head should, ideally, complement your own academic self-portrait. By providing a thumbnail sketch of an applicant's talents, achievements and interests, as seen from the classroom, the referee offers a university more fodder for its decision. A strong open reference will also show how the student's achievements measure up against those by others at the school, both currently and in the past (see sample).

She should certainly not just list the A-level syllabus a student has covered. It should also tell the reader about any wider academic interests she has shown. Is she an avid library user? Does she like to explore subject problems not dealt with at school? Is she persistent? Near the top of her class? The idea is to impress all the universities listed, but also to ensure that Oxbridge sees the applicant as outstanding and suited to its learning style.

If the student has succeeded against personal odds, but has not referred to those herself (many disadvantaged students take poverty and hardship for granted), this should also be made clear.

Generally, an able candidate requires more than a cautious

endorsement along the lines of "he is a good student and we recommend him." His teacher needs to be a strong advocate for his cause, and a few superlatives like "one of the best" will not go amiss. Pupils are legally entitled to see this document and can even make suggestions, if only to ensure that the Personal Statement and the Open Reference do not repeat the same points. If a reference is particularly tepid, I do feel the candidate deserves an explanation. The referee might be quite right about his academic potential - or quite wrong about the kind of student Oxbridge is now looking for.

I would certainly not drop the idea of applying there at this point, unless strong reasons were given. Because the Oxbridge interview counts for so much and is now complemented by tests, some clever students do get in with a less than brilliant reference.

The Open Reference should also describe the school. If it is not an average comprehensive, do add something about its educational status, intake and environment. As relative newcomers, academies and free schools may want to offer further details. If a school is tackling problems likely to affect student performance, all the universities listed will want to know.

It is worth spelling out anything of possible relevance here, above all that there is a good match between subject choice and a student's talents, interests and work habits. (Applicants who picked different courses at different universities may be asked why. Oxbridge, for one, likes to feel that the course you have chosen is the love of your life. Any dithering between the respective attractions of Maths and French can get you dismissed as a wrong 'un.)

So, what are Oxbridge admissions tutors looking for? Well, it depends on the individual, college and course, but quite a few agreed that the kind of Open Reference which would make them feel well-disposed towards a student might be a version of the one overleaf.

4. Candidate's Work Sample

As said, a university interested in a candidate may also want to see a sample of work she has done in her chosen course subject or a related one (which can mean History, if she is aiming for HSPS or PPE). Scientific or engineering models are fine, but if it's a student essay, admissions tutors like it to be marked and, ideally, done at school rather than at home. This way, they feel, one can be sure no one else was involved in writing it. Teachers whose students have no school essays to show can set the applicant a (perhaps vaguely relevant) essay topic, so they have something to send in.

John is a very bright and inquisitive student who takes an active interest in chemistry well beyond the requirement of the school syllabus. He makes impressive contributions to discussions in class, while his written work has consistently been good and outstanding at times. The GCSE and AS level marks he has obtained were the best in his year.

Project work John has undertaken has impressed staff as well planned, imaginative and thoroughly researched. He is also involved in a project by young people trying to set up their own science website. John is the kind of autonomous, interesting pupil we have not seen for some years.

Moreover, John has maintained this standard despite difficult economic circumstances. Unemployment within the family has required him to take on weekend work. This suggests that he is focused and determined, as well as bright.

Ours is a rapidly improving school which has just become an academy. Most of our intake comes from the local neighbourhood, which is one of the most deprived in our city. 50 per cent of our students qualify for free school meals and almost 70 per cent have English as a second language.

5. Application forms for pre-interview subject tests

Nearly all Oxford applicants, as mentioned, now sit some kind of formal, standardised test. Although some are tested at interview, pre-interview tests are now more common.

While some tests are run by university departments, others, including the BMAT, taken by Oxford applicants for Medicine and Veterinary Medicine, the TSA, HAT, MLAT, MAT, LNAT, ELAT, PAT, HAT, OLAT, TSA and Oxford Philosophy Test are administered by a company called *Cambridge Assessment*. Registering with it is fairly simple, but note that its deadlines are set in stone.

At Cambridge so-called *Admission Assessments* are now the rule for all colleges and most courses. Pre-registration for these tests is essential, unless they are held at interview. Details are on the university website. Cambridge Maths applicants and some applicants for Engineering, Chemical Engineering or Economics still need to first register with the admissions testing service for the STEP test.

Cambridge applicants for both Medicine and Veterinary Medicine also need to pre-register for the BMAT, which they can sit, unlike Oxford ones, in September or October of the application year.

Oxford ones are only able to sit the test in October.

While this can sound pretty confusing, links on the Oxford and Cambridge tests are found on the individual course pages. These also take you to the necessary application forms.

Not all the tests are free. UCAS charges a small processing fee, and candidates sitting the BMAT or LNAT need to check on the test websites what else they have to pay. A UK student genuinely unable to afford test fees can ask the university to be reimbursed.

Students should be aware that rules about pre-interview tests, dates and the courses requiring them do sometimes change. So, make sure to scan the Oxford or Cambridge website more than once.

CONQUERING THE PAPER TRAIL

The advice any Oxbridge don will give you about the form-filling stage is to work slowly and carefully. Check dates, data and the right place for each bit of information. Being unable to follow detailed instructions makes a very bad impression.

The long list of requirements also means that even the most motivated candidate may need help from her school. Private schools often manage the whole process for their pupils, from explaining the forms to editing students' Personal Statements. Comprehensives which regularly send pupils to Oxbridge also have a firm routine in place. They direct candidates towards the right forms, offer advice on what to write and ensure deadlines are met. One school even arranged for a pupil with unemployed parents to have his processing fee paid.

The most disadvantaged candidates, though, also often attend the least Oxbridge-oriented schools, and this is where the system breaks down. Even the few Access schemes which offer guidance on the applications process cannot change the fact that teachers may be unsure about what to write, or students unused to filling-in forms.

The good news is that Oxbridge, which used to argue that the paper trail was essential to attract "non-traditional candidates", has now acknowledged this problem by abolishing some forms. The bad news is that the introduction of subject tests has generated others.

Looking at those forms, it certainly struck me as amazing that thousands of young people every year managed to return them at all. Even more amazing is that so many of them handled the process skilfully enough to be offered a place. Perhaps this is a measure of the qualities possessed by Oxbridge candidates (one admissions tutor did think so) but, more likely, it reflects the sterling support provided by so many schools. What this book enables you to do is to maximize the value of that support, or to get by without it, in case it is not there.

9

What not to wear to the interview (and other worries)

Having received the completed paperwork, Oxbridge does a month of sorting. As long as your teenager has very good grades and A-level predictions, or managed to shine at a pre-interview test, he is likely to be offered an interview. Over 80 per cent of all Cambridge applicants are invited up for this, but less than 60 per cent at Oxford. When it comes to top courses with hundreds of applicants, the percentage at both places is much lower.

While pretending that interviews are cool, a student will be thrilled, as well as panicked by this development. You may want him to get on the net immediately and track down the cheapest fare to Oxford or Cambridge, but he has more urgent matters to resolve. The first of these concerns his appearance.

What to wear for the interview can seem like a trivial question, but if both of you are nervous about the event you might be pushed into expenses the family can ill afford. So, forget that Armani suit your son says is a must-have for the great day. Hardly anybody wears suits for the interview anymore. If the admissions tutors interviewing him really cared about designer clothes, they would be working in a place with far higher salaries than Oxbridge.

Even the message sent by a certain type of old clothes is out of date. Among the sixth formers fidgeting as they wait for their interview, there will invariably be one confident young man dressed in his father's frayed, greenish-blue tweeds, with the label of the best Cambridge tailor stitched into the silk lining. Unless, however, he also has a lot between the ears, he too will not necessarily get in.

This is not to say that clothes don't matter at all. Turning up in dirty, scruffy gear, with mud-covered shoes indicates a lack of respect for the institution you are supposedly keen to join. So, smart casual is the order of the day. This means jeans are OK but should be in a healthy state, an ironed shirt might be preferable to a T-shirt and if it has to be a T-shirt, let it be plain. Anything imprinted with an even mildly obscene message is absolutely out.

The same basic rule, of course, applies to girls. They don't have to wear skirts, suits or dresses any more, but it probably does no harm to look nice. This does not mean showing masses of bare flesh. Even the most heterosexual male don is likely to take this as a sign of desperation.

Gay men, whatever their usual style, might be wise to avoid looking wildly camp at their interview. It will only get you typecast as one of those tiresome, idle chaps hoping to relive Brideshead, Evelyn Waugh's great homoerotic novel, set among upper class students in 1920s Oxford.

A light jacket might usefully complete the outfit of someone applying for Medicine or to one of the posher colleges, such as Magdalen, Oxford, or St. John's, Cambridge. Clean hair, needless to say, is a must. I would not go into a panic about nose rings or even tongue studs at this point. Students sporting them can be seen in a few medieval quads, so clearly they are not, in themselves, a cause for rejection.

Lastly, it is crucial that once these basic principles have been absorbed, you leave the choice of interview gear to your daughter or son. It's no good sending someone off to an important interview sobbing: "I look like a prat."

MANNERS

Most people teaching Oxbridge entrance include a smattering of manners. This usually means things like sitting straight, looking (at least occasionally) at the interviewer and speaking clearly, rather than mumbling. Most academics I have interviewed swear blind that manners don't matter one bit. What they are looking for is talent, and if talent bites its nails, that's OK with them.

I am not so sure these academics are telling the whole truth. Obviously, saying "may I sit down", rather than just sinking into the nearest chair is no longer a sufficient entrance qualification. Equally obviously, a young Maths genius scratching his back as he rattles down perfect formulas, explanations or equations is rarely shown the door.

However, if your child is not a genius but is still rather bright, then sheer pleasantness may well tip the scale. After all, the interviewer will have to spend at least an hour per week in a small study with the applicant. This is a less attractive proposition if she cannot easily hear what the boy is saying, if she risks being showered with dandruff or if he does not show her respect.

THE HORRORS OF FISH

One of the key anxieties I have heard expressed are about table manners. Interviewees eat their meals under the medieval eaves of the guest college's often very impressive dining room. One girl recalled her horror when served a whole Dover sole at her first dinner there. How on earth was she going to get this dead body into an edible state?

She need not have worried. The dinners are not a test of whether you'll fit in, just a way of meeting other students. Of course, if your son takes the opportunity to get drunk and abusive instead, it might be assumed that he is not interested.

Still, for the sake of reassurance, you might want to pass on the basic rule: treat the fish like a travel bag to be unzipped; cut round the edge, throw it open so you have two fillets, one of which should have the skeleton attached to it. Lift out the skeleton with knife and fork, put it on the side of the plate and start eating, preferably with your mouth shut.

And, by the way, the slightly deformed looking bits of cutlery next to your plate are the fish knife and fork, to be used much like the other kind. If there are several knives and forks are laid out, start with the ones at the outer edge, working your way inwards, course by course. The same rule applies to the row of shiny wine glasses to the right of your plate.

Conversely, Oxbridge dons keen on wider participation might also wish to learn something new. Fish is eaten by most of the population in the form of easily dissected, breadcrumb covered fillets without bones. Perhaps the hall menu in interview week could take account of this fact. If it doesn't, note that most colleges also have a perfectly nice snack bar.

10
What to expect at the interview

Having resolved the big issues, like whether a micro-skirt qualifies as smart-casual and whether someone living on prawn crackers can define herself as a visiting vegetarian, your jittery daughter can now address herself to secondary matters. In other words, she can start wondering what on earth, Oxbridge actually wants her to go up for. Is the interview just a grown-up conversation?

To many non-university parents it seems logical that being such a grand place, Oxbridge has summoned their teenager primarily to see whether she will fit in. They will consequently advise her to be on her best behaviour and, perhaps, "to treat these great professors with respect".

If you are a teenager, you are likely to interpret this to mean that you must not talk too much, not query anything you will be told or, heaven forbid, disagree explicitly with any, however, objectionable statement. It also suggests that you should sound as posh you can and not dangle your legs in those hideous, freshly polished new shoes. The prospect is dire enough to make you want to miss the train up on the appointed day.

In fact, the purpose of your forthcoming visit is something completely different, so just forget this advice. The word interview is a misnomer which can trip up even the most talented students from non-university backgrounds. What awaits you is a verbal ability test, which might be preceded, for some courses, by a formal written test. The verbal team opposite is likely to consist of two or three people, while the test might be a pen-and-paper or computer one. The questions will have been devised by course tutors or education experts. It is easier to get into Oxbridge once you know what to expect.

Most British universities no longer routinely interview potential students. Only those whose record is defined as "borderline" are still invited in for a chat. That tense half-hour in which a terrified 17-year-old, who may have never before talked to adults outside her immediate family, faced three men in corduroy trousers sitting behind a shabby wooden desk bit the dust in the 1970s. A friend who started his academic career then and is now a sociology professor at a popular university, recalls it as a supremely pointless exercise. "What on earth do you ask somebody applying for a subject they haven't done at school?" he had asked a fellow interviewer.

"Beats me," was the reply, "but we always pick the girl with the longest legs."

Oxbridge, though, has an almost religious belief in the magic of the interview. Combined now for most courses with a test devised by education experts, it is meant to establish the candidate's ability to think. Few state school candidates, of course, get this far without such an ability, but displaying it while balancing on a 16th century armchair which keeps tilting backwards can be a different matter. Not all of us spontaneously do our best thinking among the oak-panelled set of a period film.

So, how do you cope, apart from by reminding yourself that you are there because Oxbridge was impressed by your potential? The answer will be obvious to every pint-sized boy scout: be prepared. Find out as much as you can beforehand.

DOING THE GROUNDWORK

Before setting foot in Oxbridge, it is wise to do yet another bit of light reading. Start by skimming through the essay you sent and your personal statement, so you're prepared to talk about anything mentioned there. Look at the university prospectus again, then recheck the course details given on the faculty website. You want to know where you are going and why.

Wise candidates also try to find out whether the interview might involve, say, an essay or experiment. If the invitation or prospectus does not tell you what to expect, it is perfectly OK to ask the college by email, even though you won't get a detailed answer.

Next, it helps to know that "the interview" may consist of up to three separate conversations. A candidate is usually interviewed by the admissions tutor teaching the course applied for in her college room. A second tutor may be present, especially if the candidate has mentioned a personal interest in an unfamiliar field. For instance, a History tutor expecting a candidate who has done a project on Northern Ireland may bring in an expert on the Province from another college. An English tutor specialising in Victorian poetry might ask an expert in modern American literature to sit in on the interview with a young Alice Walker fan.

An Oxford candidate can usually look forward (!) to two interviews at the college he has picked, or perhaps at a college which the university felt might suit him better. To increase a student's prospect of success, Oxford often also arranges for him to be interviewed at a second college. The fact that he is being passed on does not imply a low opinion of the lad. Tutors and colleges can have very specific approaches and like candidates to fit in with them.

A prospective Cambridge student is likely to be seen only by the college she picked. Only if she made an Open Application will she be interviewed at a college chosen for her by the university. She may have two interviews, occasionally three. Should student and college not hit it off but the girl did impress, she'll will be put into a "pool" of shortlisted candidates. Her previous interviewer may even advise another college to fish her out. Alternatively, a college with places to spare may invite her for a further interview.

Traipsing around between colleges or waiting for one's turn to be seen can be a nerve-wracking experience. So, try and remind your daughter before she leaves that her success does not, in fact, depend on her interview performance alone. The results of any pre-interview tests will certainly count. So will a good open reference from her class teacher, especially if he does not just praise her school work but also broader qualities such as motivation and a willingness to read beyond syllabus needs. The teacher should also mention any obstacles she had to overcome during her schooling.

If your daughter has attended any Access event, even if it was just a morning visit during an open day, this again will count in her favour. Attendance is interpreted as a sign of commitment, yet another quality Oxbridge dons like to encounter. And if she actually visited the same college she is about to be interviewed in and made a good impression there, even better.

Lastly, a good personal statement, crisply written and packed with details about her own interests and achievements, can direct questions towards areas in which she can shine.

TALKING THE TALK

Students may have to wait endless minutes for their interview, but friendly student volunteers are usually at hand to calm them down. Once you've walked through the study door and sat down, though, interviewers at some colleges start throwing questions at you right away: Why does ice float? How do plants and animals differ in their treatment of water? What is oxidation? Make sure you cannot just understand key subject terms, but can also define them. Then be specific in your answers: amino acids or historic documents are not "things".

If a student appears exceptionally nervous, an interviewer may start off gently with small talk unrelated to the course. This is not the moment to show off, but to connect with a stranger by exchanging feather-light bits of information. The first question, especially if the interviewer is no creative genius, might well be: "Did you have any difficulty getting here?"

All your son is expected to do in return is to keep the ball rolling. "No," by itself, is a conversation killer. "No, but it's quite a long journey up here from Sunderland, what with half the points system not working," will do fine. Such an answer allows his conversation partner to ask questions about the boy's home town, his school or the state of British railway engineering. His answers will help to make him a real person to the interviewer.

Do tell your son not to fret too much about his answers at this stage. Anything said to him while he is still taking off his coat is unlikely to be a test.

Once everyone is seated, talk will rapidly shift to scholarly matters. Interviews have become far less rambling and more academically focused, but none of the interviewers is likely to dwell on the candidate's A-level syllabus, except in maths. Instead, they may want you to discuss a project done or a school essay sent in. Questions will centre on your research, the independent reading you did and the problems you encountered.

Not only does this gives you a chance to show how you think, but it confirms that the document was really all your own work. Remember to mention what you enjoy about its course-linked subject!

Another "easy" question sometimes used to kick-start the actual interview is: "Why did you choose this college (or Oxford)?" Fortunately, the traditional answer, "Daddy spent such a wonderful three years here" is no longer good enough. Still, it is probably best to avoid total honesty, if that would mean saying: "Because you're rich enough to give me a decent hardship grant."

A better idea would be to suggest that you had heard it was best for a specialist field which you are becoming interested in, say Medical Physics or Civil Engineering. Candidates who have done their net research might even add that their interest in this field was prompted by a piece in New Scientist, contributed by one of their own dons. Remember, you can find this inside dirt on the college website!

Be cautious about bringing up your own ambitions here. Magdalen College, Oxford, has indeed educated most British Prime Ministers, but "because I want to run the next government" is still the wrong answer. While this might be true, your university chances will be far better if you focus on the academic training the college can offer. True, Magdalen has unbelievable connections and an old boy network that seems to rule the world, but to mention this would be rude, proof that you don't understand the subtle strategies needed for a political career.

There is a further reason, of course, to talk about academic work, not networking: your future dons are human beings. They like to spend their time with people who enjoy their teaching and give something back, rather than regard their tutorials merely as stepping stones to power.

In any case, such questions mark the end of the warm-up. After that, things tend to get rather pacey. Transmogrifying into a more paunchy, less well-dressed version of Jeremy Paxman, the interviewer will start checking what kind of things, in or outside your field, you can understand, explain or make sense of: what are the determinants of market failure? Why is money so important? Are equality and fairness the same thing? Question might follow question, without any feedback about whether you hit the spot.

This style can be quite disconcerting for some candidates. State schools have in the last two decades gone out of their way to communicate with students in ways that build confidence, rather than just implant knowledge. They emphasize the positive, try to be soft on delicate young egos.

Many Oxbridge interviewers, on the other hand, believe in the rapid fire approach, in tough questioning not interspersed with any reassurance or praise. After all, they have scores of candidates to see within a couple of days. By pressing on, they hope to quickly discover hidden strengths, expose weaknesses, get to the core.

This is not the moment for a candidate to feel shy. No intelligent guess or opinion is likely to harm her chances of acceptance. What matters is to take a stand, then back it up by giving good reasons or facts. Often, she will be invited to apply familiar theories or principles to new areas. A History candidate, for instance, might be asked the following question: if the appeasement of Hitler was a bad thing in 1938, would it now be wrong to appease, for instance, Kim Jong-un, North Korea's dictator?

Fortunately, the girl is not expected to issue the final ruling on this world-shaking matter. The interviewers are trying to extend her understanding of the subject by their questions, not trip her up. A promising candidate will be happy to speculate on whether the theory behind the first scenario might be effective in the second. The skill the interviewer is fishing for here is an Oxbridge favourite: lateral thinking, known to members of the computer generation as "mental cut-and-paste."

It is also important to realise that candidate and interviewer are playing a subtle game. A Politics tutor, for instance, might choose to put forward a quite outrageous proposition: "Could it not be argued that dictatorship is a natural form of government suited to some of the world's nations?"

A young candidate might seriously consider walking out at this point in horror. Are these ghastly old fogeys the people she had considered studying with? Best to suppress this emotion. This is not the time to run, but to hold your ground. Chances are, the tutor is merely playing devil's advocate. He'll want to hear why she would disagree, and will expect logical grounds and/or concrete examples. She is being invited to play intellectual tennis and should hit the ball back hard but politely.

Scoring a point here means showing that one would be responsive to this kind of teaching, has respect for its learned practitioners, is articulate and keen enough on the subject to have done some independent reading. The interview is a selection test for the ability to do academic work. Could this candidate, the interviewer asks himself, benefit from tutorials, engage in dialogue, contribute to college life?

WINNING STRATEGIES

While a student has no control over what questions he will get or how they are delivered, there are strategies he can adopt which will greatly improve his answers.

The first of these is to make sure that you have understood the question correctly. It's OK to ask for it to be repeated or rephrased slightly, if necessary. Don't spend too long wondering about the perfect answer, but it is best not to rush in either: often a question will contain subtleties that require a bit of reflection. And don't panic if you really do not know one answer or get it wrong: this alone won't fail you.

The second strategy is to always remember in what context you are being asked a vague or unrelated question, seemingly plucked from the sky. One example is: "Could you imagine the country doing without TV?"

If you are hoping to do Computer Science, you are probably expected to take this as an invitation to describe the various different ways in which electronic signals travel through air. If you are aiming at a politics-related course, say HSPS or PPE, on the other hand, this may be the moment to talk about the role of television in education or the shaping of public opinion instead. There is almost never a single correct answer here. A good answer, though, will connect the question to the course and allow you to display any knowledge you have.

The third strategy involves not being too set in your ways, a sin some of the smartest applicants are prone to. Not all of human behaviour can be explained through the writings of Karl Marx, Sigmund Freud or Virginia Woolf. Equally, great historic figures are sometimes revealed by later historians as liars or wimps. Great scientific theories, which seem to explain everything, turn out to be incomplete and are superseded by others.

So, temper your views with a good dose of scepticism. If your daughter has been holding forth on the evils of capitalism, it may be a wise thing for her to end with something like: "On the other hand, poverty might have a whole number of causes, and I'm really keen to learn more about those."

Much of this, it should be clear from the examples given above, applies not just in the arts, but also the sciences. While scientific facts are of a more definite nature and interviewers expect you to know the basic ones, you also need to be aware that assessments can change. This means you could get a question along the lines of: "What is wrong with Watson and Crick's views on DNA?"

THE APPLIANCE OF SCIENCE

A concern for the implications of scientific developments is often seen as essential. If a Natural Sciences candidate claims that her main interest is biology, for instance, she might well be asked her opinion on the possible consequences of genetically modified organisms (GMO).

Again, no ultimate judgement is expected of her. What she needs to show by her answer is that she has enough of a sound factual basis to speculate intelligently, as well as a grasp of the most important scientific principles. The idea is to apply these principles to the new information put in front of her, to notice connections, or differences, or rules.

Again, too, it is crucial to elaborate. The ideal answer to any question, no matter how short, will be long enough to show that you have a solid grasp of the subject, a positive hunger to learn more and a healthy awareness that certainty can be an elusive thing, even in science. Thinking aloud here is a good idea: this way, the interviewer can appreciate how you arrived at your answer.

Some science subjects require a very hands-on attitude and this too should affect what you say. In Engineering, for instance, a willingness to apply the knowledge you already possess in Maths or

Physics to practical problems marks out the right candidate.

So, if asked a question that starts with "Would it be possible to..." don't even think about answering yes or no. Instead, try to suggest an experiment that might work in response. If you have ever conducted a relevant one, even better. The point here is not to offer an instant, picture-perfect solution, but to show that you are willing to grapple with a problem.

Science interviewers, whether they are vets or physicists, also share a general appreciation of certain traits. High up among those is a numerical bent. So, don't just put all your answers into words. Instead, show your awareness that figure analysis is often a good way to tackle even a non-mathematical problem.

This need not be a scary prospect. Often, it just means doing mental calculations based on estimates, or suggesting a simple statistical inquiry. At other times, a verbal question may be best answered by scribbling equations, calculations or general diagrams on the nearest pad or board. But do talk about what your scribbles might mean; don't just assume that they are self-explanatory.

Is there something you must absolutely avoid doing? Well, one common student habit is said to thwart even the most well-meaning interviewers. This is answering the question you had hoped for, rather than the one you have actually been asked.

USING YOUR EARS

Knowing your stuff is little use if you don't carefully listen to the question. Note key words or key dates, as they will give you a clue to what your interviewer is hoping to hear. Is it a definition, an explanation or your opinion? Here is one example that should make sense not just to prospective historians:

"What *triggered* the French Revolution" requires you to look at a particular moment in time. So, a good answer might include rising taxes, famine, the growing privileges enjoyed by the French aristocracy and the growing clamour for universal rights and for a representative national assembly in 1789.

"What *inspired* the French Revolution?" calls for a broader picture and a longer time scale. This might lead you to mention the English Revolution of 1640 and the Boston Tea Party of 1773 in support of the American colonists' stand that they would only pay taxes to the British crown if they also sat in the British parliament.

Finally, keep in mind that interviewers can be quite elderly and so may have listening problems themselves. A whispered or mumbled answer, therefore, can be as bad as no answer at all.

ACING THOSE TESTS

To give applicants yet another way of proving they have brains (and to allay public concerns), Oxford and Cambridge started using standardised, written tests for a few courses in 2002. It took another dozen years and some outside pressure for those to become near universal, but these days interviewers for most courses can no longer put an applicant to their college just through a test of their own. Developed in conjunction with education experts, what the new tests try to establish is whether a student has the intellectual aptitude for a specific course or field.

Tests taken in advance of the official interview date matter most because only students who do well may be offered an interview. In reply to queries, Oxbridge has consistently claimed that as these are not simple knowledge tests, preparation is unnecessary. This is somewhat misleading. Basic subject facts do need to be firmly entrenched, key concepts familiar.

A willingness to consider the way in which discoveries, policies, theories or weather changes may impact on earthly life (gleaned from books and news media) can help not just with the interview, but also with essay-type test questions. Test questions in humanities-related fields often seek to identify students able to assess the validity of an argument or the usefulness of some practice. While that sounds scary, questions are more often than not based on simple, day-to-day situations.

What Maths course tests fish for is, according to many subject tutors, is creativity and the ability to think from first principles. Faced with an unfamiliar type of problem, what is the student able to make sense of? Economics applicants, too, need to thoroughly revise their school maths, as questions here can be very tough.

Applicants for science-based courses also need quite good maths and an awareness of scientific principles, theories and methods to give good written answers. A student aiming for Law or Philosophy may get logic (or ethics) questions based on a popular TV series.

"Comprehension" is the key ability sought both in many of the tests devised by *Cambridge Assessments*. What this usually means is the ability to read a text you are presented with in a critical way, understand the main ideas in it, comb through details and grasp implicit meaning. You can start practising this by reading a feature on a politician's key speech in the paper. (See also p. 132).

Because the two (slightly different) Oxbridge Thinking Skills Tests used are devised for students taking a wide range of courses, subject-related knowledge is not supposed to matter there, particularly not by Cambridge. Officially, the purpose of either TSA is instead to identify problem solving skills and the ability to think critically. This may tempt a student to rely on her natural intelligence which, given the limited time and wide range of questions, can be a mistake. What you should do is to practise hard beforehand. *Critical Thinking Skills* by Stella Cottrell has lots of useful sample questions and smart advice on how to answer them. *Think you can think?* by Minesh Tannah is slightly harder and explicitly TSA focused.

To do well in the TSA or BMAT students must also grasp the evaluation rules: both tests include two types of questions. One kind requires critical or logical thinking. The other is about solving problems often involving numbers or shapes. Problem-solving can seem easier, so many time-pressed students focus on it. However, if you answer too few logic questions, you will be short of marks. As a result, you may not be short-listed (see p. 132).

In practice, the key to handling any test question is to not blindly rushing ahead with your answer. Start by re-reading it slowly to make sure you have not missed the point. Then, reflect, calculate, evaluate, compare or contrast as appropriate. Next, write your answer in clear, simple, grammatically correct sentences, using appropriate subject terms or mathematical language.

Don't worry too much if you sometimes really cannot find a good answer: the tests are meant to be hard. A few questions may even defeat a brilliant student. How much your results will count for, exactly, neither Oxford nor Cambridge will say.

LEARNING TO WRITE

What also helps you write good test answers is familiarity with their style. A puzzling format or wording can completely throw a nervous student, so always check for sample papers available online.

You need to be both careful and fast; successful students have practised an awful lot. Too many students, having down-loaded a sample paper, merely skim it for a few minutes, or mentally speculate on the answers. This is rarely enough. See whether you can write responses of the right length and within the right time. This is not a skill you will suddenly acquire during the test.

Practice matters most for Oxbridge tests involving short essays, often with a maximum length of 500 words. Many state schools no longer set classroom essays, and their students can lose marks over this. What they have been taught is to write extended essays which require detailed, laborious pre-planning. As a result, some spend most of the time stipulated for their Oxbridge test filling pages with outlines and key points. The result will be an unfinished essay or one barely started. If you have only 20 or 30 minutes, it's better to keep things short. An outline consisting of one short paragraph or just three key points will allow you to move forward.

An essay is also the place to showcase your analytic mind. This is not as hard as it sounds. In a subject such as geography or history, for example, it means that you should make clear three things when dealing with anything from a subterranean earthquake to a Highland uprising: why it happened, what difference it made and what were the consequences. Again, keep it short!

Becoming a great interviewee

Many of my readers will, at this point, throw up their hands in despair. How can a smart but inexperienced teenager possibly cope with such a complex scenario? Do those dons really expect a 17-year-old from a comprehensive to shine in a kind of discourse they never have at home?

The answer is, of course, that it is much harder for those from non-academic backgrounds, and for the quieter kind of young person. Nor can you expect much help from Access. Only a handful of its myriad projects offers Oxbridge interview training. Some of the scheme's organisers say that this is because to do so would be unfair to other applicants. Given that almost half of those accepted will come from private schools which lay on intensive training, this seems pretty odd. Other Access staff argue that what matters more is to raise pupils' low self-esteem. The interview, from this perspective, becomes a minor obstacle, rather than a decisive event in the application process.

State schools can be very good at bridging the gap. The most crucial thing a school can do at this point is to provide enough interview practice. At some schools, sadly, the sole Oxbridge applicant, already feeling edgy about going on this jaunt, is matched up for one brief mock interview with the school's sole Oxbridge-educated teacher, who may not have been back to his old university for 20 years. This rarely goes swimmingly, leaving the candidate more anxious than before.

State school teachers who regularly send students to Oxbridge are adamant that three interviews, each of them followed by detailed feedback, are the minimum it takes.

A good mock interviewer will not just ask generic questions, but also ask about interests mentioned in a student's own statement. Feed-back should be given not merely on what to say, but on how to say it.

One young Oxford English graduate, now teaching at a London specialist school and proud of sending a steady stream of students to her old college, is clear about what is required. "My students," she says, "are encouraged to practise the long, explanatory reply, rather than the brief, correct schoolroom answer. This can involve speculation, examples, even an admission that the girl does not know enough yet about the subject to be certain she is right. I also tell them that it's fine to question something that has been said, as long as you are willing to make clear why."

The teacher admits that if a pupil comes from a culture in which you don't openly disagree with your elders or betters, this can seem an almost insurmountable challenge. Still, talented pupils faced with a sympathetic interviewer occasionally do bring it off. "Of course," she added, "it might be fairer to allow our students to acquire such skills in their Oxbridge years."

Another state school teacher, educated at a northern university, concentrates on ensuring that her well-taught Modern Languages students are relaxed enough to display their abilities. She makes sure to put a lively foreign language novel into their hands and their grammar onto firm foundations, but knows this may not be enough. Having visited Cambridge several times, not just on an Open Day, she can honestly assure candidates that "people like you" are already there. The teacher also encourages them to feel that the visit to Oxbridge is already a special treat, a reward for their hard work.

Yet another teacher, an Oxford educated scientist, tries to keep up with scientific work done in the two colleges which he directs pupils towards. This helps him to recommend papers they can read in order to show that they are interested in the "cutting edge" approach taken by their chosen college. He also prides himself on knowing Oxford well enough to always pick one feature of the place, college or course that will appeal to a specific applicant. His pupils, as a result, manage to display genuine enthusiasm at the interview.

Not surprisingly, given the quantity of ground covered above, only a handful of state school teachers manage to do all these things in between marking, class work and smoothing the path for six dozen university candidates applying elsewhere. The number of Oxbridge students going into teaching too has been steadily dropping, so pupils from urban comprehensives, in particular, cannot rely on their teachers alone.

How, then, can your state educated son walk in with a realistic hope of success? After all, being lively, brainy and enthusiastic in the presence of some terrifyingly eminent older figure does not come naturally to any teenager.

WHAT NOT TO DO (BEFORE THE INTERVIEW)

One temptation at this point, for some parents at least, is to assume that determination will do the job of preparation. In other words, if the lad will only understand just how important Oxbridge entrance is to them, they feel, he will study as hard as he can beforehand and concentrate as hard as he can on the day. Surely, this is enough to swing things?

One young man I talked to was actually told by his father, while walking him to the train, that as he was his parents' eldest son, the family's entire fortune depended on his interview. The poor man was not alone in making Oxbridge entrance a life-or-death issue: one girl recalled that her mother, a single parent who had been forced to leave university due to money troubles, spent weeks saying that she would be absolutely gutted if her daughter didn't get in.

Unfortunately, telling your teenager that you don't know how you could possibly live with the disappointment is the worst possible thing to do. She needs to be at least tolerably calm to succeed, but can't be if you keep upping the stakes. Instead, the wretched girl is almost certain to panic on the crucial day and fail, crushed by a responsibility far too great for someone so young.

THE DO-IT-YOURSELF INTERVIEW

Instead, it is best to concentrate on honing general interview skills. The interview is, above all, a talk between a teenager and a strange (in some cases, very strange) adult, so one of the most useful things you can do is to ensure that the experience is not totally new to your son.

But who can he talk to? With the demise of the extended family and the growing fear of "stranger danger", many children reach 18 without ever having talked to an adult who is not their teacher or parent. How you can solve this problem depends on the stage you're at.

A young child likes to chat in a safe place. So, invite a neighbour for tea or take the boy along when you go to see your building manager, accountant or union rep. Then encourage him to answer any friendly questions these strangers may ask. What's crucial here is to let the boy speak, not to butt in and answer on his behalf.

Later on, send him on a play scheme, to summer camp, to a youth club or to Sunday school if you can, any place in which he will have to interact with people he hasn't known all his life. Older teens gain more than just confidence from an engagement with the community. Preparing a religious service and picketing a multinational are both good for mixing generations.

Sleepovers at friends' homes are great confidence builders, too. You'll be amazed how many candidates spend a sleepless first night at Oxbridge, freaked out by staying in a bedroom not their own.

Academic talk will seem far less daunting after such enrichment activities. They may well pay off, as long as your son has done enough general work, of course, and is prepared to follow the route outlined by this book, as well as his own good sense.

While there is no way of accurately predicting Oxbridge questions, he can limber up for the interview by doing a few practice runs. This does not necessarily mean setting up a whole trial interview; even just preparing for a likely kick-off question can be worthwhile, because this will prevent him from going blank at this early, scary stage and in those unfamiliar surroundings.

But how do you prepare? Start by describing your university-geared interests. How exactly are you pursuing them and what made you consider the course? Was it a book (remember its name and author), an article or a TV programme? What insights did you gain? Are you able to describe those, using proper subject terms which you can also define, if asked? Has an aspect of your chosen field generated some intriguing dilemma or problem?

Candidates need to know their subject, say dons, but should also be clear about their motivation and interests. Much of this will already be in your personal statement, but don't count on them having actually read it.

Now, read this one-page profile to yourself. Then take the three key points, write them on a scrap of paper and, drawing only on these, try to tell the whole story smoothly. Then do it without any notes. The point here is not to become word perfect, but to know what you want to say and get used to speaking up.

GIVING THE RIGHT ANSWERS

Next, it is time for you to work out how to handle different types of questions. A growing number of interviewers dispense with the warm-up stage and shoot basic subject questions at you right away: What is history (or an enzyme, or thermodynamic flow)? How does it impact on us? Could you list a cell's molecular components?

Practise offering facts, functions or definitions. Use proper terminology in your replies and, if possible, also touch on complexities or problems.

Other questions fish for the "what and how" in a specific field. "What rights might be infringed by invasion? is one. "Which developments made genetic testing possible?" is another. Asked "Is genetic testing a positive development?" on the other hand, you are meant to give your own opinion after laying out the pros and cons.

Interviewers also like you to compare and contrast. In what

way might majority rule differ from democracy? Could you describe the difference between a virus and a bacterium?"

Yet another type of question wants you to speculate on the basis of factual knowledge. An example is "Could you suggest what might have happened had Churchill died in 1939 (or Elizabeth I in 1559)?" Unless you know the key dates of the periods you studied and the challenges Britain faced then, you won't be able to answer. It's OK to launch into a wildly imaginative scenario, as long as you can offer some facts justifying it.

Students applying for an economics-linked course should prepare for questions taking them across academic disciplines. "It has been claimed that the Greeks are lazier than the Germans," an interview might say. "How would you research this problem mathematically?" You don't need to be a maths whizz here, but could propose we compare the number of hours people in each nation work and perhaps their per capita output in certain fields. You can then display your mathematical abilities by drawing a simple graphs for your data and suggesting what (if anything) your findings mean. Look for examples of such graphs!

GROWN-UP TALK

To get used to all this, you could start by testing your answering skills on an adult, perhaps a neighbour, careers adviser or family friend (not your mother, who might feel too involved and will only make you nervous). This could be a good time to visit your old cricket coach or your aunt. Alternatively, the bathroom mirror will do.

Parents determined to help should know that practice for more detailed interview questions is best integrated into normal conversation. If your teenager would rather eat glass than converse with you over dinner, you can always ask her to explain the appeal of Charles Dickens' novels while you're driving the car.

What you need to offer, most of all, is a sympathetic ear. While some expert knowledge would be nice, it is not absolutely essential. Your limited familiarity with the subject currently occupying that teenager's brain can even prove a positive advantage.

Being asked "So, why are cells so important?" will enable the girl to contextualise her knowledge. "What problems will this make for the government, you think?" is a question that will allow a student to formulate his political ideas after you have watched a current affairs programme or even just listened to the news together. "How do you figure these robots work?" subtly challenges a potential engineering student. You may then want to jointly consult http://www.britannica.com or a specialist website.

What matters most in this conversation is that you pose open-ended (not yes-or-no) questions and listen politely to what the student has to say. You can now add a follow-up, starting with "But what about...?" This approach will not just build verbal fluency, but also foster a broader, more complex world view. Don't, however, interrupt just because the girl has stopped talking for a moment. This is her show. Moreover, a bit of silent reflection before finalising one's point can pay off at the interview.

DIGITAL LEARNING
Despite their often stern demeanour, dons conducting an interview do not perceive themselves as interrogating students but as debating with them. But what if you have done no debating before? Well, the next best thing to a real-life, fast-paced intellectual debate is a recorded one. Top of the range are the *Today* programme and *The Moral Maze* on BBC Radio 4 (www.bbc.co.uk). BBC2's televised *Question Time* is hectic and sharp.

To discover a calmer, but more academic debating style, listen to an episode of Melvyn Bragg's endlessly inspiring BBC Radio4 series, *In Our Time,* kept in the user-friendly digital archives of the BBC (262). Here, a student can learn what our best minds disagree on, from imperialism to the impact of Tolstoy on the British novel. She can also get a sense of how real academics argue their points A weekly dose of this could turn a timid talker into an intellectual bulldog.
Once a student has concluded that highbrow arguing can be fun, it is time to see how Oxbridge interviewers do it. Students who attended one of their City Conferences can enjoy a taste of this, but for those who can't, all is not lost. Clips of interviews, albeit mocked up, are now on both universities' websites.

While your own experience may turn out to be very different, as each interviewer has her own style, the clips can be helpful. Most importantly, they familiarize students with the very adult, formal terminology many dons use. A question starting with "What is your sense of..." or "Can you imagine a situation in which ..." is not meant to scare you into silence. Instead, it seeks to elicit both subject knowledge and your views.

Not just are you meant to answer at some length, but your answers may be challenged. Could there be other outcomes or interpretations? The interviewer may also check you're aware of your subject's general principles or rules. Keeping up your end now can be tough, but an able, truly interested student tends to manage it, or so

Oxbridge dons believe.

Lastly, it pays to know that some of the worst advice you can follow will also be found online, or rather in student chatrooms. Out there, privately educated students whose entire school life has been geared towards Oxbridge regularly beseech others to eschew all interview preparation. Behaving naturally is all that counts, these anonymous friends insist - and it got them in. Some persuaders are genuinely unaware that years of intense coaching by teachers who speak just like the interviewers do aided their Oxbridge success.

BECOMING A SPECIALIST

Having decided what you might say during the first few minutes of the interview, you may wonder how to prepare for more specialised questions. Should you jot down yet more detailed notes? Well, it's best to have your school Physics or the rules of Spanish grammar at your fingertips, but cramming works only up to a point. There is no way of second-guessing the interviewer. She might want to hear you talk about a subject area or topic never studied at school.

Still, if you have expressed an interest in evolution in your Personal Statement, it is as well to double-check what issues keep popping up in the literature. This will mean you can offer an informed opinion when confronted with a question like: "Should all living species be preserved?"

Arts admissions tutors in particular like to discuss topical issues, so it can be worthwhile, yet again, to read at least a quality Sunday paper in the months before the interview. Look out for relevant articles written by experts, which will be on the features pages, as well as for news. The most useful ones will have headlines asking things like 'Should we leave the European Union?' or 'Can we trust GM foods?,' before laying out the pros and cons.

Questions of this kind are put to candidates for many courses and you can prepare for them by reading a Sunday broadsheet or that useful press digest, *The Week.*

It helps to expect different types of questions. "Talk about biological success," for instance, is scarily open-ended, but this does not mean you are being asked to go on and on. Just list what you think might be its key features and then, if you feel confident, venture an opinion on whether the term is meaningful at all.

Often you'll need to decide quickly whether you are being asked to establish a fact or express an opinion. If the interviewer is fishing for facts, then try to respond in that vein. If it is your opinion which is being sought, don't just state it but give reasons too. This shows you are capable of analysing things. You'll get extra brownie points for making clear what you base your answers on: is it a theory, an observation, a principle or a book you have read?

Now give some thought to how you lay out your stall. A good answer is not a ramble. It will be fairly concise, which often means between two and four sentences long. Many interviewers also like you to use qualifying terms such as "perhaps," "in some circumstances," or "on the one hand" (don't forget the other!). So, draw up a few sample questions, no matter how far-fetched, do a quick think and practice using these phrases as you write five line replies.

Lastly, what can keep you calm is not to expect the interview to have a steady rhythm. A tutor will briefly spot-check key points but may want to dig out every single fact you know about others. So, when your turn comes, be prepared to launch into a long, detailed reply, only to be interrupted after a few words.

The point of all this is not to have a stock of perfect answers ready, but to avoid being thrown by the way in which your interviewer talks. While a sound factual basis matters, of course, so does an awareness that questions may take you outside your field or beyond your subject knowledge. If you have both and practice the Oxbridge answering style, you are bound to come across well.

On the other hand, don't bother learning how to speak without your own perfectly normal accent. You may now want to drop the teenage habit of peppering your sentences with "like", but this is not a test of whether you can pronounce your h's. One or two students have said that their voice suddenly sounded out of place to them at the interview, but they still got in. It helps to remember that nobody on earth sounds quite like an Oxbridge admissions tutor.

Instead, you want to sound keen, thoughtful and open to new ideas. The standard advice from Oxbridge is to "be yourself", but perhaps it is a more a case of being you "with added value". If you're worried about how to pronounce foreign terms like regime, risorgimento or Reichstag, go to an audio site like https:howtopronouce.com/.

There are yet more ways to impress. One very shy science candidate, whose textile worker parents had moved to Britain from Bangladesh, decided that she would field all questions by imagining she was the cool and smart Carol Vorderman. Reader, it worked for her.

THE BOOK
What, though, is the strongest factor which swings the interview for a candidate? Dons are unequivocal: it is his willingness to analyse, combined with some lateral thinking.

The successful Oxbridge candidates I talked to were just as unequivocal: it was "the book." Each of them had read (and mentioned in their Personal Statement) at least one adult work relevant to the subject they were applying for. By putting their subject into a broad, intellectual context, the book had enabled them to understand the questions and answer clearly. Reading only magazine articles or the key chapters of books produced far poorer results.

This is not to say that the candidates had necessarily read the same book, or the same kind of book, even if they were applying for the same course at the same college. The more determined ones had indeed patiently worked their way through a first year university textbook, in the case of science candidates something with a title like *Modern Organic Chemistry* or *Advanced Physics*. Others had chosen different kinds of books throwing light on their subject.

But what is the best book to read? The answer, of course, depends on your interests and course. While textbooks or something from OUP's *Short Introductions* series will help, it is often the book which focuses on a narrow period or subject angle that stays in your mind. It need not be an academic work. Students often start out with a general interest book by some lively expert. This can make for a pain-free transition to a second or even third, more challenging book.

Dons in all fields are delighted to encounter a well-read candidate and you can find some course-specific reading suggestions on the Oxford and Cambridge websites, often under "Resources". Books mentioned there are carefully picked and meant to be challenging. So, don't drop the idea of an appealing Oxbridge course just because you cannot make sense of a chapter!

Don't be put off by the cost of books either. Instead, lobby your school for a regularly updated sixth form library. It is immensely useful, even in our e-reader era. So is a trained school librarian.

Below is a small selection books that both helped and thrilled successful Oxbridge candidates. Let's start with the science ones.

Popular among biology fans were: *Genome* by Matt Ridley, *The Making of Memory: from Molecules to Mind* by Steven Rose, *Trilobite* by Richard Fortey, *The Lying Stones of Marrakech* by Stephen Jay Gould, *The Darwin Wars* by Andrew Brown or *The Human Brain: A Guided Tour* by Susan Greenfield. *The Story of Life* by Richard Southwood was thought useful for most related courses.

Aspiring physicists had read: *QED* by Richard Feynman, *The Physics of Star Trek* by Laurence Krauss, *Chaos* by James Gleick, *Mr. Tompkins in Wonderland* by Russell Stannard and George Gamow, *The Restless Atom* by Alfred Romer or *The Physics of Ball*

Games by C.B. Daish. Those interested in astronomy and cosmology read anything by Stephen Hawking.

Aspiring engineers benefitted from *The New Science of Strong Materials* by J. E. Gordon, *The Engineer in Wonderland* by Eric R. Laithwaite and *Heat Engines* by J.F. Sandford. Also useful but more general were *Engineering in Society* by M. Haigh and *Engineering: A Beginner's Guide* by N. McCarthy.

Books that can fine-tune your A-level chemistry and take you beyond it include *Calculations for A Level Chemistry* by E.N. Ramsden, *Chemistry, Facts, Patters and Principles* by W.R. Kneen, *Why Chemical Reactions happen* by J. Keeler, *The Age of the Molecule*, published by the Royal Society of Chemistry, *Genome* by Matt Ridley, *The Selfish Gene*, by Richard Dawkins and *The Chemistry of Life*, by Steven Rose.

A Short History of Nearly Everything by Bill Bryson has helped students to see the broader picture, as has *Science: A History 1534-2001* by John Gribbin. Scientific interests could also be developed with the help of a good biography, such as *Marie Curie: a Life* by Susan Quinn, *Einstein* by Banesh Hoffmann, *The Periodic Table* by Primo Levi or *Genius: Richard Feynmann and Modern Physics* by James Gleick. A fictional version of the scientific life, centred on ethical problems, was found in *Cantor's Dilemma* by Carl Djerassi.

Even certain plays can make you a more interesting science interviewee. These included: *Copenhagen* by Michael Frayn, *After Darwin* by Timberlake Wertenbaker, *Arcadia* by Tom Stoppard, *The Life of Galileo* by Bertold Brecht, *The Physicists* by Friedrich Durrenmatt and *An Experiment with an Airpump* by Shelagh Stephenson. All make great school plays!

Students considering Medicine have a wide choice. *Complications* by Atul Gawande explores the way hospital doctors learn, *First Do no Harm* by Peter Sykes looks at the key issues in NHS care and the struggle for reform. The *Man who Mistook his Wife for a Hat* by Oliver Sacks is no less inspiring than *The Invisible Enemy: A Natural History of Viruses* by Dorothy H. Crawford. For a broader view, try P.B. Medawar's *Advice to a Young Scientist* or *The Logic of Life: Challenge of Integrative Physiology* by J. Black (but only if your library has this expensive book). First, though, medical candidates must read enough science.

Young mathematicians trying to bridge the yawning gap between A-level Maths and the Oxbridge version will hugely benefit from reading *How to solve it,* the classic introduction to mathematical problem-solving by G. Pólya. Those sitting the Cambridge STEP papers also need to work through *Advanced Problems in Mathematics* by S.T.C. Siklos, an OCR collection. They could then relax by reading *Dr. Riemann's Zeros* by Karl Sabbagh.

Law candidates new to the subject's formal language and issues often start with *Letters to a Law Student* by Cambridge don Nicholas J. McBride (but warm up for this by following topical cases through reports in *The Guardian* or *The Times). The Politics of the Judiciary* by J.A.G. Griffiths enhanced students' perspective. Geoffrey Robertson's *The Justice Game* is both an account of his most famous cases and a reflection on the gap between the law and justice. *Eve was Framed* by Helena Kennedy, which deals with the courts' treatment of women, introduced readers to a specialised field (see p. 193).

In other arts subjects, and especially in languages, history, theology and philosophy, the range of "useful" books varied so widely, as did candidates' personal tastes, that there is no point in giving examples. A newspaper review or TV documentary can introduce you to an author you like or to an intriguing aspect of your course subject. With so much good material now online, you should be able to follow this up.

Lastly, English is a field in which students both have a huge choice of reading material and a lot of essential ground to cover, so this is dealt with separately (see p. 187).

HOW TO READ SERIOUS BOOKS

How, though, do you fit all that reading into the rest of your life? Time pressure, most caused by exams, now affects pupils of all ages. This can tempt some students to cut corners. Reading only the beginning and end of a novel, (or only the study guide) will get you nowhere. Also, some non-fiction books, such as *Genome* or *Chaos*, have a story ark which leaves you with a broader understanding of their subject if you stay the course.

On the other hand, picking out a few chapters in an essay collection like *A Short History of Nearly Everything* or *Bad Science* can still be worthwhile, because these are free-standing. The contents pages will help you decide. Skip the introduction, but start with the first chapter. Then go for chapters which sound intriguing or help to bridge a gap.

To explore a single point, use a book's index. As for foot notes, you can disregard those at the pre-university stage. The same often applies to forewords. Check you have understood what you are reading, but don't bother to look up every unfamiliar word. Many subject terms will become clear as you read on. Clicking constantly on

Wikipedia will stop you from getting the general idea.

Should you jot down anything? This depends on the complexity of a subject. Try to summarise a key argument (and perhaps your disagreements with it) first in your head, then in a few lines. Make a note of the evidence offered by the author.

What an interviewer will seek to do is establish whether a candidate has reflected on the texts he has been consuming. The student will be expected to voice an opinion based on his reading, to make comparisons, mention what problems he encountered and show signs of lateral thinking.

A good bookworm, in other words, is a selective bookworm. Candidates who "skim" lots of material may have a wider range of facts at their disposal, but the best books teach you to connect.

BREEDING A BOOKWORM

So, the wise parent does not assume that never looking up from one's homework is the key to getting into Oxbridge. Discouraging hobbies and restricting a pupil's reading to school textbooks, as some well-meaning, non-university educated parents try to do, can produce a very dull candidate and make family life hell.

By the A2 stage, most teachers have produced a university geared reading list, but until then a wild dash through world fiction or a solid diet of electronics textbooks can work equally well. As long as it has a spine, its presence on top of that pile of dirty washing in your son's room is probably a good thing. All sorts of books, serious or funny, fiction or nonfiction, highbrow or lowbrow, will broaden his outlook and introduce him to unfamiliar ideas, places and words.

How, though, can you support this expensive habit? The point is, you shouldn't even try. If your daughter is a serious reader, she will go through far more books than you could possibly buy. Instead, make sure that she acquires the library habit early on. Take her to your local children's library, let her pick her own books and go to the counter to have them stamped. Back home, establish a corner where only library books live, so they will never get lost. A working bedside light is not just a convenience but will protect a bookworm's eyes.

If she seems to lose interest after a while, consider that she might have outgrown the children's section, even if she is only ten. Ask the librarian for a map of the grown-up shelves. Then suggest that you might both potter around for a bit in what she thinks is the most interesting looking section. At this point any section, whether philosophy or photography, will be fine. And if your local council tries to "rationalise" library services by closing your local branch, organise a protest picket - then campaign for the opposition.

Encourage your daughter to ask for advice. Once she has worked out what books she likes, it's OK to ask the librarian or a subject teacher for suggestions. Only if the books have just come out or have been stolen from the shelves (as happens in our local library) should you think of buying. Staff working in any good bookshop love to be asked for suggestions. Book tokens make excellent, lightweight presents and show that you trust the girl to make her own choice.

If your daughter gets interested in a subject via a TV documentary, she might want to read the book of the series. Before you buy it, though, encourage her to skim through to check whether it really expands on the subject, or just offers bits of recycled text in large print plus lots of film stills.

Dramatised fiction, on the other hand, will more directly lead to top quality books. The only problem of discovering a great story in this way is that the TV version remains in the mind. So, before talking excitedly at her interview about Dr. Zhivago and how the star-crossed lovers managed to escape, your daughter had better cross-check what happens at the end of the book (the hero dies).

YOUNG OXBRIDGE

If your family's potential Oxbridge student has a younger sibling who shows similar ability, here are a few practical suggestions. You don't need to be brilliant or highly educated yourself to implement them. If the child has a good mind, these strategies will help him on his way:

1. Let him experiment with his pile of bricks without rushing in to help and without sneering when things go wrong.

2. Tell him it's all right to say "I don't know."

3. Encourage him to ask "why" or say "can you explain".

4. If you can't answer his questions, suggest that you both look for answers in a book.

5. Don't always interrupt what he is doing. It is important to eat, but it can also be important to finish a drawing.

6. Listen to his opinions with respect. He might be wrong, but has probably thought before speaking.

7. Ask his opinion about films, teachers, the state of the world.

8. Ask for advice. By ten, a child should know quite a bit more than you about computer bugs, video editing or burning CDs. By 15, he will be light-years ahead when it comes to hair dyes, online travel booking and music.

9. Encourage him to give his opinions and advice clearly and politely.

10. Teach him that there may be more than one right way of looking at major issues.

THE PITFALLS

No amount of reading can fully prepare you for the interview, and neither is it meant to. One of the key ideas behind the Oxbridge interview is the precise opposite: to discover how well a candidate will cope when faced with the unexpected. Elderly dons still fondly quote the first lines of Rudyard Kipling's poem, *If* - in this context. Oxbridge, so they imply, wants you:

> If you can keep your head when all about you
> Are losing theirs and blaming it on you,
> If you can trust yourself when all men doubt you
> But make allowance for their doubting too,
> If you can wait and not be tired by waiting,
> Or being lied about, don't deal in lies,
> Or being hated, don't give way to hating,
> And yet don't look too good, nor talk too wise...

Well, this is an impressive list, and the ability "to keep your head" was mentioned even by many dons without reference to the poem. The quality would certainly have been useful for picking a Victorian district officer who would be ruling over half of Burma or some pre-1948 Indian state with a million inhabitants and no other Queen's representative within 500 miles. Why it should be quite so crucial "to keep your head" for a future Music or Biological Science student, though, is anyone's guess.

Questioned about this by *The Independent* (1st October 2000) Susan Stobbs, the veteran director of admissions for Cambridge Colleges, said somewhat defensively: "We are not trying to catch people out. But our courses move very fast. We need to see that students can pick up and develop ideas fast."

Younger Oxbridge academics can be quietly critical of this. One female science tutor from a comprehensive insisted (off the record) that guiding a student through a set text, however complex, was a totally different process. She thought it wrong to put already intimidated young people on the spot and certainly never adopted the tactic herself.

Still, certain, often elderly admissions tutors continue to believe in the If-approach and like to make sure the candidate feels surprised. Often this is just done by a peculiar seating arrangement. One successful candidate recalls being made to sit at the far end of a very long table, while the interviewer sat at the other end, almost invisible in the gloom. Another one described how her two interviewers positioned themselves at opposite sides of the departmental office, so she could not look at both of them at the same time when she talked.

More disconcerting can be a swap between two related subjects. Sue, a grammar school girl who was hoping to read Chinese, found herself interviewed by someone actually teaching Thai, and was asked to apply her (as yet very basic) understanding of Chinese grammar to a line of Thai writing. As the two languages are closely related and she had followed her yoga-teaching mother's advice to do some relaxation breathing before the interview, the girl, somewhat stumblingly, managed to comply.

Tess, a comprehensive school pupil from a non-academic family, had applied for the Anthropology and Archaeology course after reading an article about a Japanese anthropological project. She was shaken when she found that her interviewer was an archaeologist. Her total ignorance of his subject, she felt, meant she did not stand a chance against "cleverer" applicants. Shrinking back into her seat, which was miles from the tutor's, she whispered: "I don't know a thing about this." However, when reassured that this was OK and invited to speculate, she decided she had nothing to lose. She is an articulate girl, and her off-the-cuff suggestions on how one might study a dead, rather than a living culture got her in.

Another popular tactic is the prolonged silence. This can be used in various and sometimes disconcerting ways.

Tim, a terribly well-read candidate, was faced with an elderly interviewer who failed to greet him, settled into a distant window recess and after several minutes barked "talk about your own subject" in his direction. The young man launched into an account of what he, out of nervousness, called Astrology, though he meant Astronomy. He quickly corrected himself, but felt so embarrassed he lost his thread. He stumbled on, expecting to be told when to stop, but instead was allowed to go on. When he eventually ran out of things to say, the interviewer maintained his silence. After what felt like an eternity but was, as the candidate later realised, only quarter of an hour, he was told that he could leave.

Grace, who had applied for Modern History, had the opposite experience. She had mentioned in her Personal Statement that she was the leader of a Brownie pack. One of her interviewer's first questions was about the founder of the scout movement, Robert Baden-Powell. Shaken, she admitted to having never heard of him, and prayed that they would move on to another subject.

Instead, Grace's tutor gave her a little lecture about the

famous man, which took up most of the interview. He then asked a few well-structured questions to make sure she had understood everything and could put it into a broader historic context.

(Unlike the prospective astronomer, the Brownie leader got in. What can we conclude from this? Probably only that external factors, rather than the interview itself, determined the result: she was a Shropshire working class girl with top grades and a perfect mix of brainy interests and sporting skills, while he came from an already over-represented public school.)

A more tricky approach can be deeply unsettling for vulnerable candidates. Ken, a sergeant's son, had mentioned his interest in ancient warfare, developed through books, in his UCAS statement. His interviewer though, chose to ask him about the atrocities committed by the Red Army instead. Which ideological factors, did he think, had motivated them? When Ken said that he had not studied this part of Russian history at school, his interviewer barked: "Well, just guess, then!" Ken was so angry he messed up the rest of his interview.

Maher, an applicant from a poorly rated comprehensive, did well in his written science test, although he felt that had he been less nervous, he would have started faster and done even better. But faced with a plummy-voiced interviewer whom he found hard to understand he clammed up. He had never sat in a room with such precious old furniture before. Being fairly dark-skinned, he also wondered whether making him sit at the end of the room was a put-down. Did the professor not want to sit next to a dark-skinned person? Or did he think that he, Maher, smelled?

Or take Joseph, who came from a struggling urban sixth form college. He had applied for a course based on Spanish, his mother tongue. When his interviewer explained that she did not actually teach the language, Joseph's first thought was: "So the Spanish tutor can't even be bothered to see me." Hurt and confused, he refused to play the game. He gave short, terse replies to any questions put to him, and when asked what he thought was the most exciting aspect of European culture, he just mumbled: "No idea." He had, in fact, worked as a Saturday cleaner for a small record company that promoted regional music and was interested in its work, but feared that mentioning his lowly job would demean him in Oxbridge eyes.

All three applicants were rejected, which came as no surprise to them. Their respective teachers, though, were absolutely furious. Each of the boys had been carefully hand-picked by his school as an outstanding student.

So the result of such an über-clever approach, although perhaps designed to transcend subject coaching and create a more level playing field, is often counterproductive. It is bad enough being in an unfamiliar environment with someone speaking in a superior accent without being asked about a subject one knows nothing about. Almost invariably, the applicant's residual doubts about whether this venture into other people's world was a good idea will click in. The suspicion that he is undergoing a deliberate humiliation, rather than a fair test, may paralyse a student intellectually, so that he might fail.

UNWISE THINGS TO DO AT YOUR INTERVIEW

- Assuming that your interviewers' earnest demeanour means they dislike you.

- Rambling on when you have already realised that you are on the wrong track.

- Dismissing a tough question with a "Don't know", rather than think hard, then have a stab at the answer.

- Answering the question you hoped would come up rather than the one you were actually asked.

- Thinking it's enough to say what happened in a lab, country or period - without adding how or why.

- Mistaking the interview for a quiz and answering much too fast.

- Solving a maths problem in your head, rather than showing the stages by which you got there in writing.

- Trying to guess the interviewer's views on a contentious issue rather than giving your own (well substantiated) views.

- Hoping to wing it when asked to comment on a book you have not actually read.

12
Paying to shine
at the interview

Active self-preparation works for many students, but for those in the money there is one obvious way to make the Oxbridge interview a cinch rather than a nightmare: this is to go there from the right school. While creating Oxbridge entrants used to be a mission restricted to a few top public schools, fee-paying parents now expect this from every private establishment. They also tend to obtain it, and not just in terms of the intensive, small class teaching by qualified staff which the schools officially emphasize.

One such establishment, once mainly known as a supplier of officer cadets to Sandhurst, includes in its weekly time table for Oxbridge entrants amongst other things:

- a 40-minute tutorial taking pupils through old Oxbridge entrance papers;
- A short essay on interview questions former pupils had been asked;
- Verbal interview training;
- A talk on an interview-related course subject given by an expert brought from outside;
- Short talks given by pupils on their individual academic interests;
- A problem-solving session;
- Guidance on how to research a project to be mentioned;
- "Six of the best" book club sessions in which pupils and teachers discuss the half dozen books listed as mandatory holiday reading etc.

The effect of all this has, for many decades, been to create what one young ex-Oxbridge lecturer now teaching abroad referred to as "a Sparkler", meaning a candidate who shines brightly at his interview, but might soon fizzle out.

The Sparkler would deliver all the "right" answers from the start. Asked why he picked his course, he would launch into a little monologue suggesting that he embodied all the qualities and skills admissions tutors were fishing for.

To show you what this could mean until the gradual Oxbridge interview reforms, here is a (mildly satirised) version of the Sparkler's performance:

"Well, I thought a lot about it before deciding. I was very impressed with your general academic reputation, of course, especially in Historic Anthropology (my housemaster told me about it), but I became really interested in the family structure of medieval Provençal villages when I went to the local museum near our French holiday home and found some old land records (actually, the careers teacher recommended that I go there, having steered me towards this unfamiliar subject. I am currently reading *Provencal birthing rituals* by Dr. Deepthought who is teaching here. It is absolutely fascinating.

Actually, I was so keen I started a Provençal Society in our school, and one of my friends has already become a member (after I agreed to join the Latin Grammar Society he founded, so it could go on his personal statement).

Then, of course, there is the recreational side. Your team usually wins the inter-collegiate rugby final (my PE teacher translated the prospectus reference to 'lots of Rugby Blues' for me) and I am quite a keen forward scrum (actually, I find rugby terrifying, but it was mandatory at my boarding school and the headmaster claimed that playing the game went down awfully well with Oxbridge. I'll drop out of matches in the first term)."

Eager, motivated and academic, the Sparkler seems to be the answer to even the most sport-hating don's prayer. But is he? The answer lies in the mixed intake of most fee-paying schools. While some parents opt for private schooling because they hope it will stretch their bright, fast-learning child, other parents see it as a way of giving a struggling learner the best chance in life.

So, a Sparkler could be anything. The best Oxbridge entrance training makes it impossible to tell whether you are dealing with a gifted youngster who will excel once on the course, or a carefully tutored but middling pupil who will struggle to keep up once his support system is gone and will finally leave, having narrowly scraped a Third.

Now contrast this with the (again mildly satirised) answers given by another candidate when asked why he chose the college:

Fred: "Well, I was told it was not too high up the league tables, so it might take more state school pupils. I wasn't too sure about this place at first, what with most of the buildings being so old, but apparently the student rooms are in a new block, so I figured that would be alright.''

Interviewer: ''Anything else?''

Fred: ''Well, of course that I could do Archaeology here. I got the idea from seeing 'Raiders of The Lost Ark', and then I read a magazine article about what archaeologists do in FHM. My local library also found me a book that was mentioned there, even though I had to wait for three weeks, but it was really interesting.

Not quite as good as history, mind you, which is what I like best at school. I even got to read out my holiday essay on Scottish war songs on local radio. Only Oxbridge History is supposed to be really difficult to get into and so my teacher suggested I settle for Archaeology instead. I'm halfway through the introduction he lent me. There's quite a bit of history in your course, isn't there?''

Interviewer: ''Arguably so. But archaeology is still hard work and requires excellent time management. Do you combine your reading with anything else? Rugger? Rowing?''

Fred: ''Not really. My mate and I used to bum off for a fag when the rest got on the minibus to the sports centre at the other end of town. And we don't have any rivers in Luton. Mind you, I've heard that you got your own, full size football pitch. Would it be OK to have a bit of a kick-about later?''

Well, who sounds more like a potential Oxbridge student to you? The answer is not quite as clear-cut as it seems. A handful of colleges do now have an intelligent, motivated, honest student like Fred. What makes the huge parental investment in school fees seem worthwhile, though, is that so many admissions tutors, including state school educated ones, still go for the Sparkler.

While Oxbridge is not unaware of this problem (first raised by the author in 2003), no satisfactory solution has quite yet been found. Sports now counts for much less, interviewers ask far fewer personal questions, and standardised tests can provide further information about a student's grasp of facts and thinking skills. However, the language used by dons and the knowledge base expected can still trip up ordinary students.

INTERVIEW TRAINING

So, what options do parents have if they cannot afford the fees that would transform Fred into a Sparkler? Until the appearance of this book, which was put on this earth to do exactly that, the answer has been precious few.

The cut-price option has, for the last decade or so, been a bit of interview training offered by an Oxbridge graduate doing home tutoring while he waits for his dream job, or a group of sessions offered to outsiders by some private A-level college. Alternatively, such training can be bought, in the form of about a week's coaching plus some general guidance, from a small number of expensive outfits specialising in this field.

Oxbridge absolutely hates these paid interlopers. Mentioning that interview training courses were now held in Oxford itself, one powerful admissions tutor told me with almost a hiss: "I am appalled to think that some genuine colleges here would agree to have their premises used by such people."

Anthony Smith, the President of Magdalen College, Oxford, went even further when he described the staff of one interview training company whose success in placing pupils had been much in the news as "just a bunch of grasping, meddling, money-grabbing young men" (*The Times*, 29th May 2003).

This is a quite extraordinary reaction. After all, the headmasters of most private schools are welcome guests at the dreaming spires. So, if a man who charges parents £20,000 a year to (amongst other things) get pupils into Oxbridge is regularly invited to dine at the dons' high table, why is the chap who offers to do this for a more affordable sum, between £250 and £1,500 a throw, treated as socially below a pimp?

There are two possible explanations for such a reaction. One is that interview training companies, or at least those which work on the basis of a no-win-no-fee basis, will only accept the kind of students who would get in anyway and therefore, as Magdalen's President has also suggested, "make their money out of parents' social anxiety about Oxbridge."

This would indeed justify the Oxbridge disdain, if it were not for one thing: some dons are claiming the precise opposite. Far from agreeing that all those evil, venal young men always get their pupils in, they insist that interview training never works. They are convinced that they can always spot its signs (unless, presumably, it is done by a private school) and that this leads them to dismiss the candidate's own abilities.

In other words, just a tinge of snobbishness about the kind of training which is acceptable, as opposed to the kind which is not, might be a more likely explanation.

But if you buy, will you get value for your money? You certainly might. While interview training cannot impart a knowledge of facts, it can help a student decode the often mystifying questions asked by Oxbridge dons. Ways of neatly structuring your answer may also be taught. This may be enough to shift the balance in favour of a bright, well-taught applicant from a non-academic home.

Problems can sometimes arise. One of these is that interview trainers who prepare large groups of students for Oxbridge during a very short time may blur their individual style. This can make it too obvious that a candidate has been coached.

And, if parents only pay an interview trainer if their son or daughter gets in, that target can end up overriding others: pupils might be subtly encouraged to lower their sights in order to improve their entrance chances, for instance by considering less competitive fields than Law or Medicine. Alternatively, they might be directed away from the most academically renowned and hardest to impress colleges, in favour of the old "housemaster's route" outlined earlier.

The less popular a candidate's course and college choice is, after all, the more likely the candidates are to get in and the interview trainers are to get their money. The result of such a strategy could be an unsuitable course, or a miserable time at the wrong college and a career that does not live up to one's expectations.

However, there is no sign that any of this is happening, on the whole. Instead, students who had paid interview training are often delighted with the results. If there is a real problem with interview training, it lies elsewhere. Many parents cannot possibly spare several hundred pounds, never mind several thousand, just to help a top university recognise their teenager's ability.

MORE SMART INTERVIEW TIPS

While you cannot fully predict interview questions, here are the top strategies that will counter-act interview panic and enable you to give strong, convincing answers.

Spell it out
Don't ever answer an interview question with just yes or no. This has to be followed by a reason. Which scientific fact, moral principle or past event are you basing your answer on?

Listen carefully
Unless you do, you won't know whether the interviewer is seeking a definition or an example, a fact or your opinion.

Breathe deeply and reflect before answering
This helps because interview questions can be complex: you may need to look at a topic from more than one obvious angle, or consider more than one possible explanation.

Have a strategy for handling bewildering questions
Think for a bit, then decide whether any part of the question is familiar. Now work forward from that. You might have to offer an informed guess, but check it fits the situation or data. If a question does not make sense to you at all, it's OK to ask dons to clarify it or explain an unfamiliar word.

Know that even short questions may require longish answers
Faced with something simple like "What is genetic mutation (or an internal combustion engine)" it is tempting to give an equally simple answer. However, you are usually also expected to say how it works and why.

Show that you can think
Remember that some questions may require an answer based on logical reasoning, not facts.

Practise doing your sums
If your subject has any mathematical element, make sure your mental arithmetic is up to scratch, as you may not be allowed to use a calculator.

YET MORE SMART INTERVIEW TIPS

Think logically
Logical thinking is a key quality dons seek. So, ensure that the reasons you offer for, say, climate change or religious strife might indeed explain it. Alternatively, try to think through the logical consequences of a new policy or law.

Qualify
Remember that not all questions are geared towards making you state an absolute truth. So, think whether you need to qualify your answer with words like "occasionally" or "in most cases".

Compare and contrast
A good answer often involves doing both of these things, or at least one. This can mean looking at other countries or incidents. It's a nice way to show that you have a strong knowledge base and a flexible mind.

Draw on what you know
Asked a question like "What if we had chosen to remain neutral in 1914?" many students assume that they must imagine a completely new world. Actually, it's fine to draw on real-life scenarios from other periods or places. Just make sure you recognise a key date!

Be objective
Some questions offend some students. When asked whether it may be alright to torture animals or take drugs you are not meant to just give your personal view. Look at the issue in the course context, i.e. from a legal, medical, scientific or ethical angle.

Be aware that the questions change somewhat each year
So, learning old interview questions by heart is fairly pointless. This is why this book gives you answering guidelines instead.

Honour the English language
When asked for written answers, make sure your English is concise and correct (no text speak!). Practise writing half-page answers to sample questions – by hand, not on your laptop.

13
Grading the interview

Oxbridge students tend to be very positive about the interview process. After all, it enabled them to join "the brightest and best" in their delightful mini-world. Unsuccessful candidates, who went into the interview cold, are quite often more bewildered than cross. "I just couldn't work out what they wanted from me," was a phrase heard more than once.

Outside experts can be more critical. Professor Deborah Eyre insists that identifying those who will benefit most from a top academic education is an expert job. As the director of the National Academy for Gifted and Talented Youth she set up an enrichment programme based on first establishing students' intellectual profiles through a whole portfolio of evidence, including a battery of scientific tests. The Oxbridge interview, to her, is "a very unscientific way of testing ability, made even more arbitrary by the variation in practices by individual admissions tutors and colleges".

Much of this is due to the fact that dons used to be given no formal preparation for interviewing at all. They could ask a candidate whatever they liked and, if the spirit took them, with both eyes shut. After protests from a humiliated interviewee in the 1990s, it was agreed that interview talk must not be offensive, but there was no rule against it being obscure. Only the admissions tutors for the Oxford medical course were somewhat restricted; their questions had to cover specific areas, listed on a task sheet. How to cover them, though, was up to the interviewer.

Having fiercely defended this policy for decades, Cambridge started to coach newly appointed admissions tutors a few years ago and Oxford announced in September 2008 that all its interviewers would now be trained. Even trained dons, though, don't always grasp the mysteries of accessible behaviour.

In December 2008, one bright student I had mentored found himself opposite three men in black gowns who stared at him for 30 minutes with fixed grins, while bombarding him with very formally worded questions. The idea, presumably, was to put him at ease, but the young man, who lives on one of London's scariest housing estates, found the scene so disconcerting he could not display his skills. He was not offered a place at the college, but other students I knew who were interviewed there did well.

The interview, then, remains a bit of a tombola; those candidates who get in and those who don't may have totally different interviews despite university guidelines.

Professor Eyre is also concerned about the distorting effect public school training has on interview outcomes: "What we see is that children in the private sector seemingly over-achieve. They are trained up to the limit of their potential, then groomed to come across as exceptional, whether they are that or not."

Nor is she happy about the fact that the blame for failure is so often attributed to a lack of self-esteem. "Some interviewers," she says, "are overbearing, and some young people just do not like to be interrogated. They find the encounter unattractive, whatever their ability."

Made a decade ago, Eyre's point was substantiated in 2012, when a comprehensive school student interviewed for a place on a Law course at Magdalen, Oxford, sent the university a very public rejection letter. In it, Elly Nowell argued that she had found the "traditions and rituals" at her interview so off-putting they made her laugh. The "grand formal setting" was, she claimed, distorting the academic potential of students like her. While this candidate's interview took place at a particularly traditional college, hers is a legitimate view.

Another problem has been pointed out by Joan Freeman. "The talented are not a homogeneous group," insists Britain's veteran expert on this group. She wants interviewers to be aware that a gifted young writer and a gifted young scientist will behave quite differently, and individuals within each group may do so too. The "brightest and best" can be dozy or sparkling, quick witted or ponderous.

No testing system is entirely value free either, warns Professor Freeman. This is true of the Oxbridge one, as well as of the standard IQ test and the American-type SAT. The shorter a test is too, the more the values of the tester will affect the outcome, and the Oxbridge interview is often very short indeed.

The new aptitude tests introduced for specific courses have also failed to reassure some experts. The Schwartz Report of May 2004, commissioned by the Government, warns that preparing and travelling to additional tests can interfere with a student's classroom work. Deborah Eyre feels that having subject tests that also vary from university to university "makes life more difficult for the student, parent and school". A set of generally accepted ability tests might, both suggest, work rather better. There is indeed some progress towards this now in Oxbridge Medicine and Law.

Foreign academics, while admiring the intellectual glory of Oxbridge, are amazed at its entrance process. Graduates of top US universities like Harvard and Princeton, or of the Paris Sorbonne, are renowned within international organisations like the UN for their analytic minds, articulacy, lateral thinking and all the rest of the Oxbridge wish list, but they have not been entry-tested for any of this. Instead, a great university seeks to gradually develop these great qualities in bright applicants.

This is why American universities grade all applicants by a standard academic ability test, the SAT, which is regarded as fair, though you can bone up for it. The candidates with the highest scores are offered places in the top institutions. Applicants to even the most renowned French universities need only to have done well in their baccalaureate, an extended form of A-levels.

A VIEW FROM THE STAFF ROOM

How does another group, the teachers, feel about Oxbridge entrance? One group of sixth form teachers I spoke to were clear about the problem faced by large schools like theirs, with a mixed and often disadvantaged intake. It is not just that they cannot possibly provide the intense interview training offered elsewhere. Oxbridge also wants a candidate who is positively bubbling with enthusiasm about his subject and is actively pursuing it beyond syllabus requirements.

Now, although comprehensives seek to get all their bright pupils into university, ''Oxbridge qualities'' are a minority trait and pupils exhibiting them too publicly risk trouble from their peers. Winning a prize, or even choosing to compete for one can, in some schools, set the bullies on you. So can speaking up too much in class or knowing much more about various subjects than your classmates do. Not until the A-level years, when these pupils are taught separately, does the classroom become a place in which it feels safe to show off intellectually, or to openly pursue unusual hobbies.

If a pupil has an articulate, educated family, this will balance outside factors and no damage is done, said the teachers. For many bright comprehensive school pupils, though, the interview becomes a place where they are suddenly expected to do what instinct told them to carefully avoid: show wild enthusiasm for their subject, be quick-witted and sparkle. The deliberate underplaying of their abilities perfected over the years now backfires. They undersell themselves.

To illustrate the outcome one teacher quoted the feedback he had received after the rejection of an outstanding pupil by a Cambridge college. The boy, the admissions tutor wrote, ''got an A for his written exam, is serious and passionate about his subject. Unfortunately, he was nervous at the interview and overly defensive.''

The head of the department, who had sent seven other pupils to various other Cambridge Colleges that year, all without success, quoted similar feedback from the university. His candidates, he was told, had been too tense and not fluent or expansive enough at the interview. To this was added the usual sop: ''We had so many very able candidates this year.''

A teacher at a more successful school nevertheless concurred with her colleagues. Oxbridge was clearly trying to broaden its intake, but there were still ''social'' entrance qualifications. Far too much, she felt, hinges on a pupil's ability to sustain a long, clever verbal exchange with a well-spoken, highly educated adult.

Oxbridge success must not remain merely the responsibility of schools, insisted the experienced teacher: ''There is a need for a Joint Working Party made up of dons and sixth form heads in order to work out what precise qualities Oxbridge colleges can reasonably seek. It also needs to consider how entrance can be made a fairer process, given that some of these qualities just cannot be fostered in a large, mixed ability state school.''

WATCHING THEM RUN

Recent changes in the interview process could be an attempt to forestall such intervention. Questions have become more subject-centred and an admissions tutor can no longer single-handedly grill two dozen students in a day. Now there are usually two interviewers present, both to guard against prejudice and against the exhaustion that might cause the talents of the last poor soul ushered in to be overlooked.

As a veteran Oxbridge mentor, I know the difference such changes can make. But will they be enough? Contrary to popular belief, it is not just outsiders who are wondering. Writing in the *Times Higher Educational Supplement* of 13th January 2006, Oxford don Alan Ryan questioned the weight attributed to verbal interviews compared to written tests. ''What students do at university is write'', argued the Warden of New College. ''What they get a degree for is performance in examinations. You'd have thought that the way to decide which applicants to accept is to see how well they do what they will do at university. If you were picking a team to run in the Olympics, you wouldn't interview them about running; you'd watch them run.''

The recent growth in written Oxbridge tests, imperfect as some are, suggests that Alan Ryan's views are spreading.

14
Going for it

Despite all the criticism voiced of it in recent years, the interview remains the most crucial part of the Oxbridge entrance process. Most dons insist that although it may not be totally value-free, it is essential to help them find the right students for their unique face-to-face teaching system. Those found now annually include a (slight) majority of state school students, some from very poor backgrounds. Passing the interview means that you will be offered an internationally coveted university place, subject mainly to the kind of A-level results very able candidates can expect.

To a bright teenager setting out for Oxbridge, these points should provide enough reassurance to carry her confidently past those manicured lawns, shiny iron gates and freshly painted stone walls into a room full of people wearing bicycle clips. Parents still toying with the Valium, though, may want a slightly more detailed summary, which goes roughly as follows:

That the interview structure does not compare like with like there is no doubt. There is just too much difference in pupils' academic and social background. Equally, there is no doubt that it does pick up on real talent in all sorts of candidates, and that many interviewers genuinely seek to broaden their course intake, albeit in oddly unscientific ways. Even if there is prejudice among some, this cannot be allowed to determine general outcomes. While the university bench marks set to expand the proportion of state school students have never yet been met, they must be striven for. The alternative could be a (periodically threatened) cutback in Government funds.

As a result, interviewers can be surprisingly nice, and those whose fierce or peculiar manners flummox outsiders are gradually being reined in. Responding to criticism from headmasters, one admissions tutor argued that the treatment of applicants had been ''a great deal more savage'' in the past.

It should also be said that while some candidates find the interview nerve-racking, others actually enjoy the rapid verbal to-and-fro and get an unexpected thrill from being able to show off their mental skills. For many a junior thinker, there is nothing quite like a famous senior thinker's quick, almost imperceptible nod of approval after a good reply.

Leaving you for the 8.43 train, your son should therefore take heart. Not only is Oxbridge committed to taking someone like him, but you and this book are on his side. Guided by the information given on these pages, he need not feel at a disadvantage compared with posher and seemingly more confident students. Quite of few of them will fail, because even the most meticulous coaching and the greatest familiarity with ancient buildings is not a substitute for a well-focused brain. If you are blessed with the latter and have followed this book's advice, you stand an excellent chance.

The important thing is to be both optimistic and prepared. Confidence based on wise choices, well-planned school work, focused reading and an understanding of the interview process begets Oxbridge success. So does the realisation that much of this is just a game with mirrors, played by clever young people and sometimes not so smart older ones. You can join this game and win, if you understand the rules and draw on all available help. There is nothing spontaneous about the Oxbridge entrance process, and you need not comply with that absurd claim.

ONE FOR THE ROAD

If you have come this far, you have probably absorbed enough information to get through the interview, or to prepare a teenager for it. Still, just in case it all seems too much, here is a basic summary in the form of ten simple commandments:

Rule 1: Be prepared to answer questions about your interests, activities, subject, course or college choice.
Rule 2: Accept that you might not be asked about any of this.
Rule 3: Treat the interview as a conversation in which ideas may be thrown back and forth. Unlike in a quiz, there is not always a single, correct answer.
Rule 4: Say not only what you think but also why you think it.
Rule 5: Give longish, considered answers.
Rule 6: Speculate, compare and explain.
Rule 7: Don't expect the interviewer to tell you whether you were right or wrong.
Rule 8: Express curiosity and a willingness to learn.
Rule 9: Don't be too dogmatic: the more you know about the world, the less certain things look.
Rule 10: Don't panic if you are being asked about a topic you have never thought about: this is not a disaster, but a way of giving you a chance to improvise.

Or just try to remember one phrase in which a state school headmaster I knew used to sum up the interview to his pupils: ''The interview explores the ability to reason and to support an argument with constructive thought - and the skill of thinking on your feet.''

15

Oxbridge Medicine

Parents and students often view an Oxbridge medical degree as the most glittering of all prizes. In this, they are both right and wrong. They are right, because Medicine is the only Oxbridge course which almost guarantees you a job, and a well-paid, prestigious, and often highly satisfying lifetime one at that. As one young doctor I interviewed put it, it was great to be in a profession which combined science with human interaction: "You get up in the morning and you don't know what will happen. The joy of medicine is that your bleeper goes and your day changes."

However, people are wrong in that Oxbridge Medicine is not necessarily a better route to professional glory than a degree from, say, Newcastle. While Medicine involves a huge amount of academic learning, the success of a medical career depends first of all on a doctor's work record. What matters is how skilled you are in practice and how well you get on with colleagues. As a result, students rise to the top from any good medical school. The bright, enthusiastic (and privately educated) young doctor I quoted above was, in fact, rejected by Cambridge, but is, nevertheless, shooting up the career ladder. His friends, who made it into Oxbridge Medicine, have similar, but not actually better jobs.

There is, of course, something special about Oxbridge Medicine. Penicillin, the drug that continues to save millions of lives each year, was developed at Oxford in 1940 by two men, Australian medical scientist Howard Florey and a German Jewish asylum seeker, biochemist Ernst Boris Chain (although the compound had been discovered in 1928 by Alexander Fleming, who worked and trained at St. Mary's Medical School, London).

Cambridge can take credit for a more theoretical discovery. In 1953, British scientist Francis Crick and two Americans, James Watson and Rosalind Franklin, decoded the "double helix" structure of the DNA molecule, which carries the genetic information from old cells to new ones, in a Cambridge lab. Few individual discoveries have so quickly ushered in so many fundamental advances in so many fields, from genetics and evolutionary theory to biochemistry and medical research. Today's students attending the Oxbridge courses have yet more reasons to feel privileged. They don't just enjoy some truly brilliant staff and labs, but also have the opportunity to mix daily with contemporaries involved in quite different academic fields, which makes for a vibrant social and intellectual life. Medical students elsewhere tend to live, study and party within the far duller confines of a teaching hospital.

As a result, the competition is fierce. Oxford gets eight applicants for each place, Cambridge around six. (In most other subjects, the proportion of applicants to places is about four to one.) After years of bitter criticism over their selection procedures, these have been much restructured. No longer can a bright young chap expect to get in thanks to what older medics quaintly recall as "trial by sherry".

In fact, Medicine was the only Oxbridge course to have a formal entrance test in addition to the interview for several years. This was used by all colleges. Cambridge eventually followed suit, but each of the two universities had its own test, devised by its own medical staff. The tests were designed to test not so much to probe an applicant's background or IQ as their aptitude for this particular course.

However, there was concern that both exams favoured public school pupils because of their broader knowledge base and special coaching, and so both were eventually scrapped. A more ability-based exam, the Biomedical Admissions Test (BMAT) was first introduced in November 2003 for medical candidates applying to Oxford, Cambridge, University College (London) and Imperial College. While still not perfect, it has been much improved since.

So, how do you prove that you have what it takes? The answer, at least partly, is by doing some research.

MEDICAL SCHOOLS AND COURSES

For a subject which has generated so much public debate, Oxbridge Medicine is surprisingly small. Oxford admits around 150 new undergraduates a year, Cambridge around 260. (Their graduate medical courses for people with other degrees are even smaller, with some 20 places each.)

The first concern of many students is which of the two undergraduate courses to pick. Dons at each of them will earnestly assure you that their own is by far superior. Both medical schools are certainly world famous. A high proportion of their students will become consultants, that is medical specialists, and combine treatment with medical research. Others will spend most of their professional lives in the computerised labs of hospitals, pharmaceutical firms or medical schools. There they will pioneer new treatments, identify new diseases or develop new drugs.

While this means there is an awful lot to learn, Oxbridge medical students are not expected to do so primarily by sitting in large lecture halls or by doing practicals. Instead, their course is tutor-based. A medical lecturer will work through the material with two undergraduates, sometimes even one-to- one. Students read stacks of books, but their content is filtered through personal discussion. Tutor and student may remain together for three years.

Not only does such personal attention allow students to take in large amounts, it also enables them to follow their personal interests with encouragement from their tutor. There is a flipside, of course. A student really needs to be brave enough to ask questions, speculate on answers and risk being wrong.

Candidates also need to grasp that medical training at Oxbridge is more theoretical than elsewhere, at the beginning at least. "It suits the academic mind," as tutors put it. You are expected to show an interest in scientific theories and research, so don't say in your application that you picked the course because you want to help people. Patient care here is just one of several challenging study areas.

There are differences between the courses, too, if mainly in structure. Oxford teaches medicine in the most traditional way. While some top universities move their students' knowledge forward through a problem-centred approach, for instance by taking them through all possible causes of a bad headache (Manchester, Liverpool) or by a systems-based one, for instance by teaching students "all about the lower limb" (Edinburgh), the Oxford curriculum is taught discipline by discipline. Students gradually work their way through anatomy, physiology, biochemistry etc. In their first two years they don't see very many patients.

At Cambridge, the emphasis in the early course years is on imparting medical knowledge areas by importance, rather than by scientific discipline. Once students have a good grasp of anatomy, they explore everything from the body's self-regulatory systems to the molecular basis of cells, from the way diseases progress to the role of drugs. After that, they learn about human reproduction and human behaviour in a medico-social context. They also encounter real-life patients quite early on.

HOW DO I GET PICKED?

Winning a medical place is hard. On average, around 10 per cent of applicants do so at Oxford, and around 19 per cent at Cambridge. While state school students make up a slight majority of their annual intake, students from the smaller independent sector have a higher success rate. "Diversity is not sought", as one medical don somewhat huffily put it. "What we seek are those students who will do best in our school." He is training life-savers and knows that a bad doctor can kill.

So, what does make a good candidate? An open mind is essential. Students who are really curious about the way human bodies work and interested in statistics, social factors or the NHS find it easier to get through the course. To get through a doctor's working day, you need resilience. Medicine is hard work, and so interviewers are looking for tough people, for "grit and determination".

You also need to know that Oxford and Cambridge ask for somewhat different qualifications and that their broader selection process differs. Once you got the full picture, you can start preparing for it. Here are the details:

GRADES

Oxford and Cambridge ask for a high proportion of top grades at GCSE, while making some allowances for disadvantage at this stage. In 2018, Oxford was expecting three A-levels, all taken in one year, and resulting in grades of A*AA. Cambridge was expecting A*A*A in most cases. There is some (very slight) flexibility on this in case of disadvantaged candidates or struggling schools.

Current subject requirements vary between the two universities. Oxford applicants must have at least an A-grade in both chemistry and one of biology, physics. Cambridge applicants need A-levels in chemistry and one of biology, physics, mathematics.

In practice, though, most applicants have at least three full science/maths A-levels. Some Cambridge colleges ask for this or even for a specific A-level subject or two. Do, therefore, check with a college before applying there.

Both medical departments say they admit students with a third non-science A-level, but their success rate is tiny. Also note that the entrance requirement for Medicine can change from year to year.

READING YOUR WAY FORWARD

If you're applying for Medicine, being science-oriented means reading avidly alongside your A-level work. The Cambridge Medicine website contains a list of key scientific concepts which will make this much easier. You could start with a scientist's book about cells, then pick a handful out of an Oxbridge Medicine list of recommended academic texts and a guide to medical ethics.

Round this off with a monthly trawl through *New Scientist* and perhaps *Student BMJ*. Also, look out for press reports (some are linked to in my tweets) about new drug treatments, new insights into the cause of a disease or yet another NHS reform. Then think about the possible consequences. What ethical dilemma might a new drug create for NHS doctors? Should every medical condition be treated? Practise expressing your views in more than one sentence.

MULTIMEDIA STUDIES

For light entertainment, your laptop will let you access some brilliant medicine programmes from BBC Radio or TV via the BBC iPlayer. You should also listen to one of the inspiring radio programmes on medicine found in the archive of that excellent BBC Radio 4 series "In Our Time". Lectures on medical topics that a smart sixth former will be able to understand can be found not just on U-tube but also on both Oxbridge websites.

Try to go slightly out of your way in order to learn more. This can mean signing up for an OU science module delivered online or travelling to a STEM event outside your school. Meanwhile, keep checking your chosen university's website for home page news on medical discoveries. They have been put there for your benefit.

HOMING IN ON YOUR TARGET

State school students attending a Medical Summer School held at Oxford in 2009 were said to have had a 40 per cent success rate when later targeting its Medicine course. Even though rates have considerably fallen since, it's worth exploring this promising avenue.

If you do not qualify, go to a Medicine Open Day, or to one of the Student Medicine Conferences now jointly run by Oxford and Cambridge. Lectures given there are later put on the university's website, but if you attend you can ask your own questions. There are book suggestions on the course resources page. If you email a Cambridge college you like, it will send you a full reading list. You can also ask for more study advice.

Cambridge, especially, feels that attending one of its events is proof of engagement with your subject. Applicants are expected to be "active learners", which means finding out as much as you can about Medicine yourself. This can seem unfair, as medical candidates at some schools are intensively coached. The Cambridge reply is that students who lack such coaching still get in.

The Oxford book list can be found on the University's

"Courses" web page under *Introductory Reading and Resources>Medicine,* like the reading for all other courses. Unfortunately, this particular list is terrifyingly long. Although its authors warn that students "should not rush and buy" everything, it will still deter poorer students. Many of its suggestions, moreover, are far too advanced for sixth formers, as well as too expensive and unlikely to be found in any public library; they were clearly designed for students already admitted and thus able to use their departmental library. You'll find a much shorter list suitable for grappling with in the holidays under *Read all around* it (see p. 27).

WORK EXPERIENCE

A medical candidate will learn much from trailing a real doctor in a real hospital, from hearing her diagnose a patient during her ward round, and from being bossed about by nurses. Keeping your eyes and ears open, though, is not enough. You must be brave and ask questions yourself (not of the god-like consultant you are trailing, of course, but of the nearest junior doctor).

Make your questions short. How do doctors work out the cause of chest pain? Why does team work matter? Try to also get a sense of the management structure. Who has the real power, doctor or hospital manager? Note down the diseases you've encountered, then look them up at home and think about the challenges they may pose.

Students determined to find a hospital placement need to type *NHS Volunteering* Placements into Google, then go to *Gaining Experience,* a page full of useful advice for both job seekers and student volunteers. Alternatively, they may want to contact *Volunteering England* or just phone the HR department of any large Hospital trust.

Another option, shadowing a GP, will enable you to observe perhaps less exciting but more common medical conditions. To arrange this, just phone or email any of the local surgeries listed on *NHS Choices.*

A local care home will do fine too. Check first if the place employs a full-time doctor (it will be better for you and the residents if it does), or if you can shadow a visiting one. Also find out if the nursing staff speak English. Observation here again needs to be backed up by conversation, even if it is mainly about physical hardship, low pay or residents' often stressful demands. Which problems do staff face when caring for people with multiple illnesses? Practise explaining what you've learnt by button-holing your gran.

If you have acted as a carer for a relative, this too counts as a medicine-related experience, but you must reflect on it. Do carers have needs of their own, and how can they be met? In which way may the illness of one family member impact on others?

Even if all you can get is an ordinary job, don't give up. You can still explore health-related issues in your work environment: pollution, the non-observation of health and safety rules, dangerous machinery or shift work all have medical implications. You'll also find lots of exciting books about killer diseases and about life as a doctor in the medicine section of your local library or bookshop.

EXTRA-CURRICULARS

The perfect spare-time activity for an aspiring doctor is being a volunteer for St. John's Ambulance. Being involved in a support scheme for young people with disabilities will provide you with equally valuable insights. So may becoming a hospital visitor on behalf of a local charity or religious group. If none of these are an option, acting as a trained counsellor or first aider at your school can also help. Just keep in mind that what matters here is not so much what you do as what you have to say about it.

You no longer need to play rugby or tennis to prove that you will fit into a medical team, but consider some physical activity beyond logging into Facebook. After all, anything from running to dancing has potential medical implications. Can you work out what might cause a Marathon runner to collapse? Or why classical ballet is quite so painful?

WRITING A MEDICINE-GEARED STATEMENT

As a potential medic, your personal statement needs to be carefully structured and fairly conventional. The tale of your growing love for medicine, your scientific and medical interests, the books you have read and the research you have done deserves a wide audience. Towards the end, try to mention both a medicine-related hobby and an unrelated but demanding one (both genuine, of course!) as proof of your capacity to multi-task. Wrap it all up by spelling out why you, personally, might make a good doctor. The above list will give you ample raw material for a draft.

I would only add one bit of advice: think first before mentioning your dream career. It can be wise to avoid the most popular, most telegenic medical specialties. Admittedly, babies are cute, but does the only possible future for you really lie in paediatric cardiology? After all, those most in need of doctors are the chronically sick and the old. So, could you find it in your heart to treat gall bladder problems or diabetes?

THE BMAT

Taken many weeks before the interviews, the Biomedical Admissions Test (BMAT) lasts for a continuous two hours. Those who do best in it are students with strong science and maths who also have good writing skills and a quick, logical mind. Test guidance on the BMAT website has much improved, and what can further raise your score is working through its sample questions. Make sure you also read the answer keys. It is even more important for state school students to practice writing BMAT essays of the right length and on topics used in the past.

A detailed description of the test contents is not available, but part one usually assesses your ability to reason and think in numbers or graphs, often with reference to a real world situation. Students may be given figures for incidences of multiple sclerosis and for the altitude of towns, then asked to interpret it.

Watch out here for the difference between a medical cause and a correlation. A cause here explains an illness, a correlation just means that the illness exists alongside another factor, causal or not. Candidates are meant to note the connection, but not jump to conclusions. For instance, Aids in the western world largely correlates with male homosexuality. However, homosexuality does not actually cause Aids.

Part two of the BMAT seeks out the scientific mind. While no medical knowledge is expected, candidates now need to be armoured with the background facts of GCSE science, including Physics and Maths. Knowledge of basic structures like cells is essential.

Part three is a choice of essay topics. Each requires some interest in theoretical ideas, although it's OK to substantiate your points with practical examples. The essay tests whether a candidate understands a concept, can express herself, can see both sides of an argument and can offer some sort of analysis. Make sure you answer the actual question and write in a clear style.

While this can be a chance to shine, students who do often have essay skills beyond those taught in most comprehensives. To improve yours, study the BMAT sample essays, or get help from your English teacher.

How important is the BMAT? Once it comes to drawing on it, the two universities differ. In recent years, Cambridge has interviewed well over 70 per cent of those who sat the test. Oxford, which has greater trust in the BMAT but also a much smaller course, tends to interview on average just 28 per cent of its medicine applicants. Neither department has a formal commitment to increase its intake from under-represented groups, but Oxford will upscale the BMAT score of a student who has outperformed others at her own and similar schools at GCSEs. Students on the Cambridge *Extenuating Circumstances* scheme may be offered a post-BMAT interview at some of its colleges.

THE MEDICAL INTERVIEW

A few weeks after the test, invited candidates travel up for the next stage. Once they have snacked for free in a college hall or cafeteria, it's time for their medical interviews. At Cambridge, a student tends to have two. An Oxford medical candidate is generally first seen by two sets of interviewers at the college of her choice, then by a second college picked by computer, so she may get up to four.

So, what might you be asked about? If there are any warm-up questions, they may involve your reasons for choosing medicine. Or, having read the account of your medical placement, an interviewer may want to seek out further details. A student who has reflected on her own abilities and motives will now gain confidence as she speaks.

The next stage at either of the two universities will probably be a battery of straight science questions: How are messages sent around cells? Can you describe to me the key factors in evolution? Do scientific facts exist?

These may be followed by questions about aspects of Medicine: Will you talk about the role of GPs? Should the NHS treat self-inflicted illnesses? Here the student must define terms and give examples. She also wants to show an awareness of the moral problems doctors face.

Another interview feature is the "show and tell" question. To test your knowledge of human biology, you may be given a picture of some body part and asked to first identify, then talk about it. You are being invited to make an intelligent guess and to spell out clearly how you got there.

So, the right answer would go something like this: "It's a heart, judging by the shape and the valve. No, actually, the valve is at the bottom, so it could be a kidney, and then the valve would be connecting it to the ureter, which connects to the bladder. The kidneys filter out the waste from your blood to make urine. Then urine passes from the kidneys into the ureter which drains into the bladder. That's right, isn't it?''

You might still be wrong, but you will have shown that you have grasped the process of arriving at the truth.

The opposite of an intelligent guess, adopted by some panic-stricken candidates, is the stupid guess. After a long silence (bad if you only have 20 minutes to impress the tutor) one desperate candidate, I was told, finally whispered: "It could be a penis." Asked to explain why, he replied crossly: "I don't know, I'm just guessing."

Was he prepared to guess again, asked the tutor. "Not much point," he snapped, clearly regretting that he had ever taken up the invitation. As you may have guessed, he was turned down.

So, the ideal medical interviewee is someone willing to think, and to think aloud. She should also be calm enough not to panic if she doesn't know something; she must at least try and analyse what's put in front of her.

Much of a candidate's interview success is due to attitude. Be willing to engage with the questions put to you, even if they are about something totally unfamiliar. Some do not have any definite answer. Interviewers like students who follow clues and pick up on hints.

Don't go into disaster mode if you get something wrong - candidates are often accepted even if they do. Be prepared to have more than one try and, above all, don't keep mum.

Basic good manners also help, though this need not mean upper class speech. Again, don't make assumptions about Oxbridge only wanting posh students. The grander the college, the more likely it is these days to need a few working class applicants to stave off public criticism. So, don't mumble "I don't know, we didn't do that stuff at my school," if you are stuck. Instead, say "I don't know a lot about spinal vertebrae, but I'd really like to find out more, also for family reasons: my father has a lot of problems with his spine because he's a warehouseman."

Allow for the fact that the interviewer herself may well have gone to a state school. Accents do fade over the years. While there is no point in worrying about your own accent, "you need to be a bit formal," as one Medicine interviewer put it. What this mainly means is wearing a jacket, using polite phrases like "would you like me to" and, of course, not smoking.

There are also a few human qualities that go down well. Cheerfulness is tops. Medicine will give you traumatic experiences and encounters with people who need reassurance. It also involves lots of exhausting teamwork. So, no tutor wants a young Victor Meldrew.

Modesty can be another useful trait. Interviewers really do hate arrogant candidates who seem to believe that they have a right to get into Oxbridge just because they are smart. Almost all Medicine candidates are.

Being well informed can matter too: having kept up with news stories about changes in government health policy and their impact will enable you to field topical questions.

Lastly, this is one subject in which the otherwise rather imperial demand that candidates must be able to "think on their feet" may well be justified. After all, that is what doctors faced with a new patient or slide of some diseased organ do every day. The fancy name for this, done on the basis of lots of scientific knowledge, is "diagnostic skills".

While you will leave exhausted, note that your interviewers will have worked hard too. To prevent bias, medical dons at both universities now undergo preliminary training, interview in pairs and must cover certain subject areas. They may not even be told whether the applicant has chosen their college. At the end, interviewers fill in a score sheet, to be evaluated by a committee.

The score sheet, designed to establish whether a candidate's intrinsic qualities can carry her through, is a fairly recent innovation, even more recent than the written test. It ensures that the interview result cannot be skewed by an admissions tutor's preference for tall public school boys or cool Irish girls.

Like the centrally devised BMAT, the score sheet tells us something important about Oxbridge: while its dons will always argue that admission procedures are as perfect as can be, they will manage to make them just a little fairer and less idiosyncratic when there is enough outside pressure.

HOW DOES ALL THIS PAN OUT?

After their adrenaline-charged interviews, candidates can spend the rest of the day kicking their heels, being intimidated by the seeming confidence of Oxbridge students and wondering how people living in such a beautiful place can have such atrocious dress sense.

Meanwhile, a bit of academic horse trading goes on. Each college will rank its candidates in order of perceived ability. GCSE scores, BMAT scores and interview scores will be added up and compared. At Oxford, no allowances are made for a student's background when it comes to interview performance. It is assumed that "people will rise to the occasion." However, both colleges a student has been seen by can now make her an offer, which does improve her chances of a place.

At Cambridge, once it is clear who the very best candidates are, dons may sift the next best group "by fairness". A very good candidate whose chosen college cannot take her is sent to the Pool. Not all colleges have the same ideal candidate in mind, so she might still get in, but only if another college still has a vacancy after the first admissions round.

In the end, almost all the candidates that a medical department can accommodate will be offered a place at a specific college, conditional on them getting the stipulated A-level grades. A handful will get an "open offer", which means that their college cannot yet be specified. Where they will end up depends on the candidates who were dropped because they did not get the right grades.

So, how much fairer is the outcome of the medical admissions process today, almost two decades after the Laura Spence story? Well, there has been a slow but profound change. In 2017, almost two decades after the brilliant state school girl from Whitley Bay was rejected by Oxford, just over 60 per cent of UK medical students admitted by both Oxford and Cambridge came from UK state schools. Also, both state and private school applicants now have roughly the same 15 percent success rate. Making a fuss can work.

When it comes to other categories, the picture is uneven. Oxford medical school has consistently admitted a slightly higher proportion of women and of students of Asian origin than there are in the general population. However, while it admitted 18 black medical candidates between 2015 and 2017, those from African families are rather more likely to get in than those of Afro-Caribbean origin. The latter's success rate is disproportionately low.

As for working class students, a category Oxford and Cambridge do not use, comprehensive school teachers complain that when it comes to Oxford Medicine, the success rate of even their very best students remains disappointing. Many of these are very poor young people taught in poorly equipped schools, who find it hard to gain the right entrance qualifications.

Working class boys with the right grade predictions may also lack the formal manners that carry you through. They are likely to be gruff rather than polite, macho rather than balanced in the way they express themselves. While these are useful qualities in their current environment, they might well shed them in a different one. University students almost invariably do. By judging them purely on what they are at this point, the Oxford medical selection system does not really work for them.

Despite slightly different selection criteria, the same problem is said to still exist at Cambridge. A sixth form head at a London comprehensive crammed between two housing estates bitterly recalled how he had sent one of his very best students to a medical interview there. The teacher had spent lots of time encouraging the boy to take this frightening step and had carefully picked a college the school had some carefully nurtured links with. The applicant, who came from a large working class family, was rejected nevertheless. When the teacher asked for an explanation, he was told that the main problem had been "nervousness in the interview, a lack of ability to hypothesize, expand on points, a lack of verbal articulacy and of interview skills."

Things are gradually improving. As applicants become aware of the need to prepare and admissions departments are made to reveal more detailed break-downs of their intake figures, the odd disadvantaged pupil does get in.

Does it matter if the vast majority of Oxbridge medical students come from nice homes? I think it does. People in the lowest income groups have a different life-style and are more prone to certain diseases. Also, the bulk of patients are the elderly poor. Forget all those media lies about pension-rich baby-boomers causing Britain's economic crisis: millions of people in Britain live on the basic state pension, currently £6,549.40, a year. So a doctor who knows their world can be useful.

Interestingly, one disadvantaged group of medical applicants breaks the mould. Today's working class girls often do well in the interview, though it is not clear why. Perhaps being polite and formal comes more easily to them, or perhaps interviewers are more sympathetic towards a timid girl than a sullen boy. It is hard to tell.

DOES COACHING WORK FOR MEDICINE?
Tutors admit that quite a few of the students they see have probably been coached for the interview, but feel that it would be unfair to reject a good candidate on those grounds alone. One tutor actually suggested that such preparation did, after all, suggest a commitment to the medical profession.

Some coaching is informal. Quite a few candidates in both the state and the private sector are doctor's kids and will have had a chance to talk through likely questions at home. Alternatively, a doctor friend, relative or neighbour might be roped in. While interview questions do not cover medical treatment, questions about structures and problems can favour students with links to the medical world.

On the formal side, many schools in the private sector also run

179

a brief course, usually called something like "how to get into Medicine", which is especially geared toward Oxbridge. In addition, private schools often have science societies in which their students may discuss reports of medical discoveries or explore health related issues with adult guidance.

Well-off state school parents can also often buy in academic help. Quite a few private revision colleges now also offer far-from-cheap interview training for a wide range of science subjects, including Medicine.

Do interview training courses work? One of the medical dons I spoke to insisted that he "could not believe that the organisers of such courses could possibly deliver on their promises." Others felt certain that they would be able to spot a candidate who had been coached. They also seemed unreasonably sure that they had not encountered such a candidate yet.

Some short courses primarily introduce A-level students to aspects of medical practice. Teenagers whose parents can afford the substantial fee learn about medical terms and practice, get guidance on the university admissions process and have a mock interview. One such outfit, called *Medlink*, even let them treat Harvey, a state-of-the-art dummy, for a variety of conditions.

Although a strong grasp of science is vastly more important for Oxbridge success, such an immersion process may enable a bright candidate to "talk the talk" and meet the requirements set out above. This should not make a student feel that such a course is essential.

If you are a parent, here is one final bit of advice: encourage the lad to arrive at his college the night before the interview, if college accommodation is offered. Medical interviews are intense and it is not a good idea to walk into yours breathlessly after getting up at 5am and standing for two hours on a train. Better to have a relaxing stroll first and meet other students.

The above points should cover just about everything done in "entrance training courses" for potential medics, except for the treatment practice. Candidates are never expected to have treated anyone before.

At both the beginning and the end of this process, though, you must also do something else. You must get across that Oxbridge, in fact, does want some candidates from an ordinary, non-medical background. So, your son has nothing to hide and should try to mention his origins. If we ever get a regulator determined to ensure a fair distribution of university places, of course, Oxbridge might suddenly discover great promise in more young people like him.

16
Other ways of healing the sick

Medicine, especially in the era of the TV serial, offers bright young people an almost irresistible dream. The dreamer, dressed in a crisp white coat, is bending over a pale, rapidly fading patient. He then straightens up, furrows his brow and proceeds to deliver a brilliant diagnosis or to prescribe the perfect drug. The patient recovers in a jiffy and is full of gratitude. Colleagues standing near the doctor glance up at him (or her) with total admiration (or unbridled lust).

Waking up from such a dream can be tough but is often inevitable. Medical applicants, despite their sharp minds and top science A-levels, have some of the lowest UCAS success rates. Competition means that most will not get any of their four university choices. Reaching for another, last minute option, perhaps abroad, can be unwise. Many non-EU medical courses are not accredited in the UK, so graduates cannot work here.

Fortunately, a sixth former determined to heal the sick has another attractive option: pure science. This is because when it comes to finding out what ails people or to curing them, the leaders in the field are often not doctors at all. They are scientists working in a rather wide range of related scientific disciplines or in various cross-disciplinary ways.

By opting for a career in Chemistry, Biology, Biochemistry, Biomedical Sciences or Physics, the young idealist can improve the health of patients all over the world. She can also earn an excellent salary, become world famous and, sometimes, even wear a white coat. Given the range of medical problems still in search of solutions, the opportunities are endless.

Despite this, a bright student's prospects of getting into one of the Oxbridge pure science courses are not bad at all. Oxford applicants for Biochemistry in 2017 had a success rate of 24 per cent and for Biology of 26 per cent. For Biomedical Sciences, a popular course often wrongly seen as a stepping stone towards Medicine, the figure was 15 per cent. Cambridge Natural Sciences used to admit a third of all applicants but, with numbers rising, the success rate for this world-renowned course has dropped to a (still reasonable) 25 per cent.

It seems strange, therefore, that relatively few students apply. For a brainy Year 12 keen to both do good and do well, one of these science options seems an obvious and often very satisfying choice.

CHEATING DEATH IN THE LAB

Students' reluctance to apply is often rooted in popular culture. While scientists are highly respected elsewhere, their image in Britain has often been that of dangerous madmen or unworldly boffins, engaged in weird, pointless experiments. So, if you are still wondering what actual contribution these people have made to our lives, here is a very brief list.

Take our ability to explore a patient's insides without surgery. This was first made possible by Marie Curie, whose research into radioactivity led to the development of the X-ray machine. Curie, then went on to discover two medically useful new chemical elements, Polonium and Radium.

Magnetic resonance imaging (MRI) has given us a safer, more detailed way of looking inside the body, avoiding even harmful x-rays or dyes. The MRI scanner, which uses magnetism and radio waves, is now a standard medical tool. It is based on research by Peter Mansfield, a physicist, and Paul Lauterbur, a chemist.

Even non-scientists have heard about the decoding of the double helix, the structure of the molecule which determines DNA. Carried out by the physicist Francis Crick and the zoologist James Watson, it has had a huge impact on medical progress. Genetic research is based on it and keeps moving forward: by revealing the structure of large complex molecules such as insulin, penicillin and vitamin B12, the crystallographer Dorothy Hodgkin made possible the development of drugs that have saved countless lives.

Aids research was much advanced by the work of Kary Mullis, a chemist and champion surfer, whose discovery of the PCR test made possible viral load counting. Chemists Sydney Brenner and Robert Horvitz, together with molecular biologist John Sulston, subsequently discovered the key genes that regulate organ development and programme cell death. This, too, has proved crucial to the study of Aids.

By discovering RNA interference (RNAi), a naturally occurring process for switching off specific genes, mathematician Andrew Fire and Craig Mello, a biochemist, pioneered a genetic technique making possible radical new treatments for incurable disorders from blindness to heart disease and diabetes. The research findings of Paul Nurse have given doctors a way to understand, and hopefully alter, the deadly process of cell division in cancer.

You might also like to know is that the reward all those hardworking scientists reaped has not just been moral satisfaction.

There is also celebrity status: almost every single one of them won a Nobel Prize for their work. The exception is Marie Curie, who won two, one for Physics and the other for Chemistry.

Research success can have further attractive benefits. Paul Nurse, a London-born biologist who was the first person in his family to attend university, told reporters in 2001 that he had spent some of his £800,000 Nobel Prize money on a 500cc Kawasaki motorbike. As he also received a knighthood, its parking space outside his Cambridge lab is labelled Sir Paul Nurse.

CREATING A HEALTHIER EARTH

Chemists, biologists and physicists might even be able to heal our sick planet. Not only are they steadily increasing their grasp of what is causing ecological change, but they are identifying cures that can be administered with a very large spoon. Research done on ozone depletion by Nobel Prize winner Sherwood Rowland, an expert in atmospheric chemistry, led to the 1995 world ban on the use of CFCs in aerosol sprays.

Rowland is one of several hundred world experts who form part of the Intergovernmental Panel on Climate Change, the UN body which released the first comprehensive report on the problem in February 2007. Global warming, it concluded, was 90 per cent likely to be due to human activity. The consequences would be higher temperatures, a rise in sea levels, hurricanes, droughts and famines. Having named the guilty and spelled out the world's dire prospects, the IPCC scientists are now exploring options for adaptation and mitigation.

In other words, the survival of humanity (as well as that of the world's luxury motorcycle industry) may depend on experts like these. With an Oxbridge degree in one of the natural sciences, you could be joining them.

17

Other dream courses

A small clutch of Oxbridge Arts courses are hugely popular among school students. PPE, Economics and English together attract well over six thousand applicants each year. Even the best of them, though, are often unfamiliar with the interests, knowledge base and activities which course admissions tutors seek and so fail to gain a place. Here you'll find out how to become a strong candidate.

PHILOSOPHY, POLITICS AND ECONOMICS (PPE)

Oxford PPE is a rare and fascinating course with huge career potential. Its graduates, it seems, can walk into any job and rise rapidly. They are perceived as super-smart, and even the performance of our disproportionately PPE-educated political class has yet to dent that impression.

But can smartness alone get you in? It certainly helps, as all three PPE elements require a sharp, flexible mind and a capacity to learn fast. Even at the first hurdle, the UCAS statement, students need to perform a delicate balancing act: as most will also be applying for different courses (there are only two more PPE courses in the UK), they need to convey a love for this one without alienating other departments. This matters because most universities no longer interview; their offers are largely based on grades and statements. Oxford, on the other hand, continues to interview all realistic PPE candidates.

A student must also not rave in his statement just about one PPE element, such as Politics. After all, the Oxbridge admissions tutor finding it on her desk may not be teaching the subject.

Linking all three PPE elements in your statement is another wise thing. It is generally enough to have read seriously around two. Do a quick recce of the third, then write briefly about any great ideas or interesting questions prompted by your reading. Oxford also seeks proof of hard work and persistence: PPE students are in for three extremely pressurised years.

Faced with some seven applicants for each place, dons take A-level grades of AAA for granted. Quite a few of their students have achieved A*A*A. Oxford's pre-interview TSA, though, matters far more. Here too, you need excellent writing skills and basic maths. An AS level in maths, if the subject is not taken at a higher level is therefore also thought essential. Even a real gift for logical and lateral thinking has to be fine-tuned to PPE standards. Keep tackling sample papers with an eye on the clock. Now check not just that you got the answer right, but that you have understood why you did or didn't.

It is the thought of the PPE interview(s), though, which makes most applicants shake. How do you prepare? First, learn how to define and use basic concepts, which will help you when showered with questions like these: Can a country still be democratic if only one party can campaign? Is inequality natural? Does the internet have its own ethics?

If a student has expressed a particular interest in politics, she needs a sound grasp of current affairs, either in Britain or another country. She should also be familiar with (at least modern) history. Applicants don't have to show knowledge of political or economic theory, but may be asked questions touching on it, such as whether privatisation is always a good thing, or how you would develop a Third World country. Give some good reasons for your views, even if based on personal experience.

Candidates new to Philosophy, and most are, may only get non-specialist questions, something like "What makes us good, the outcome of our actions or our motive?" While this is answerable off-the-cuff, you will do much better if you first read *Think* by Simon Blackburn. *An Introduction to Political Philosophy* by J. Wolff, will draw academic strands together. The BBC's *In our Time* podcasts on democracy, the Social Contract or free will liven up the subject.

When it comes to researching a personal interest, don't feel obliged to use academic tomes. General interest books dealing with topical issues such as recession economics or the Arab Spring may do fine. The online London Review Bookshop has a great, well described selection and helpful staff.

News stations and BBC programmes such as *Analysis* or *Question Time* will keep you in the loop. Broadsheets offer more detail, but note that papers like *The Times* and *The Guardian* may prioritise different news and suggest different solutions. So will journals like *The Economist* and *Prospect. The Week* gathers in articles from all sides. If your focus lies outside Europe, do also consider a monthly trawl through the English edition of *Le Monde Diplomatique*. Fortunately, online subscriptions have brought down costs. Daily papers can be found in your library, too, if that has not been closed.

Is the selection process fair? Well, students from top schools (state and private) and from high achieving, well connected families remain somewhat over-represented. Success rates for both school types, though, are almost equal now, and state schoolers make up 57 per cent of the intake. Also, more applicants from ordinary comprehensives are slowly getting in.

Moreover, some PPE students are entirely self-made. What sets them apart is that they were thinking ahead. PPE is not a good course to apply for on a whim at the very last moment. Successful candidates may have been regularly reading the broadsheets at sixteen. By seventeen, they had started on non-fiction books and by eighteen they were pursuing a demanding interest of their own. This also makes it harder to succeed if you apply very young. A post A-level application can sometimes make sense here.

What can move applicants further on is belonging to a network in which burning issues are discussed. Some PPE students I met had been members of the United Nations Youth Association or the UK Youth Parliament. Others had been involved with a political party, trade union or foundation. A few had been campaigning with activist groups. Some school clubs and societies also foster the right skills and profile for this hugely popular course.

You get no credit for any of this, but it is here that the ability to think logically and speak clearly is often forged. If you would rather develop them within your school, try to start a student book club. Take turns in choosing a book, then explain your choice and its value before throwing open the debate. Alternatively, talk about an article you liked with a teacher.

In short, independent reading is the key, but you must also discuss it. Doing this will enable you to confidently tackle ideas put to you and to express your own. Lastly, keep in mind that PPE interviewers don't always seek the "right" answer to their questions. They prefer students to address problems in a creative way. If that sounds like something you might actually enjoy, go ahead and apply.

ECONOMICS

Every autumn, yet more top-grade students enter Oxbridge Economics courses eager to learn about the secrets of wealth creation or (less commonly) poverty reduction. What they will actually be doing much of the time is maths. This is because undergraduate Economics at both universities, like elsewhere in the UK, emphasises Neoclassical economic theories. Championing smaller governments, free trade, private sector deregulation and fiscal responsibility in government, many of these are based on mathematical models. Keynesian Economics with its greater stress on the role of the state in fighting recessions and fostering stable economic growth is given less space.

This does not, though, make Economics a narrow field. Not only does it span the arts and the sciences and is intellectually bracing, but it opens up a huge range of public and private careers.

Entry barriers are high: while Economics A-levels are not required, most applicants do have them. Teachers sometimes say that if the A-level is offered by your school, disdaining it implies a weak subject interest, but students do get in with other hard subjects. What Cambridge does ask for is A-level Maths at A*A*A (and at some colleges for A*A*A*), as well as A-level Further Maths. 90 per cent of those admitted there have full A-levels in both. Oxford so far just asks for A-Level Maths at A*AA, but likes AS Further Maths.

Keeping up with your course certainly requires a firm grip on algebra, especially calculus and differentiation. A strong applicant can show on a board exactly how he arrived at the answer to a maths-based question and is not stumped when asked to draw curves or interpret statistical data. Students without FM need to spend a lot of time on the NRich Maths website. If you can offer enough Maths, though, you can combine it with almost any other hard A-level.

You need to work hard to beat the competition: in 2017, both Oxbridge courses had a success rate of roughly 7 per cent, and intakes are relatively small. Cambridge Economics has 155 places, Oxford's Economics & Management course just 83.

Students also need to be clear about the differences between the two courses. Oxford's Economics & Management, co-run by the Saïd Business School, is the one with the corporate slant. Beyond economic theory, students focus on how large organisations and economies work, how decisions are taken and resources allocated. Students analyse business structures, government policies, the practices of financial institutions and the huge changes in countries' economic systems.

The Cambridge course is broader in scope and a bit more theoretical. "This is not a business studies course," is how one economics tutor I know starts his schools talk. While taking you through core, pure and applied Economics, the course also draws on ideas and techniques from History, Sociology, Politics, Statistics and Maths. Applicants still keen on Management will be pleased to hear that this can be added from Year Two as an optional subject.

Before choosing, do read not just the course descriptions but also the advice on the departmental websites. If aiming for Oxford, check out its Thinking Skills Test (TSA), which you must pass to get an interview. Cambridge hopefuls are put through a different test, the Cambridge Admission Assessment for Economics, taken at interview.

The advantage of the latter is that you won't just be rejected sight-unseen, if you don't shine in the test. Try answering as many mock questions as you can during your preparation and don't skip the harder ones, because you need high marks.

Knowing some modern UK economic history also helps in the admissions process. With topical questions increasingly common, though, following economics-related news stories is more crucial. However, you must now go beyond the free sheets and thirty second TV statements about the country's economy made by politicians at election time. Instead, listen to some top economic experts. Radio4's *Today* programme features many of them, as do BBC TV's *Newsnight* and *Analysis*. Also worth watching are Ed Conway at SKY News and Robert Peston at ITV. Paul Krugman's blog, recommended by admissions tutors at both universities, is not just useful for American economic affairs.

Many sixth formers also like *Prospect* or *The Economist* because the weeklies tend to explain complex new economic developments to newbies, albeit from a Labour or Conservative angle respectively. *The Times* and *The Guardian* which, again, tend to prioritise different news and suggest different solutions, are strong on the link between economics and politics. Saturday's *Financial Times* covers economics, politics, business and management issues, while *New Internationalist* documents the harmful impact which even well-meant economic policies can have on people in the Third World.

Fortunately, online subscriptions have greatly brought down costs, and there is often free access to key articles. Dailies and weeklies may be found in your local library, too, if that has not been closed for economic reasons.

Still, given the breadth of the subject, you eventually need to move on to books. Students are generally advised to start with *Economics: A Very Short Introduction* by P. Dasgupta or with *Economics* by Begg, Fischer and Dornbusch. To this, both Oxford and Cambridge in 2017 each added a terrifyingly long list of suggested reading. Before deciding whether you will have to sell the family dog to afford even half of it, note that these lists were originally meant for offer-holders and first years. Even very strong Economics applicants have usually read at most four or five of the books. Staff in a good bookshop will help you make a choice.

It is at the book-reading stage that A-level students often realise that economic theory and economic reality can be quite far apart. Don't rush into strong views after the first chapter: you may yet discover that economic doctrines can be rooted in political ideas, mathematical models may not work in real life (as shown by the derivatives scandals), and that theories can easily become outdated: Milton Friedman's view that state regulation just molly-coddles people with negative effect came to look rather less convincing when an under-regulated banking sector started to crash.

Eager young economists may also have noticed the emergence of new economic strands, from behaviourist economics to more leftwing ones. They can be worth mentioning, but make sure here not to over-state what you've learnt. Your interviewers are certain to know hugely more about any of this than you do and may actually have written the seminal books.

What may benefit you is taking a broader geographic perspective. Knowing something about major US policies matters, if only because the Neoliberal economic theories behind them, which seek to make away with the role of the state in economic life altogether, are spreading from there. In their spirit, company taxes are now being slashed and individuals must take responsibility for their own economic survival. It is a huge and to many economists very exciting experiment with potentially massive consequences.

What this means is that there is a lot of ground to cover. So, rather than playing Minecraft as you sit on the bus, you could be listening to Economics podcasts. Try some of the BBC's *In Our Time* ones, fronted by Melvyn Bragg, in which Economic experts discuss key issues in their field. A good one is about Game Theory: not only will it tell you what this is and does, but also what it cannot do. This is quite a good way of looking at Economics generally.

Come the interview, make sure you can define terms like protectionism, outsourcing or supply-side economics and recognise common abbreviations. A smart candidate knows the difference between tax avoidance and tax evasion, even if some of our business leaders don't.

Expect interview questions across a wide range. Many economists are as interested in the poor as in the rich, even if their students often end up in finance: why is low inflation good, but high inflation bad? What effect does the market power of supermarkets have on suppliers and consumers? Why does the government seek to regulate the amount of sugar in my food? Can you give an example of a Keynesian policy adopted by a UK government?

Questions get harder as you move along: how might migration impact on an economy? Does the benefit system help or discourage job seekers? Who should pay for negative externalities? Since pensions, education and the NHS are the main areas of public expenditure, is there a way of reducing their cost? US trade policy is undergoing major changes; are import tariffs or free trade more likely to revive an ailing economy? Can you find the height of a regular tetrahedron with side length 1?

A management interviewer, meanwhile, may ask whether high rewards for creating a high level of profits can be bad for business, or want you to talk about the factors determining at what price a clothing retailer might sell a new type of jeans.

Keeping up with events and thinking logically matter here. Economics may be a stand-alone subject at university, but it is anything but in reality. Don't, therefore, just read the business pages. Corporate concerns, environmental issues and a government's social or education policies all hugely impact on an economy. So do wars, uprisings, and religious shifts (think of the oil price).

What can be just as important is an awareness of the fact that economics is beset by controversy. Its practitioners virulently disagree on key issues like the economic effect of the free market or welfare state, and on the role of trade unions or banks. Is the availability of easy credit good or bad for economic life?

There is a lot of thinking to do, and not just about how soon you'll be able to buy a Lamborghini for yourself or a house for your mother. Oxbridge Economics graduates don't actually have the highest starting pay: they are piped to the post by graduates of Oxbridge Maths, who can expect initial salaries of around £38,000 in the financial world and £42,000 soon after. Oxbridge Computer Science graduates can do even better. A top Oxbridge degree in Economics may earn you £32,000 in your first year, but even that is not universal. So, make sure you picked this demanding course for the right reasons.

Meanwhile, what else might improve your chances? I would not obsess about getting a pre-university internship. Admissions tutors don't expect you to, though students who worked in an economic environment (which can mean corporate, small business or public sector) do sometimes find interview questions easier. You could also try your luck in the annual essay competition run by the Cambridge Economics Society. Even if you don't win, taking part will sharpen your subject knowledge.

What interviewers really seek are students who will enjoy economics as an academic discipline and like the tougher kind of Maths.

ENGLISH

Endlessly popular, the two non-identical Oxbridge courses attract candidates from all backgrounds. English students always say that what won them a place was their enthusiasm for the subject, but this was backed by voracious reading. You won't get in by just knowing the books of your favourite author and the extract of Romeo and Juliet you were handed at school.

Good candidates engage with different periods, genres and styles. Make sure to read at least one Victorian novel to develop a feel for the language. Don't watch the DVD version beforehand: it is far harder to get gripped if you already know the ending. As you read, think about the means by which the author conveys the feelings of her characters or perhaps creates a sense of dread. A library journal called *English Studies* (Routledge) can tell you how to do this and much else.

It further helps to have some sense of a novel's historic or social context. How was Great Britain changing? What was the status of women? An interest in quality non-fiction such as biographies or travel writing is fine, too.

There are no set books at this stage. You'll find a useful list of 20th century classic novels written by dead white males online. Great books by modern women writers include *Angel* by Elizabeth Taylor, *The Handmaiden's Tale* by Margaret Atwood, *The Bell* by Iris Murdoch, *The Bloody Chamber* by Angela Carter, *The Colour Purple* by Alice Walker, *The Hundred Sacred Senses* by Amy Tan and *Beloved* by Toni Morrison.

Great books by contemporary male authors include *Empire of the Sun* by JG Ballard, *The Remains of the Day* by Kazugo Ishiguro, *The English Patient* by Michael Ondaatje, *Waiting for the Barbarians* by JM Coetzee, *Metroland* by Julian Barnes, *Catch 22* by Joseph Heller, *The Wasp Factory* by Ian Banks and *The Buddha of Suburbia* by Hanif Kureshi. Although the Cambridge course, unlike the Oxford one, largely focuses on British authors, going beyond those now is fine.

Don't feel obliged to read just classics, as experts don't agree on the meaning of the term anyway, but look for books with complexity and depth. If you can tell everything about a book's protagonists from a few stock phrases on page one, there is nothing to learn. Oddly, some Oxbridge English Lit. graduates write such books with huge success.

When asked in an interview what you like about a novel, don't focus on the personal. It's nice to hear that Elizabeth Bennet's family in *Pride and Prejudice* is almost as embarrassing as your own, but this does not yet qualify you to become an English Lit. student. Try to describe what makes a book stand out in terms of language, plot or descriptions. How does the author make her characters come alive? How does she heighten your expectations? What is the story you have been reading really about?

Be prepared to compare and contrast short extracts from fiction or non-fiction texts. Familiarity with subject terms matters here. Look up irony, satire, allusion or allegory if you need to. Know what an unreliable narrator is, or intertextuality.

Short-stories are another pleasant way to progress. Some of the best are by Elizabeth Bowen, Catherine Mansfield, Virginia Woolf, Alice Munro, Doris Lessing, Sarah Maitland, Conan Doyle, Rudyard Kipling, Edgar Allen Poe, James Woodhouse, James Joyce, Raymond Carver and Ernest Hemingway. Think about how this type of story may be structured. What does the writer do to hold your attention?

Poetry is hugely varied, so it's not enough to dip a toe in it. Go through a poem by an author you like. Read slowly. Whose voice(s) are you hearing? Are there strange words? Is there any significance to varying line lengths or breaks?

Now choose an anthology with different poets, periods and styles. Students often browse *War Poetry* (OUP), edited by Jon Stallworthy, or *The New Penguin Book of English Verse*, edited by Paul Keegan. Make sure you understand what the "close reading" of a poem involves. How do you tell what kind of poem it is? Can you talk about imagery, metaphor, rhythm or meaning? Which words or phrases are important here?

If your A-level work has not focused much on poetry, ask for personal guidance at school. English teachers love to talk about it.

Do also make sure to read at least one of Shakespeare's sonnets, know what a sonnet is and can define an iambic pentameter. It helps to write a few such lines of your own.

This brings us to the great man's plays. Read a few of them, and don't be afraid of the verse. Once you've watched a Shakespeare play on your screen and listened to the actors, all will make sense. Can you describe the techniques which make parts of it funny? Is there another way in which it could be staged?

Try not to think of these plays as just belonging to a bygone age. Many resonate with modern concerns. *Hamlet* is about a teenage boy in conflict with his step-father; *Julius Caesar* explores political struggles; *Richard III* is the story of a cunning, violent dictator. Which universal questions might be raised by others? There is excellent material on Shakespeare and his language on the website of the Royal Shakespeare Company.

If you have a strong interest in drama (which is not mandatory), you should also explore some more modern plays. Key ones include *A Woman of No Importance* by Oscar Wilde, *Journey's End* by R.C. Sherriff, *Death of A Salesman* (and *The Crucible*) by Henry Miller, *Look Back in Anger* by John Osborne and *Waiting for Godot* by Samuel Beckett.

Having explored English Lit., you can now make an informed choice between the Oxford and Cambridge course by reading their course websites.

Come the written test, watch your spelling, grammar and punctuation. The questions tend to be manageable, as long as you disregard a bit of advice offered on the website of the English Literature Admissions Test (ELAT). It assures Oxford applicants that "this is not a test of wide reading," which is utter bunk.

LAW

What draws students towards Oxbridge Law are its intellectual challenges, as well as the career prospects it offers, and not just in the legal field. A top Law graduate can realistically hope to one day become a banker, NGO head, crime writer or Prime Minister. As the course covers a discipline which has evolved over hundreds or, arguably, thousands of years, entrance criteria are high. Admissions tutors look for people with an eye for detail, an ability to rapidly absorb lots of information, strong writing skills and verbal articulacy. Having a mind which enjoys intellectual sparring and/or a desire for justice are personal qualities sought. Unlike in films about legal eagles, though, you won't be rushing around playing the private detective in your spare time.

A-level grades of AAA at Oxford (plus a C/4 grade in GCSE Maths) and of AAA* at Cambridge are the base line. Oxbridge accepts a range of hard A-level subjects in various combinations, but many successful students have English, History and Maths. Even a science is fine, as it can be useful in business cases. A-level Law is not seen as challenging enough.

Offering early proof of your writing skills is important. If you were not required to write essays at school, ask a teacher to set you one and mark it. Alternatively, it helps if you can point to any impressive writing you have done in a school magazine or online. Showing in your statement that you are a keen reader of (specified) quality fiction or non-fiction will suggest you are already expanding your vocabulary and knowledge of the world.

An active engagement with the legal world is next. Most applicants attend at least a couple of trials, one perhaps in a civil court and another in a criminal one. This too can go into your statement, but you must expand on it. Is there anything that you learnt from the experience or that surprised you?

To learn more, look out for press reports of current court cases in the public eye. *The Times, The Guardian* and most Sunday broadsheets will describe not just the crime, the proceedings and the defendant(s), but also the broader issues raised. A defence barrister, for instance, may argue that his client, in court for making deeply offensive public statements, was merely exercising his legal right to free speech. The prosecution, meanwhile, may take the view that the law against incitement to racial hatred could be pertinent here.

The outcome can hinge on the quality of the arguments produced in what one hotshot corporate lawyer has likened to a football game: You can only have a good defence if you can respond to - and anticipate - the likely attacks." High-earning barristers, certainly, excel at both rhetoric and research. Undertaking an extended research project of your own may therefore benefit you.

NEED MORE HELP?

Some schools run debating clubs in which you can hone your own rhetorical skills or even stage mock trials to improve students' understanding of justice-related issues. If your school doesn't, any organisation in which issues of the day are a discussed will benefit you, even if it is just a youth club.

SmartLaw, an organisation backed by the Law Society, also runs two much praised annual events, a "Magistrates Mock Trial Competition" and a "Bar Trial Competition", designed to develop teens' understanding of the justice and legal system, as well as helping them to grasp that the law touches every aspect of our lives. Students enter it via their schools, and the benefits include greatly enhanced speaking skills.

A student planning well ahead, moreover, will be able to apply for a place at an Oxbridge Law summer school, a Cambridge Law Masterclass or one of the annual Oxbridge Law conferences for sixth formers, all very useful.

What, though, should you read? *Letters to a Law Student* by Nicholas J McBridge is still probably the best general introduction to the Law, even if bits of it may be too hard as yet. *Eve was Blamed* by Helena Kennedy addresses a highly topical concern. *Is Eating People*

Wrong? Great Legal Cases by Allan Hutchinson shows the link between legal and social issues. (See also p. 193.)

While Oxbridge claims that no actual knowledge of the Law is required for its tests, familiarity with Britain's legal structure and a keen interest in the quandaries people in the legal field face still matter for the interview. Students keen to sharpen their minds for all parts of the admissions process may therefore also want to read *Critical Thinking Skills: Developing Effective Analysis and Argument* by Stella Cottrell.

THE LAW TEST

Tests and interviews remain the key hurdles Law candidates must jump. Formal tests, introduced fairly recently, partly to whittle down candidate numbers and partly to change a course history of admitting mainly private school students and others from well-educated middle class families, are now a key factor in determining who gets in. Student diversity has already improved.

To do well in the Law Aptitude Test, the LNAT, used by Oxford, or the Cambridge Law Admission Assessment, though, you must do lots of trial-runs first. Read through the mock questions found on the LNAT website (or, for Cambridge, through the sample tests on its course pages) well in advance and try to answer every single one; don't just dip in to find some easy ones. If you get an answer wrong, check why.

Students who get high marks in either Oxbridge test are able to read a text about an unfamiliar topic both very carefully and quite fast, then work out their answer with the help of their book-enhanced thinking skills. One key essay skill is the ability to write to the required length. Try to find out from the mocks how many short but crucial points you can make in, say, 500 words without over-running. Doing a big cutting job on an essay in a test situation usually takes too long and can leave you with unanswered questions.

Quick thinkers tend to do well in the question part, as long as they keep calm. Beware of rushing through the questions or being sloppy in your answers because both seem simple on first sight. Law test Q&As rarely are.

What sets apart the Cambridge test is primarily that it is taken on the interview day rather than weeks beforehand. This is important because it ensures that you at least get the chance to impress admissions tutors in person. Moreover, while Cambridge questions can be quite similar to Oxford ones, they are more based on ordinary life.

Note, too, that individual Cambridge colleges can vary in the importance they attach to the results. Because of the preparation gap between applicants from different types of schools, colleges sometimes rely less on the test and more on interviews, grades and other indicators of aptitude for the course.

TALK LIKE A LAWYER

The Law interviews at both Oxford and Cambridge are often feared by applicants because they are still new to legal matters and language.IN fact, interviewers try to word their questions in non-specialist terms. If a question does require legal knowledge, such as the definition of a law, it is provided on a sheet in advance.

Interview structures vary. Some interviewers like to discuss just a single court case from various angles while others cover a wide range of topics. Here are some examples of the latter:

Are there any factors which might deny people access to the Law? Why might sentencing young offenders to community work often work better than imprisonment? Could it ever be right to disobey the law? People are entitled to practice their faith, but what if that faith requires them to deny this right to others of a different faith?

While some questions based on events in the real world may refer to those only obliquely, news followers should be able to base their answer on an example once they have practised on those:

Can you think of any new legal issue raised by the spread of internet technology? If some members of a neighbourhood gang have committed a crime, is it just for all of its members present at the time to be tried for it? Does the existence of a legal system guarantee justice?

Note that the point here is not always for you to offer a definite answer, but to show that you are aware of the challenges or dilemmas faced by people in the legal field. As that can be quite hard, give yourself time to order your thoughts before answering. You also want to make clear as to whether you are speaking from a moral or legal perspective.

If you are looking for more examples or to get accustomed to legal language, there are also Law mock interviews on both Oxbridge websites. Also note that Cambridge has put Law lectures on particularly interesting court cases and general advice on YouTube at https://www.youtube.com/playlist?list=PLy4oXRK6xgzHukYwMI80 6wyHrLBoL9K0v.

Students seeking yet more preparation support should be aware that major law firms are often willing to send an Oxbridge educated member to conduct mock Law interviews at a school on a 'pro bono' basis. Do look up this useful term!

WORKING YOUR WAY INTO LAW

Work experience is not really expected by Oxbridge, though you could write to local solicitors' firms, asking for a chance to shadow a staff member or become a holiday intern. Some students volunteer at a law centre, but other activities also count. Helping out at a food bank or homeless shelter will show you how changes of the law can affect ordinary people's lives, while getting involved in environmental campaigns can teach you how to lawfully advance public demands. One Oxbridge admissions tutor reportedly praised a student keen on criminal law who had walked into his local police station and volunteered to take part in police identity parades.

While all this adds up to quite a lot of extra-curricular work, being clear about what lawyers really do can make you a much more confident candidate. It will also help you to understand that although much legal work revolves around minor financial transactions or petty crime, it is crucial for the smooth conduct of business and the safety of the public.

Other legal work can be morally rewarding. The barrister who obtained a guilty verdict against a husband who had violently assaulted his estranged wife is likely to make her way home on a high. So, too, could the solicitors who in 2018 successfully advised dozens of Caribbean-born black Britons threatened with expulsion, although they had legally lived and worked in the UK all their adult life.

While many Oxbridge Law graduates spend their professional lives drawing up million-Pound contracts in shiny corporate towers, others find satisfaction in very different areas of the law.

OXBRIDGE PREPARATION CHECK LIST
(YEAR 12 OR EARLIER)

Part I: pinning it all down

1. Start thinking about which degree subject to choose well before you enter the sixth form.

2. Pick at least two hard A-levels in the arts or sciences (or three STEM ones if you are considering a science course).

3. Go to the Oxbridge prospectus websites to see which courses are on offer there beyond those taught at school.

4. Explore at least a couple of promising options by reading through the full course description, including entrance requirements and future careers.

5. Once you have found the most appealing course, check whether you qualify for a free, course-specific Oxbridge summer school. Booking usually opens in January and places fill up fast!

6. Come spring, check the Oxbridge *Open Days and Events* pages for other course-related activities. These, too, will be free but are best booked right away.

7. Check whether other Russell Group universities have Taster Days geared towards roughly the same course, as these events will be open to all and may not require booking.

8. Ask your teacher or an academic you meet at an event which introductory book they recommend. The Oxbridge course websites list lots of (somewhat harder) books.

9. Set aside a fixed time for course-related reading, at night or on weekends at least, and stick to it.

Cont. /

OXBRIDGE PREPARATION CHECK LIST
(YEAR 12 OR EARLIER)

Part II: getting good at it

A. Read at least one course-related book in the Christmas, Easter and summer holidays, or start problem-solving on a challenging maths site such as NRich or Meiklieriggs.

B. Check out subject-related news in an online journal or science magazine. If you're applying for politics, economics, law or geography, a Sunday broadsheet, or the daily *Guardian* or *Times* will keep you up-to-date, as will BBC Radio4.

C. Jot down a handful of notes on each useful article or book you've read, including the title and author's name.

D. Look up key subject terms you come across, so you can define them if asked.

E. Get used to the way academics talk by watching some lectures at YouTube, Ted Talks or Gresham College. Listen also to a couple of the taster podcasts produced by Oxford and Cambridge.

F. Hear academics discuss exciting aspects of their field in podcasts of IN OUR TIME, a BBC4 radio series.

G. Try to book yourself into an Oxbridge Masterclass, a science workshop or a Law or Medicine Student Conference.

H. Find a course-related BBC programme you like and listen to it regularly. Good examples are TIME TEAM, QUESTION TIME, ANALYSIS and SCIENCE.

I. For the real thing, visit a historic site, science lab, law court, theatre or course-related exhibition.

(For links see p. 276)

18
Aftershocks

What comes after the admissions process is another long wait. Only in early January will most offers and rejections arrive and your daughter needs to keep up her spirits until them. Even if she left her interview in tears (a sure sign that her interviewer was an amateur) she might well find an offer in the post.

If she does, it is time to go into top gear for A-level study. Oxbridge is not very flexible once a grade offer is made, and the tutors I spoke to could only recall two cases in which a candidate had been accepted despite failing to reach the offer level: the first was a girl who had fallen seriously ill. The second candidate had been evicted from the hostel in which he lived.

So, it is time for the study plan, revision course, and a (partial) withdrawal from the endless social whirl that is teenage life. It is also time to withdraw from paid work. If contacted by a totally broke, self-supporting A-level student, Oxbridge might help. There are a few small study grants for disadvantaged candidates, which the college bursar can tell you about.

Let us next assume that the bright girl actually got in. What this means is that you can look forward to several months of mutual incomprehension. Dropping in after her first term, she will confuse you by talking about weird things like formal hall, mods and prelims, and you will shock her by failing to understand existentialist philosophy. Her school friends will wonder who gave her the haircut from hell. When she tries to talk about her new life, her brother is likely to tell the poor girl that her accent stinks and her sister might accuse her of being stuck up.

Unlike students elsewhere, she will rarely come home at weekends. Oxbridge workloads and college social life do not allow for it. Those who see their parents every Sunday are perceived as odd.

After the first giddy year, though, an Oxbridge student and her family usually rediscover their common humanity, or at least a shared liking for Becks. By now, the dizzy girl might have learnt to appreciate your cooking and the fact that money does not grow on trees. She will also have become bilingual: she might still talk posh for a day, but will then switch out of it. Knowing that she managed to cope with an initially terrifying study schedule will have calmed her. She'll be smug but sympathetic. She might even go bowling with the younger kids. Holidays will no longer feel like a battle zone. This is the moment for you to rejoice in your Oxbridge work, and for her to help repaint the flat.

AMONG ALIENS

The bad news is that even if your teenager has got in, the Oxbridge dream can still go wrong. What if your visiting daughter confesses that she has unpacked nothing but her teddy bear after three weeks of Oxbridge life, because she does not fit in? She hates the place, made a terrible mistake and is planning to drop out as soon as she finds someone willing to feed the poor little tame rat she adopted.

That Valium suddenly seems a good idea, after all. What are you supposed to do? Offer to drive up so she can collect her stuff? Or should you just tell her that the feeling will pass and that she ought to pull herself together?

The answer is that it would be a good idea to know more. The first sight of student life anywhere can be exhilarating for some and terrifying for others, and student life at Oxbridge comes with added medieval pomp. Most students adjust fast, often by doing all the things you warned them against. This may not happen if they encounter situations they are ill equipped to handle alone. A student in this predicament might become depressed, feel unable to study or decide to drop out. Some Oxbridge students in every year do. Mercifully, suicides are very rare and happen mainly at the finals stage.

Given these frightening possibilities, you should try and get your daughter to explain what exactly bothers her. Sometimes the mere act of pouring out all her small initial failures or disappointments will make everything all right.

Chances are, your fears will prove unjustified. The problem is, more often than not, a disappointing grade, a tutor who speaks too fast or the discovery that nobody else in her year likes Tinchie Stryder. The best thing is to let her rail on uninterruptedly, even if your roast burns to cinders. After three to four hours of woes, she might suddenly jump up, grab her backpack and run for the next bus back because she has just remembered that there is a college entz (club night) at ten thirty.

The girl has just been letting off steam, which is normal for students. So, don't rush in with advice, or agree that going to Oxbridge was perhaps a mistake for someone from a background like hers. Still there are areas of Oxbridge life that can give rise to real grievances, and students and their parents need to know about them.

19
Women's troubles

"When I walk home through the quad at 2am and see the moon rise above the college battlements I can't believe how lucky I am, and I really hate the idea that just two years from now I got to leave again," one girl from a South London housing estate last year wrote to a cousin she was encouraging to apply to Oxford. She is not alone. Female students of all backgrounds often fall in love at first sight with their beautiful old university.

This love has not always been reciprocated. For the first six hundred years of Oxford and Cambridge, women were banned from both universities. Their sheer presence was deemed unacceptable. College fellows (researchers and lecturers) were not allowed to marry until the end of the 19th century, and while a man could do so once he had reached the status of professor, many had lost interest by that stage, wrote Vera Britten in her history, *The Women at Oxford*.

Women's attempts to gain at least partial access to higher learning were greeted with contempt. Even liberal figures like John Ruskin, who served as Oxford Professor of Art, declared in 1871: "I cannot let the bonnets in, on any conditions, this term. The three public lectures will chiefly be on angles, degrees of colour-prisms (without any prunes) and other such things, of no use to the female mind and they would occupy the seats in mere disappointed puzzlement."

After the first female students were admitted to Oxford in 1879, the Canon of Christ Church, Professor Edward Pusey, described women's colleges as "one of the greatest misfortunes that have happened even in our own time in Oxford".

In order to save male students from distraction, female students could not initially attend lectures or enter any of the men's junior common rooms in which much of the university's intellectual life took place.

Even when the lecture halls were opened to women, it was not in order to enable them to qualify. They were still denied access to the all-important degree at the end of their course. Without this document, of course, the few dozen exceptionally bright and determined women who had been accepted could contribute to society only as volunteers. Eleanor Rathbone became an outstanding social reformer, while Gertrude Bell joined her ambassador uncle as an unpaid assistant and went on to create the new state of Iraq out of various tribal territories.

Another graduate, Margery Fry, fought to improve the conditions for prisoners in British gaols, organised war relief for Europe during WW1, founded the National Council for the Abolition of the Death Penalty and became a governor of the BBC.

Those who needed the official qualification in order to get paid work had a very long wait. Oxford only started to issue degrees to its women graduates in 1920, Cambridge in 1947.

Women students remained outsiders for decades. They were banished to colleges far from the main university facilities, which initially lacked all basic amenities, from bathrooms to libraries. They were also condemned to an almost prison-like existence. Female students were not allowed out, even to the shops, without being chaperoned by "a respectable, elderly woman". During lectures, the chaperone would sit in the back of the hall knitting until she could take her charge home again.

The female principals who ran the women's colleges tried hard to gain acceptance by being as unfeminine as possible in their meetings with male academic colleagues. "Not a word was wasted, not a charm nor a wile exercised," a biographer approvingly wrote of Emily Penrose, the first principal of the Oxford women's college, Somerville.

Students too were expected to conform to almost unearthly standards of perfection. Elizabeth Wordsworth, who founded Lady Margaret Hall, suggested that it should be named after Lady Margaret Beaufort, the mother of Henry VII: "She was a gentlewoman, a scholar, and a saint, and after having been three times married she took a vow of celibacy. What more could be expected of a woman?"

None of this was enough to change male students' preference for someone who could shoot grouse. Public misogyny was rampant. In 1926, the majority of Oxford Union members voted in favour of a resolution which stated: "The women's colleges should be levelled to the ground."

Widely reported, the resolution caused some embarrassment to Oxford in the outside world. Its male students were perceived as having gone too far, as being out of touch with the modern world.

Things improved gradually for women students after that, though not to everyone's satisfaction. "The presence of women at Oxford was now a deterrent for friendships between men," one male college head recalled peevishly in his 1940s memoirs. Lest this deterrent should completely scupper the chances of the lonely male don, the number of women students at Oxford and Cambridge was formally restricted to one sixth of all students until 1957.

MODERN TIMES

But all that is history now. Oxbridge is about learning and this could not be restricted to academic fields. so, it gradually came to agree with the anonymous don who had warned in the *Oxford Magazine*: "The young men and young women are not going to spend their lives here, and we make it difficult for them to learn a very important part of human behaviour, how to conduct oneself in relation to the opposite sex. We isolate the problem, give it more thought than it is worth, enact regulations which, if they are effective, postpone till a later age adjustments which have to be made some time and somehow. The world is not a world of chaperones, of perfect vigilance..."

Equal opportunities legislation did the rest to turn Oxford and Cambridge into something other than the rowdy boys' towns of yore. Today, all colleges and facilities are open to both women and men. Total numbers of female students admitted is up and in 2017 even exceeded male ones for the first time ever. More importantly, perhaps, it's fun to be a young woman at Oxbridge. All the female students I spoke to made that absolutely clear.

For a start, living in a smallish town dominated by students can make young women feel safe. Although neither Cambridge nor Oxford are crime-free, many praised the physical mobility they enjoyed by being able to cycle or walk almost everywhere, day and night. "I really love working my way through a pile of books until I have totally grasped something, and here I can stay in the library all night and walk home at 3 a.m," one girl said enthusiastically.

There are other advantages for those who have different plans for 3 a.m. The academic atmosphere, plus the presence of so many bright young male students can create new rules of attraction. Elsewhere, talking to a really clever girl can make quite a few men nervous, but at Oxbridge female brains qualify as a turn-on.

And, when it comes to careers, highly paid employment often beckons after graduation. Oxbridge women do notably better than women from other universities, just like Oxbridge men do.

SIX FOOT IRRITATIONS

This is not to say that Oxbridge is a gender-equal utopia. While most academics are very careful to observe equality legislation, and some can seem positively delighted at the progress of an especially bright female student, this is not a universal rule. Some very elderly dons can be awkward or subtly dismissive when forced to tutor a girl. After all, these strange creatures have been wandering among the college walls a mere hundred and forty years.

Even male fellow students can be irritating. Girls from single sex grammar schools, which are very brainy places, often complain that far less bright boys will hog the conversation in a tutorial, seminar or burger bar. As a result, getting into Oxbridge can be the beginning of a new kind of battle if you are a girl.

Oxford Student Union Vice President (Women), Melanie Marshall, points out that there are considerable inequalities when it comes to university and college spending on sport. Women's sports are invariably under-funded. Far more money goes on facilities for cricket and rowing than on those for aerobics or yoga. There is also an assumption that what women do in sport is less important; the men's boat race and its outcome are reported in the national press. The women's boat race, an equally annual event, barely gets a mention in the college rag.

The imbalance, Melanie explains, is a leftover from the university's men-only days, and it helps to make male students feel a sense of ownership of the place. This sounds terribly abstract until you look around and see a few young men happily throw about a ball on a manicured college lawn, while two or three girls stand around awkwardly as if someone still needs to hand them a script.

When asked to recall a case of individual discrimination, though, Melanie couldn't come up with one, however hard she tried. What there is of gender injustice is clearly not grave enough to leave any indelible trauma. We parted following her promise that she would consult her archives, in case they contained any striking cases, and that was the last I heard.

THE BRAIN RACE

Academic inequality is a different matter. Female students almost invariably found it harder to get in than male ones when applying to the majority of courses, though the gap was gradually narrowing.

Nevertheless, Oxford's male PPE applicants in 2015 still had a success rate of 15 per cent, versus a female one of only 13 per cent. In Maths, the rate was 18 per cent (male), versus 11 per cent (female), and in Physics 17 per cent (male) and 14 per cent (female). The success rate for Medicine was 13 per cent (male) and 9 per cent (female). This kind of gender gap was seen as perfectly normal. Almost no top Oxford course offered women as good a success chance as it did to men.

The good news is that this is now changing. By 2017, female PPE applicants had a success rate of 22 per cent, as against 20 per cent for male ones, an unprecedented development for this course, while success rates in Physics had become an identical 16 per cent for both genders. In Medicine, male applicants, who had a success rate of 15 per cent, were now less than half a percentage point ahead of female ones with just over 14 per cent. In Maths, though, the male students' success rate of 15 per cent still topped the 12 per cent one of female ones.

It is important to understand that such outcomes are not just determined by the quality of each year's applicants but also by the publicity they generate. To give an example, the male success rate in the hugely popular Oxford Economics & Management course in 2009 had been a typical 9 per cent, as against a female rate of only 4 per cent. However, after this was pointed out in the 2010 edition of this book and echoed by other media, course applicants of both genders in 2011 magically, and for the first time ever, enjoyed the very same success rate, just 8 per cent. It has remained pretty equal, with the odd dip, ever since.

Still, imbalances like the ones described still exist in a few Oxford courses. The gap can be especially big in the small but popular combined ones.

Nor does Cambridge seem gender-neutral. The success rates for its Medicine candidates were 17 per cent (male) and 13 per cent (female) in 2011, and 22 per cent (male) and 17 per cent (female) in 2017. Cambridge Maths applicants had a success rate of 20 per cent (male) and 11 per cent (female) in 2011, as against 21 per cent (male) and, yet again, 11 per cent (female) in 2017. The gender gap seems stable from year to year, although girls get better A-level grades.

Magic, however, also sometimes happens at Cambridge. While the success rate of its male Economics candidates had been 13 per cent in 2011 and 15 per cent in 2015, versus 12 per cent for female ones, both genders in 2017 did equally well for once, sharing a 15 per cent success rate. That this was also a year in which feminist issues were much in the news was presumably a coincidence.

There is also a gender gap at the Oxbridge degree stage. Every year, almost without exception, male students at both universities get far more Firsts than female ones. This is an outcome extremely rare outside Oxbridge. One key factor pointed to has been the encouragement received from a student's academic supervisor. This, apparently, is more easily given to young men whose aggressive ''intellectual muscle flexing'' is often taken as a sign of excellence.

Oxbridge colleges, too, can have consistent gender preferences, although not all of them prefer the same sex. Somerville, an Oxford college, clearly has a high opinion of the female mind because women made up 51 per cent of undergraduates there in 2013. At Keble, female undergraduates only constituted 40 per cent, one of Oxford's lowest proportion.

Actual discrimination mainly affects women working at Oxbridge, though the gender gap is narrowing here too. While female academics in 2002 constituted just over 20 per cent of academic staff at both universities, mostly as lecturers, that figure had risen to over 30 per cent by 2016. Female professors, though, remain a small, if growing minority. Oxford, where they made up just 9 per cent in 2012 (half the national average in higher education), by 2018 proudly revealed that this had risen to 24.2 per cent. Cambridge female professors, meanwhile, still constituted a mere 17 per cent in 2016, the latest year for which figures are available.

This has financial, as well status consequences. In 2006, the pay gap between full time male and female academics had been 16 per cent at Oxford and 19 per cent at Cambridge. While women academics earn less everywhere, such gaps were among the highest in the country. At Bolton University the pay differential that year was 1.5 per cent. For female Cambridge academics this situation has not changed much, but the Oxford pay gap has gradually shrunk. However, its female academics were in 2017 still earning just 86 per cent of what their male counterparts were being paid.

Women have done better with top Oxbridge posts. Cambridge has had a female Vice Chancellor, Professor Alison Richard, since 2003, while Louise Richardson was installed as the first-ever female Oxford Vice Chancellor in January 2016. Each of the universities also now has eleven female college heads. However, this still leaves two thirds of colleges headed by men.

Most female academics still work in the current or former women's colleges, especially in St. Hilda's at Oxford and in Newnham and Murray Edwards at Cambridge. Oxbridge is an ambitious world in which men are often that little bit more ambitious, but at least if there are only women to fill the jobs, women get them.

Even the honorary jobs held by students, much contested because they will look good on future job applications, tend to fall to the more pushy, namely men. Take the role of the president of the junior common room (the college union). Despite there being almost as many female as male students at Cambridge, most JCR presidents are invariably men. Oxford, where women used to hold at best a third of such posts, saw the ratio change for the first time in 2012.

Ratios like these matter because female staff might pick students by more women-friendly criteria. Interviewed about sexism at

Cambridge a few years ago, the feminist writer and English don Germaine Greer complained that whenever a women's college had taken on male staff, they had shown a worrying preference for admitting "fluffy blondes", rather than earnest and sometimes plainer girls with an obvious academic bent.

Equally, female academics can be more sympathetic to women-centred projects. A female student who proposes to do her degree research on, say, maternal needs in public housing, is likely to elicit more support from a female don than from her male equivalent.

WOMEN'S WORLDS

As a result of such differences, current students, old girls and the female staff at the remaining women's colleges have made sure to protect their single-sex status whenever a change was put to the vote. After all, they can offer a roll call of successful women.

St. Hilda's College, Oxford, which educated prize-winning scientist Susan Greenfield, former Tory Education Secretary Gillian Shephard, poet Wendy Cope and broadcaster Joan Bakewell, decided in 2003 against going co-ed. The defenders of the status quo argued that not only are the opportunities there better for women than in mixed-sex colleges (there are no all-male ones anymore), but that the atmosphere is better. Many female graduates describe it as more collaborative, supportive and conducive to lasting friendships.

So, would your daughter be best off in a place like that? Well, it depends. Those with academic ambitions should know that women at mixed colleges get more Firsts than those at women's colleges. There are several reasons for this. Women's library facilities may have caught up since their foundation stage, but the most highflying academics tend to be attached to mixed colleges. Also, the old Catch 22 problem remains: as fewer of the women's college staff are eminent enough to be involved in setting the exams, fewer of their students get the best possible exam preparation.

In addition, the students who attend the women's colleges are no longer mainly the bookish, hardworking spinsters of yore. The outcome is that exam results are middling at best. St. Hilda's languishes towards the bottom of the Norrington table, the informal ranking of Oxford colleges by degree results.

A student would be very wrong to dismiss the lovely college nevertheless. St. Hilda prides itself in taking interesting students from a range of backgrounds. Not all are potential academic stars, but they often contribute new ideas, not just to the college but to society.

Also, the general atmosphere is not totally female anymore:

male friends come to visit and one women's college, Newnham, now has male lecturers too. The odd boyfriend from another college even stays the night. It is hard to imagine now that all girls from this college had to be tutored in pairs until well into the 20th century, as a female student could not possibly be left alone with a male tutor.

Today's female concerns are of a different kind. The Cambridge women's officer proudly talks of the improvements she has made in contraceptive facilities. Female pressure also resulted in the introduction of a university night bus, funded by Goldman Sachs, which takes female students safely home to their colleges after clubbing. After a long debate, it was decided that male ones could hop on too.

On the other hand, tutorials and seminars in Newnham and Murray Edwards remain women-only. The same holds at Lucy Cavendish, a college solely for mature female students. For girls educated at a mixed comprehensive (as are most state school pupils) this can be quite a shock. Student life, after all, is not just about work. They are young women and most fully expect to have torrid love affairs with young men at their own level in their student years.

This can still happen, of course: lectures, university societies, voluntary work and (ahem) pub crawls bring the sexes together, but finding a boyfriend could be harder work for the girl who does not knock them out at first sight. She might not relish sitting in the JCR or college bar surrounded mainly (or, depending on the day, only) by other girls. Cycling through the pouring rain into the distant town centre to lectures, the superior main library and one of the livelier pubs can make some female students envy those more conveniently housed.

So, why do a small majority vote to keep things as they are every time? The main reason, I was repeatedly told, was ambition. You do get to try your hand at more things than you would otherwise. Want to be captain of the football team? Edit the college paper? Be president of the JCR? At a women's college, no bossy, overconfident public school boy will snatch these things from you. Even a small, speccy girl might get her chance.

Students also have fewer temptations to just skive off and do nothing. There is some excellent teaching, notably in Newnham. Girls from very religious or traditionalist backgrounds also find the environment more congenial, or at least their parents think they should.

The main reasons why today's women's colleges are not seen in a positive light, though, is that many of their students have arrived there involuntarily. One of the few criticisms I heard from the otherwise terribly positive Student Access volunteers about the entrance system was that it advised girls from "non-traditional backgrounds" to not specify their college choice. Far too often, they said, this resulted in them being shunted off into a women's college.

Was it so bad then? I asked. "No, of course not," was the invariable reply. "They are quite pretty places, less draughty than some of the older mixed and formerly all-male ones. Seminars can be great too. But it's harder to have real fun there." It is arguments like those, I suspect, which made St. Hilda's students finally decide to go co-ed in 2008, after all.

So, if your daughter is at one of the few remaining women's colleges, expect the occasional complaint. Don't, though, accept that this is a reason for leaving. Inequalities exist at other universities and students at any Oxbridge women's college make great friends, complete interesting projects, obtain Firsts and end up in fabulous jobs.

And, as mentioned before, no student is obliged to drink her nightly glass of Hooch or Perrier in her own college. One girl from a northern grammar school consigned to a women's college spent all her evenings at the bar of the mixed one attended by her older brother. Not surprisingly perhaps, she is now living with his closest university friend. Whether you regard this as a happy ending depends, I suspect, on whether you are a parent or a teenager.

20

Race

Every picture tells a story. But so do numbers. The publicity material posted by Oxford and Cambridge shows young people of all different skin colours studying and hanging out together. The pictures are real enough and so, by all accounts, is the happy student experience.

What can make the reality less rosy are the attitudes of others. The days in which blatant, in-your-face racism was tolerated in Britain are long over. It is hard to imagine now that in the 1960s it was possible for pubs to display signs saying "No Blacks, no Irish", or that some grammar schools would not admit Asian students. Such acts are illegal now and public attitudes have changed well beyond the law.

Ethnic minority students, though, can still feel left out even if this was not anyone's conscious intention. People often just assume that anyone not white must be profoundly different. As Pria, a Muslim Liverpudlian of Pakistani origin told me with a shrug: "The fact that you're wearing a headscarf does not mean you don't want to be asked along when the rest of the girls go shoe shopping."

Chima, an extremely bright and outgoing black first year student from East London, loves her Cambridge course but says with slight exasperation: "It's not that anyone has ever been hostile, just that it is always me who has to start the conversation...And not wanting to step on anyone's toes can make people edge around meaning."

Chima was not imagining her problem. Since Oxbridge students tend to come from middle class schools, whether state or private, some have never talked to a black person before. "We do have one black chap on my course, but he rather keeps to himself," a first year from a rural boy's public school told me in reply to a question, then went on slightly nervously: "S'ppose one should make more of an effort, but I'm just not sure what kind of things he'd be into."

At other times, the assumptions made can be deeply offensive. Jad, a well-dressed black student, was quietly sitting in his JCR, when a passing female college worker threw him a suspicious glance, before inquiring politely: "Are you lost, dear?"

During his first weeks, the son of an eminent black pastor, attending a highly ranked college, kept being asked by fellow students whether he used to be a gangster.

A seemingly funny remark may also sting. The white student who takes his black fellow tutee to a club, but then quips: "I thought you people had dancing in your blood," is not just being silly. He is stereotyping her.

For some reason, asking someone "do you cheer for the West Indies, then?" is still regarded an OK question over a post-game drink in a few colleges.

Many ethnic minority students are also irked by hostile remarks on immigration and asylum. After all, many of their parents arrived in Britain by this painful route as, of course, did the people who founded such very British institutions as Marks and Spencer, ITV, the Glyndebourne Opera Festival and the RSPCA.

As a result, a student may return from college in the first weeks tense and unsure. Black male students, in particular, can react badly to their first encounter with Oxbridge life. They may feel they are not being treated with respect and almost every year a few of them drop out.

If your son is actually considering this, it will not help to remind him of the long-term pay-off in terms of opportunities and careers (which can be impossible to focus on if nobody at his college has yet invited him for coffee). Nor will it do much good to say that black students have reported similar experiences at Britain's other top universities, so a switch may not help. The best thing to do, probably, is to ask the lad to defer judgment a little longer, at least until the end of his first year.

At this point, having struggled to get into Oxbridge and then to fit into life there, everything often suddenly falls into place, at least for those black students willing to persist in their initiatives.

Chima, who had struggled in her first term to even keep a student conversation going, six months later had a rich social life involving students of every colour and background. She was vice president of the Cambridge University English Society, social secretary of her college badminton club, a theatre critic for her college magazine and active in the Target Schools campaign seeking to encourage more black applicants. Despite her earlier experiences, she had no doubts at all that going to Oxbridge had been, for her at least, the right choice.

This is not to say that ethnic minority students should passively accept racist behaviour. All universities, including Oxford and Cambridge, now have strong anti-racism policies and will act on reports of racist incidents. The problem can be that a student, may not feel that her experience was bad enough to mention. A study by the

Cambridge student union, CUSU, suggested that one off the cuff comment in the college bar may be enough to cause tremendous upset but not seen as worth reporting. Besides, how do you react to something that was probably not meant to be a snub?

One way of reacting is by getting support from within your own group, and far more of this is now available than there was even five years ago. Sometimes, this just means a club in which you can meet other ethnic minority students from different colleges. This is often supplemented by events designed to spread information about your minority group.

At Cambridge, the African and Caribbean Society seeks to bridge the gap through cook-outs, lectures and what its members say are the best parties in the university. Others, like the Hindu society, organize regular talks and films, as well as a widely popular, colourful Diwali ball.

A few societies are more overtly political. Oxford Black and Asian Caucus (BAC) targets racism, which it regards as a real problem, through its education activities and a large and varied programme for Black History Week. In addition, it each year runs a lively cultural festival of African music, poetry and dance. The society's aim is to "promote equality and celebrate diversity, helping to make the university a tolerant and supportive place".

CUSU puts much effort into campaigning for the same aim, but also insists that the atmosphere in colleges and faculties is broadly anti-racist. Most incidents reported to its officials involve racial taunting on the football pitch. This is not exactly a practice confined to Oxbridge, but most students find it deeply objectionable and their union is determined to stamp it out.

All these bodies, plus BAME (The Black, Asian and Minority Ethnicity Project) at Cambridge, seek to emphasize the positive about their culture and about the university's efforts, so much so that, as one young white anti-racist put it to me, you sometimes wish they would just draw up a checklist of the things they absolutely hate!

These societies often meet more urgent needs. According to one activist, the benefits of membership are that "it gives a sense of security, it motivates you to discuss things and to deal with it. It gives you mutual support and counselling...We are in a white institution, we have to encourage each other to be proud. We are role models."

There is no longer a shortage of those. Rahul Mansigani, a Londoner of Indian descent, was elected President of CUSU in 2011. Pav Akhtar, a Muslim, had been the first non-white student to hold the post a decade earlier. Asked to comment on his election, Pav had said he was optimistic: "I didn't think that it was a place for me, a lower class Asian northerner, but the university has accommodated me...It's by coming here that we will change things."

GETTING THE NUMBERS STRAIGHT

The social experience of ethnic minority students is not something Oxbridge used to take much interest in. It was implicitly and sometimes openly assumed that these people had no right to fuss; they were expected to be grateful for the opportunities offered.

Many present day academics feel quite differently and will go to great length to put an individual black student at ease. However, when you mention student numbers to certain Oxbridge dons, these rugged individualists utter an almost identical reply: "Actually, we have a slight over-representation of Asians in certain courses. Some people, you know, have complained about this."

Oxbridge statistics really do not justify such complacency. Students from the UK's main ethnic groups have never found it equally easy to get in. In 2009, the success rate of white Cambridge applicants was 29 per cent. Chinese applicants had a success rate of 22 per cent and those from the Indian subcontinent of some 15 per cent. To some, this will make sense, as minority students are often less well off and therefore less well coached.

Black success rates are a different matter. Newspaper reports suggest that a black sixth former considering Oxbridge needs to be not just smart but optimistic. In 2010 the Labour MP David and former Higher Education Minister David Lammy revealed in *The Guardian* that Oxford, which did not then publish ethnicity data, had admitted only one (!) Afro-Caribbean student the previous year. At Cambridge the equivalent number was six.

Altogether, some thirty black students, mostly from African families, had got into each university in 2009. In total, 475 black students had applied, which made for a general black success rate of roughly 11 per cent, barely changed since 2001. "Applications are being made," commented Lammy, "but places are not being awarded."

Before dismissing Oxbridge dons as a bunch of racists it seems only fair to hear their side of the story. Oxford has argued that young black people are disadvantaged from a very early age. Even black candidates with the right grades have most often done the "wrong" A-level subjects or go for over-subscribed courses. Over a quarter of black applicants most years try for Medicine, compared to 7 per cent of whites. Others pick Law or Economics. Candidates' success rates for other courses are twice as high.

These are points students, parents and teachers ought to take on board. Still, they arguably don't absolve the university from the duty to offer its top level education to the top layer of ability, whatever its colour. If a black student is flagged as exceptionally able by her school, rather more flexibility over A-level grades and even subjects might be in order.

Instead, what has already brought about change, slow as it might be, is public exposure. Having its embarrassingly low black intake exposed in December 2010, Oxford suddenly found merit in seven Afro-Caribbean applicants and offered them all places a month later. As a result, thirty-two new black students entered the university in 2011, the largest number ever. Since then, numbers have risen further, although only slightly: from 38 in 2015 to 48 in 2017. That year, the success rate of black applicant was still only 12 per cent, compared to 20 per cent for all applicants.

Moreover, colleges vary in their attitude to black students. A Freedom of Information request, submitted in early 2018, again by David Lammy, revealed yet more shocking facts: one in four Oxford colleges had failed to admit a single black British student every year between 2015 and 2017. Also, three of Oxford's most famous colleges, Balliol, University and Magdalen, had each admitted fewer than three applicants from this group in the same period. Yet another, Corpus Christi, had not admitted a single one.

Conservative Universities Minister (and Oxford graduate) Sam Gyimah chimed in by condemning the Oxbridge diversity failures as "staggering", a view echoed by much of the British press.

The picture looks slightly better if we look at a broader group, consisting not just of students with two black parents, but also of "mixed-race" students with one black parent. Members of this statistical group also tend to define themselves as black, and between twenty and thirty of them annually entered Oxford between 2012 and 2016, in addition to some twenty students of African origin.

Still, what this means in practice is that most colleges have a single black student at best. Being in such a minority can be a hugely psychological strain and should really not happen at all.

A similar data set to Oxford's is not available for Cambridge, but the success rate of black students of any geographic origin there was an average 16 per cent in 2015 (versus 26 per cent for white students) and an average 15 per cent (versus 29 per cent for white students) in 2017. Students of mixed black-and white parentage had an average success rate of 23 per cent in 2015 and 20 per cent in 2017.

In actual numbers, Cambridge in 2017 admitted a total of 58

black students out of 250 who had applied. The year before, applications by 302 black students had resulted in just 39 places. The only substantial group of black and mixed black-and-white students at the university is consistently found at King's College, Cambridge.

TEA FOR TWO

None of this means that improvements in the admissions process have had no impact at all. They have doubtlessly helped to increase the number of black applicants and raised their chances of getting an interview. Getting rather more of them in, though, is another matter.

Explanations for this offered by Oxbridge, mostly in terms of the broader disadvantages suffered by black Britons, are not entirely convincing. Education is indeed a factor, but should not be overestimated. Schooling in many poor black areas has much improved due to extra funding and most black parents now try to send their children to good schools. Grades, moreover, are rising, although few families have clocked the bewildering fact that high GCSE grades are almost more crucial than A-level ones when it comes to a student's Oxbridge chances.

Nor is the problem always poverty. By now, quite a few black families are headed by female graduates, mostly of the new universities, who are in well-paid white collar jobs, not doing manual labour. In any case, contributing to social mobility within a population group, rather than just bemoaning the low rate of it, has always been part of a top university's remit.

More relevant to black students' Oxbridge success or lack of it are often admissions tutors' attitudes, especially at the interview. Some dons can be just a little less welcoming towards a black candidate than a white one. This need not be a conscious process, but it may still scupper a tense student's performance. Even good manners don't always hide low expectations. Those accepted are less likely to have had a chilly reception.

Unrealistic expectations also do harm. Admissions tutors may say that they would love to admit more black students, but their choices reveal that they really want a young Barak Obama. That's not likely to be the student without a room of his own to study in and with an after-school job.

There are other problems. While some interviewers try hard to find merit in black applicants, others struggle to discern ability in a candidate speaking "black" English or just having a "black" pronunciation. When meeting black Oxbridge students, one cannot but notice how many speak in a "white", middle class way. Such speech tends to be equated with articulacy, seen as crucial for many courses.

Nor do all interviewers realise that a very bright candidate may still refuse to engage in a mannered but very rapid response dialogue. Instead, he may prefer to slowly ponder a complex question. As the American psychologist Alexenia Y. Baldwin puts it in her study *The Gifted and Talented: Development Perspectives*, gifted black teenagers do not necessarily "present the classical intelligence or achievement profile that is equated with giftedness."

While the standard tests now used by both Oxford and Cambridge can make up for some of this, they don't work so well for those unfamiliar with the mental gymnastics required. Practice much improves results, but you need to know this. So, the official advice that there's no need to prepare can again be really harmful.

Some teachers would like to see more formal scrutiny, as the current situation discourages applications. The more confident black students are in their abilities, the more they insist that they will only consider a university which appreciates minorities and the contribution they can make.

Teachers often try to counteract this Catch-22 factor by promoting Oxbridge as a top student's natural home. Whenever they hear a bright black pupil say, "I won't go where I'm not wanted," they try to change this fatalistic maxim to "I deserve to be there". However, this does no good if the applicant then fails to get in.

Chris Bland (not his real name), a Maths teacher, told me how he had, some years ago, sent two of his students for an Oxbridge interview. One, a boy with a white and an Asian parent, was a sound mathematician, good rather than brilliant. The other, an Afro-Caribbean boy, was considered by the school to be absolutely outstanding. Guess who was accepted? The black student's Maths teacher, although prone to cynicism after years of sending out Oxbridge candidates, was still livid at the outcome.

So, teachers of black pupils can, not surprisingly, err on the side of caution. Why expose their student to a likely rejection?

Oxbridge dons are horrified if you suggest that anyone at their university might be racist, but the problem persists. Someone does need to explain how the average don finds it so much easier to see intellectual promise in a polite, blond home counties chap or a delicate, soft-spoken Indian girl than in a hulking Afro-Caribbean boy.

By accepting that talent can be found where genteel white manners are not, the best American universities educate huge numbers of brilliant black students: black applicants to Harvard were in 2017 offered altogether 284 undergraduate places out of a total number of 1,962. Black Oxford applicants, on the other hand, were offered a bare 48 places out of a total of 3,270, and Cambridge ones 58 out of a total of 3,497 places. Different relative population sizes alone cannot account for this.

Even within Britain university attitudes are changing. Inner city teachers were full of praise for the ability of top institutions like Imperial College London, UCL and Manchester University to identify top potential in all sorts of young people.

The academic powerhouse of Oxbridge, though, remains set in its old ways, which means that black students, especially, can spend their first months feeling odd, home-sick and cross.

Having said this, one must also point out that many black students at Oxbridge are actively trying to improve the situation. Aware that their key problem is gross under-representation, they put a lot of volunteer effort into Access projects aimed at communities and schools with large black population. This itself can raise a black Oxbridge student's mood, though it would be nice if it met with more success. Perhaps a dialogue with the two universities' admissions departments about the problem may be more fruitful at this stage.

Meanwhile, none of this should be taken to mean that the improvements in the admissions process have had no impact at all. Black students from low income families and poor neighbourhoods are now more likely to get an interview. Also, if their grades are identical to that of a white student applying for the same place, the black student may be offered it on contextual grounds. Getting in, though, remains hard.

THE CULTURE GAP

Asian students, who are only slightly underrepresented, can face a different problem, rooted in British youth culture. This is that the two key student leisure pursuits, in Oxbridge and elsewhere, are drink and sex. For Muslims, the fact that they reject alcohol can be a serious barrier to the initial bonding process. Sipping your coke while others are on their fifth, hilariously funny pint of Grolsch can make you feel an outsider, as well as terribly bored. For Asian girls, Muslim or not, the more casual approach to sex taken by their white fellow students can be quite shocking.

Abstinence can certainly slow down integration, giving rise to comments like "he doesn't pull" or "she's a bit of a prude." Luckily, this stage tends to be short. Even in the face of great cultural differences, shared tutorials and the shared worries about seminar tasks or impossible essay deadlines create real bonds. Future doctors working long hours in the lab rapidly conclude that they have far more in common with one another than with any of their fellow students outside Medicine, perceived as idle slobs.

And there are other ways of meeting people. One young doctor from a Punjabi family I interviewed recalled that she really enjoyed hanging out with the Christian Union students who shared her moral stance. A Bengal-born London girl, now a young executive, had a wonderful three years as an active member of the Pakistani Society, the Islamic Society, the Iranian Society and the Oxford Union, all without ever touching a drop of alcohol or uncovering her knees.

Two male Arab students I spoke to admitted, somewhat shamefacedly, that they did drink in their first month, "because it helps to get to know people". Once they had bought the required number of rounds, though, both reverted to water. Those awkward first term nights in the pub enabled them to meet a wide range of potential friends, and those they picked had interests that could be pursued sober.

An Egyptian-born writer, now approaching forty, recalls that he enthusiastically took up football and rowing, but avoided rugby "which was for drunks". Coming from a political family, he spent the rest of his free time arguing about Palestinian rights with fellow students. One of the lifelong friends he made in the course of this is now a London newspaper editor, the other a (Jewish) professor of Politics. If you are confident in your own culture, you can clearly get away without drinking.

To sum up, an ethnic minority student seeking a happy social life often needs to do three things. One is to be aware that the dominant culture among Oxbridge students is anti-racist, another is to take lots of initiatives, and the third is to be reasonably flexible. As one female Indian undergraduate said to me: "We girls get on fine but quite a few Asian men wander around all on their own. And when I ask such a chap whether he has joined any societies or mixed much with people from other colleges, the answer is always no. 'You know, how busy us science students are,' one young man said to me. That's quite true, but most of the white students still belonged to something like the boat club or the film society. You can be too cautious, I think."

A DEGREE OF DIFFERENCE

It would be tempting to stop on this positive note, if there were not another, rather crucial fact worth being aware of. This is the degree results. In 2003, a four-year study commissioned by Cambridge revealed that nearly a quarter of white and Asian students got firsts, while only about 3 per of black students did. The percentage of firsts bestowed on black students at the university has gradually risen, but by 2017 it had still reached only 10 per cent. At Oxford, 8 per cent of black students got firsts in 2017, while the figure for white students was 32 per cent.

How to explain this disparity? Some of it may be down to schools. The "better" his school, the better prepared a student will be for Oxbridge in terms of working habits and background knowledge. Unless an undergraduate is quickly helped to catch up, his performance will not match his ambitions.

Well-meaning tutors often adopt an informal approach to this problem, if they acknowledge it at all. Faced with an under-achieving student, they may just reassure him that he must intensify his efforts. If there is a large gap to bridge, this is rarely good enough. Without more grammar skills, calculus or the historic background to British fiction, even the brightest student may conclude that he is stupid and allow himself to coast.

There are, in fact, basic books, short courses or websites which can move him on but, living on a higher realm, a tutor may be unaware of their existence, yet she is expected to be the student's first port of call. Also, a student has to be quite clear what his own "known unknowns" are.

Black students who do well have often built a close rapport with more than one member of the teaching staff. This creates a circle of approachable people who can point them in the right direction. Too many Oxbridge dons, it seems, do not know how to communicate with their black students effectively enough to offer them the necessary support.

What this suggests is that such people might benefit from is a compulsory staff course in diversity training. Such courses, designed to throw a spotlight on subconsciously racist behaviour, are now routinely provided for public sector employees. In the course of writing this book, I asked most academics I met whether they had had any such training. I might as well have asked for their favourite sexual position. No reply was ever forthcoming.

Still, Oxbridge is forever changing, also when it comes to race. Not only are admissions figures crawling upwards at a few colleges, but others are intensifying their relationships with predominantly black schools. Real change, though, is likely to depend on two key drivers: continued public concern and pressure from the government bodies providing most Oxbridge funding.

BAD NEWS AND SOME VERY GOOD NEWS

Despite the rather mixed experiences of black students at Oxbridge, many black parents remain keen to improve their young people's chances of a place. Not only are they highly clued up about the differential achievements of local schools, but ready to spend a good chunk of even very low earnings on recommended books or extension activities like museum visits. Better off black families pay for extra tuition in the hope of good grades, or even for private schools. A growing number of black community groups and churches also run study clubs designed to help their young people access top Russell Group universities. After years of almost no Oxbridge success despite all this, though, more than one community member has been known to comment bitterly: "It's just racism, isn't it?"

This might be the end of a troubling story, were it not for one fact: just before this book went to press in the summer of 2018, Oxford and Cambridge announced that they had now hired a small recruitment company run by black graduates to roll out a preparation scheme for highly able black sixth formers. The scheme, called *TARGET OXBRIDGE*, offers 160 state school students in Year 12 regular, structured support designed to help them meet the requirements for a successful Oxford or Cambridge application.

Participants are advised on A-level and degree course choice, get academic guidance and then learn about Oxbridge interviews and tests. High point is a three day stay at an Oxbridge college and a chance to talk to course tutors about what those are looking for. The scheme is completely free to students, and those who completed its pilot had a success rate of around 40 per cent.

While this is just a partial solution, of course, and one currently just open to students living in the Greater London region, it shows what can happen if the will is there.

IS IT WORTH THE HASSLE?

Ethnic minority students who had come for the academic buzz of Oxbridge, for a carefully picked course or for contact with a special academic expert, definitely did think so. So did students who were keen to get practical experience in fields like drama, public speaking or journalism. The semi-professional Oxbridge societies offering such experiences actively welcome them.

Nor does this mean that you have to pay with loneliness for these benefits. All the ethnic minority students I spoke to had made close friends from different backgrounds at Oxbridge, if sometimes after a hairy start. Quite a few did not feel totally integrated until the beginning of their second year, unlike most white students, but the college system usually worked its magic in the end. Black and Asian students, if they stay the course, tend to leave Oxbridge not less embedded in the Oxbridge network than the rest.

Oxbridge also remains the place for moving you beyond your own world on the careers ladder. Black Oxbridge graduates, especially, seem to go on to top jobs in the higher civil service, the arts, media and politics more easily than other educated members of their communities.

Academic prospects are a different matter. Should your gifted son stay if he cannot be sure to get a first from Oxford or Cambridge? Well, he should certainly be given a fair chance to. It is important to remember, though, that in the end most students at both universities get seconds, not firsts, and that still makes a graduate extremely employable. In fact, some bosses prefer Oxbridge seconds.

What if they do worse in the exam stakes? Well, Zadie Smith, whose first novel, White Teeth, won just about every literary prize in Britain and was an international success, got a Third in her Cambridge part-one exams. Her old college, King's, now lists her on its alumni page as one of two prominent contemporary British writers. The other writer listed in its official publicity material is one of its 1960s graduates, Salman Rushdie.

21
Working class heroes

There have always been some working class students at Oxbridge. Hand-picked for truly exceptional ability by the local parson or schoolteacher, sponsored by a gentleman through grammar school and encouraged to sit for the pitifully few full university scholarship places, the son of a skilled, respectable working man occasionally managed to get in. In a good decade, there could even be two such students. Careful not to presume and grateful beyond belief, these young men posed no challenge to Oxbridge.

Tension only arose when workers' aspirations increased. The introduction of free, compulsory schooling in 1870 had created a hunger for more education. Demand for the right to study at university also came from those with political ambitions. Working men now had the vote, and the Labour Party was concerned that its leaders should be men with the best possible education; so should the teachers who would raise up the working class and the trade unionists negotiating with employers.

In 1897, the TUC resolved "that the workers...should not be satisfied until the highest educational advantages which the country affords are within reach of all." This was followed by more concrete demands for access to "the deep draughts of knowledge" which only Britain's two oldest universities, so it was felt, could provide.

Cambridge offered a handful of places, but what many talented workers sought was a chance to study history, politics and economics at Oxford. This remained out of their reach, both because they lacked the right kind of schooling and because they could not afford to pay.

"We want Oxford to open wide her doors to the best of our people and take them in," declared J.M. MacTavish, a Labour member of the Portsmouth Town Council, in 1907. If the university only realised what enthusiasm there was amongst ordinary people for this education, it "would sell its plate" to help fund it, he argued, adding that such access would benefit both sides. If workers were admitted, "a true view of social questions would be taught... Although we are supposed to have no recorded history, without us all history was and is impossible."

CLOSED GATES

Gradually, the tone became less conciliatory. When told that Oxford could not accommodate working class students, campaigners angrily asked whether it was the true function of a university "to train the nation's best men, or to sell its gifts to the rich?"

There was some minority support for this stand within Oxford. A handful of dons already travelled for miles once a week to teach extension classes to men who had just completed a ten hour working day. Some of these academics had no doubt that their best pupils ought to be continuing their education at the university.

The dons were not entirely alone in supporting this aim. Charles Gore, later Bishop of Birmingham, stated in the 1908 Toynbee Report that he hoped for "a great displacement of rich or well-to-do young men who wanted to have a good time, by serious students who would come from all classes but in large measure from among the workers".

Still, when a few of the 29 Labour MPs who had been elected to Parliament in 1906 suggested that Oxford should admit at least a tiny number of outstanding working men who had prepared for this with infinite patience at the night schools of the Workers Educational Association, the response was hysterical.

Writing in the Fortnightly Review, F.C.S. Schiller, a Philosophy don at Corpus Christi College, Oxford, warned that "the workers know what they want, and what they want is destructive of progress in knowledge...What they want is an education for their purposes, an education specifically adjusted to their needs, to wit, a study of economics, politics and history... Of course, the spokesmen of the workers fail to understand the aesthetic function of Oxford... the athletic aspect of the university is equally unintelligible to them... Work people cannot understand that men whose chief interest seems to be 'play' should be allowed to remain at a University... a demand for social equality is included in their demand for 'equality of opportunity and it would almost seem that they were snobs enough to find a chance of slapping a Lord on the back in their cups one of the indispensable attractions of College life."

In any case, the reputable don argued, all clever men already had access to Oxbridge. For this reason "it is becoming more and more difficult to believe that there exist untapped reservoirs of intellectual ability among the workers. This is not to say, of course that there is no practical ability among them..."

Where that ability should take itself Schiller had no doubt: "It ought to be much easier for the new universities to satisfy the legitimate educational aspirations of the 'workers' and so to save the lily-likeness of Oxford from the hands of the uprooter.''

And thus Oxford was again ''saved'' from the workers. Only after WW1 were the entry requirements marginally eased. This was too late for many aspiring students, but talent still won out in a few cases. One of the trainees in a 1908 extension class taught by a sympathetic Balliol don was A.P. Wadsworth, who went on to edit *The Manchester Guardian* (now known simply as *The Guardian*) without the benefit of an Oxbridge degree.

PICK A NUMBER

It is the folk memory of that ugly debate which has dogged working class entrance to Oxbridge. Young people from working class homes remain deeply uncertain about whether they can get in and fit in. ''It's not for the likes of us,'' is a common view. Having arranged for the year's best student to attend a day school at Cambridge, a teacher at an inner city sixth form found himself faced with a cross, miserable lad who kept asking: ''What's the point of it? Must I go?''

The point, of course, is that working class pupils do get in. In the course of researching this book, I have talked to one Oxbridge student who was the daughter of a care worker and another who was the son of a cook. I have met young Oxbridge graduates whose fathers were lorry drivers or plumbers and an Oxbridge-educated professor whose father was a tailor. Most found university life a positive experience and a great help with their careers. ''It's wonderful that someone like me can hope to get a job in the city,'' a girl whose father was a print-worker told me with shining eyes. Those 19th century campaigners for working class access would turn in their graves at the thought of ''their'' graduates becoming investment analysts but, heck, times do change.

The question remains how much else has changed. Just how rare a bird must a working class student expect to be once he has unpacked his CDs and bought his cap and gown? The answer matters not just because it suggests how fair the entrance process really is. It also determines how comfortable such students will be at Oxbridge. Oxbridge dons can be remarkably vague about student proportions, as was exposed by a very public spat between Margaret Hodge, the Lifelong Learning and Education Minister, and the University of Cambridge on 4th February 2003.

After Hodge had remarked during a visit that the university ought to do much more to attract youngsters from working class backgrounds, the university's vice chancellor, Sir Alec Broers, responded with a strong statement. "It is simply not true that only 'rich kids' are accepted into Cambridge. Last year, 23 per cent of home students at Cambridge did not pay any tuition fees and were therefore eligible for the full student loans and for the bursaries offered by Cambridge."

Fee rules have changed since, but eligibility for financial help is not a good guide. Many a self-employed businessman can, with the help of his accountant, produce a perfectly legal income-expenditure balance which qualifies his middle class children for all there is. On the other hand, a working class couple raising three children while doing lowly paid PAYE jobs may qualify for very little.

Another measure suggested has been the number of undergraduates on free school meals at a university. Oxford former Vice Chancellor Mike Nicholson does not agree. He has pointed out that while around 10 per cent of his students are from families with incomes below £16,190 (the eligibility criteria for free school meals), only very few actually did claim them. He is technically right, of course (and figures are similar at Cambridge). However, 10 per cent is still a much less impressive figure than 23 per cent.

DO THEY REALLY EXIST?

Most dons agree that a wider range of backgrounds in the student population would be nice, but they usually refuse to define the issue any further. They certainly don't like to use the "c" word - class. Academics involved in Access projects often proved to be the ones most adamant that there is no longer any such thing as the British working class, though there were, of course, deprived people.

Student Access campaigners employed in university-sponsored projects take a similar line. When I asked one how to contact working class undergraduates so I could find out how they felt about being at Oxbridge, the response was a long silence. I might as well have asked the poor girl what sanitary towels she used. When she finally spoke, her embarrassment was so profound I could almost watch her blush over the phone: "We can't actually... you see, we don't define it like this...how would one measure it really...it is really an outdated definition."

Did she not know which students were working class, I asked, trying to relax her. "Well, not really...you know, it's not that, though," came the nervous reply.

What was it then? "It's just that it would be wrong to single out people as working class, you know, we never ask them anyway, so nobody knows."

"Surely, the students themselves would know whether they are working class and might actually want to talk about it," I finally snapped, getting exasperated. "Perhaps," was the reply. "But you can't be sure, and I don't really want to go down that route. I'm afraid I cannot help you."

Was the girl unique? Clearly not: another Access campaigner I contacted insisted that even to mention the term working class in her Access group circular would be insulting.

So, what term did Student Access use? The answer, here too, was that vague and all embracing one, "non-traditional", which covered several other areas quite apart from class.

It took a great deal of persistence to get beyond that point and a special appeal to the university's press officer but, a clutch of emails later, I was told that a face-saving category had been found. Although nobody would tell me what it was, students started to email me. This was my chance to add to the sample I had contacted by other means.

The wait proved thoroughly worthwhile. I met yet more outstanding young people who had no regrets about their university choice, but also no doubt about their identity. They were, despite a range of accents that ranged from Estuary to mildly posh, all working class, and proud of it.

One of the most interesting things that emerged from my research was that even their interviewers had not necessarily known this fact. Universities might theoretically strive for "wider participation", but practically they operate in a void. Oxbridge does not have the detailed UCAS information on the social class of an applicant's parents. Unless deliberately mentioned by the school, admissions tutors can only guess at this key fact.

Learning of all those formal and informal obstacles put in the way of meaningful student identification, it was quite difficult to feel optimistic. The admissions process sounded a bit like trying to hit a target with a sack over your head, and while doubting that the target was actually there.

BEING AN "ONLY"

Still, 10 per cent is a substantial figure, a sizeable chunk of any small town's population, and it was puzzling why working class Freshers were so often uncomfortable at Oxbridge. Surely, their accents would be everywhere, even if they themselves could not be picked out; thanks to youth culture, all classes dress much the same.

Those students I did manage to meet were indeed of obvious

working class origin. They had strong local accents, fathers who were truck drivers and mothers who did piece work on their sewing machine. They were also adamant that they were unique.

All recalled how they had looked around for "people like me" at their colleges and on their university course, only to find that there weren't any. Lizzie, a third-year student in a small college which had 300 students and a reputation as sympathetic to state school pupils, was adamant that she was the only "real" working class person there. Nobody else came from a housing estate and everybody else had parents who were much more educated than hers.

If Lizzie was right, and given that she had by then spent almost three years in the place I have no reason to believe she was not, then this would make her one in 300, or well below one per cent. Quite a different proportion.

So, where does the official figure of 9 or 10 per cent come from? Detailed research I undertook led to a unexpected discovery. Its sole source is the UCAS form, in which all applicants under 21 are asked to put in the occupation of the highest earner in their household - the very information not passed on to admissions tutors.

Using this figure can lead to considerable inaccuracies, as a friendly UCAS statistician explained to me. The first of these is due to the fact that 19 per cent of student applicants (almost one in five) actually leave this section blank. Others give an occupation that cannot later be classified.

A specific job title too is not enough to ensure a correct statistical outcome. An engineer, for instance, can be either a skilled worker or a middle class graduate.

Even if accurately defined, one parent's occupation is not enough to define a family's class. The "highest earner" in today's Britain may well be married to a low-earning middle class partner, an electrician to a teacher, or a carpenter to a writer.

To complicate matters further, there is no category called "working class". Instead, UCAS divides householders into eight categories. In place of the three old categories of "skilled manual," "partly skilled" and "unskilled", there are now four at the bottom of the list, called "lower supervisory," "technical occupations," "semi-routine" and "routine".

It is from these not very helpful data that the Higher Education Funding Council (HEFC) deduces the number of working class students at Oxbridge.

Oxbridge itself has, as stated before, responded in recent years to public concerns about unrepresentative intakes by finding out a little more about its applicants or, as it is always put, "to contextualise achievements". Oxford started doing so by taking note of an applicant's post code as it might indicate economic disadvantage. Cambridge gathered education data from the supplementary form sent to applicants after their UCAS application is received. This allows it to identify those who have obtained high GCSE grades despite attending a low achieving school.

Since 2017, the universities have also been using new, more detailed categories known as POLAR and ACORN. These expand the pool of applicants slightly further by identifying students living in run-down neighbourhoods which may also show low participation in higher education. However, this does not work well for bigger towns: in places like London, Manchester or Leeds grim housing estates often border on plush Victorian villas. Media reports on the horrific 2017 Grenfell Estate fire in the London Borough of Kensington and Chelsea revealed that the high- rise estate nestled among some of the most expensive properties in London.

In any case, a student seeking a place at either university still needs the right A-level grades, meaning anything from AAA to A*A*A, depending on the course and, at Cambridge, also the college. Despite their Oxbridge commitment to contextualisation, both universities have remained inflexible on grades.

Unfortunately, top A-level grades are most easily obtained by having private tuition, attending a high-aiming private school or being lucky enough to live near an outstanding state school. This is particularly true of "hard" A-level subjects such as physics or maths in which there is a shortage of qualified teachers.

There is also a regional imbalance. According to yet more research by David Lammy, who is emerging as a champion of under-represented groups, between 2010 and 2015 Cambridge took a larger number of students from four Home Counties than from Britain's (more working class) North East, North West and Yorkshire combined. Oxford in the same period admitted eight times as many students from the leafy London borough of Richmond as from Salford, Middlesbrough, Stoke, Hartlepool and Blackpool combined.

As a result, the proportion of non-middle class students at Oxbridge has been slow to rise. What this means is that your teenage Fresher may be in more of a minority than he expected to be and feel out of sorts. So, don't just tell the poor lad he should count himself lucky for getting in. Show some sympathy. He is in an unexpectedly alien environment and this can spell trouble.

SPECIAL HURDLES

Vaguely recalling that Oxbridge used not to want working class students and definitely finding himself in a minority, the lost lad may respond by withdrawing - mentally at first. Why bother to speak up? Students like him, he may have concluded, are expected to lie low, put up with what they are offered and hat-check their culture at the college gates. Such beliefs can affect not just his social life but also his studies.

What can make this worse is the likely discovery that his course is not pitched at comprehensive school level, and even less so at the level of even the brightest students from disadvantaged schools. Some of this can just be a matter of cultural references. The frequent use of classical imagery in science, as well as arts courses, often stumps those who grew up without any mention of Greek gods.

Luckily, this is an obstacle fairly easily overcome. One Hackney student finally ended three months of unhappy puzzlement over references to Zeus by buying a paperback encyclopaedia of classical myths.

The generous use of Latin proverbs by dons may also grate. So can being unable to understand the inscription on one's own college gate. Although no comprehensive student can read Latin, those with educated parents sometimes manage to work out what is meant and, if they can't, seem remarkably unbothered. A working class student often worries far more and needs to understand, as they do, that his education is not threatened by this.

Another handicap can be not knowing that academic help is often available as long as you ask. Paul, a working class student keen to do a course option involving European History in his second year abandoned the idea when he realised that this required a knowledge of German. A middle class student fancying the same course just discussed the problem with her supervisor, who revealed that the girl could acquire the basics of the missing language at the university language lab. There was even the possibility of a vacation grant that would enable her to get some practical language experience.

Other solutions can sometimes be found if a poor student faces what may seem like an insolvable problem. June, a very able English student, found it impossible to study in the holidays, as her family lived in one of Britain's urban war zones. When she explained to her tutor that "it's a bit difficult to read Paradise Lost when people are committing GBH outside," he suggested she should stay in college next time. Told that she could not possibly afford the £8 per night it charged outside term, he just nodded.

A week later, June's tutor mentioned that some funds might be available. When she pressed him for details at the next tutorial, he told her where to go. In the end, June got a hardship grant and spent most of the next holiday in college.

So, much can be done to smooth a working class student's study problems, but that student really needs to be clear about her needs and quite persistent. The more eminent her tutor, the more vague he might be about the basic facilities available. Requests may have to be put to the college bursar. Another useful starting point can be the student union or college JCR. In fact, Oxbridge is so well equipped that almost any course-related request can usually be met, at least if put forward well in advance.

THE MANY AND THE FEW

With only (perhaps) 10 per cent of new undergraduates being working class, social life for them can still be tough, at least at the start. Several students I met revealed that they had hated Fresher's week, because they felt everybody talked so much posher than they did and seemed so much more confident.

While public school pupils all seemed to know one another and even middle class kids from comprehensives often formed little groups, a working class student from a struggling school had usually arrived alone.

Even the getting-to-know-you chitchat in her college seminar can make a poorer working class student feel outside the norm. One girl said that what she found hardest at first were those endless questions about "what did you do in your gap year?" Another added that she just wished people wouldn't talk so much about their foreign holidays. Her family did not travel abroad, and before coming to Oxbridge she had never even been outside London.

Having less experience of academic work can cause insecurity too. Dave, a shop worker's son, accepted by Cambridge for his outstanding potential, remembered that when he was given four books to read for his first Geography essay, the task was so terrifying he could hardly open them. There had not been any books in his home and he was unused to writing long essays or to reading outside the syllabus. He was convinced that all the privately educated students were far cleverer than him. Only after the first term did he accept that he might be any good.

By the time I met Dave, he had become a quite outstanding student, but he still worked extremely hard, sometimes to the extent of making himself ill. He admitted that he was worried that he might not impress otherwise. He knew several other working class students who behaved in the same way. Most of the time, he said, "they all think they are impostors."

This is not to say that Dave has any regrets. As he put it: "Studying elsewhere is probably less stressed, there is more balance in one's life. Cambridge is very competitive. But then other universities would not have challenged me so much. It is harder to excel elsewhere. Here there is so much opportunity and such good expert supervision which develops you. I know that if I can cope with demands here, I can cope with anything."

There is no doubt that many of the working class students were not just bright, but far brighter and more resourceful than many other students at Oxbridge. One girl worked out all there was to know about the Oxbridge application process herself, after her teacher warned her that it might be too complicated. Another responded to the problem of being asked at her interview about knowledge she did not have by firing back lots of intelligent questions. Her interviewers were duly impressed.

Still, once in, students in this group can be stressed out by having to adjust so much or feeling that their specific needs remain unmet. In response, some of them in 2018 founded a new support group called *ClassAct*. Based at Oxford, it describes itself as a student campaign for low income, working class, first generation, and state comprehensive educated students. It organises social events, but also raises issues of concern in wider university forums and holds networking evenings fronted by successful graduates from working class backgrounds.

THE HOME FRONT

Meanwhile, though, working class students may also have to contend with challenging family attitudes. One girl I spoke to had been warned by her mother not to tell any other relatives that she was sitting for Oxbridge, in case she was mocked.

Often even a well-meaning working class family was unable to offer support to a student coming home after a stressful term. This was the case even if there were no external problems, such as crime. Parents and siblings might find it hard to talk to her and would watch for any signs of "uppertiness". On visits, the student might be expected to constantly play down her "other life", except when put in front of relatives to show off.

Ruth, a SPS student with particular interest in sociology,

commented that working class families often seemed unaware that a young person who moves away from home will change, wherever she might go, and might indeed develop opinions and ideas different from their own. As a result, the student's new identity is sometimes taken as a personal insult. The result can be serious family fall-outs. This is a price not exacted from middle class students.

Still, none of the students wished they had made a different choice. June remarked how wonderful it was to live without the TV blazing away, to discuss issues and develop theories, all things she had never done at home. At Oxbridge, she said with a smile, nobody gets angry if they disagree.

The main problem, though, was living in quite such a middle class set-up, in which your behaviour and speech patterns always stuck out. Unlike ethnic minority students, white working class boys, in particular, seemed initially stunned by this. They had had some concerns, but nothing in their own lives had prepared them for being outsiders. On the other hand, many did, thanks to time and obvious effort, completely blend it.

Those white working class students I spoke to certainly still loved Oxbridge, usually for its intellectual buzz and the opportunities it had given them, rather than for its social customs. All of them also wished that there would be more people like them, so they could feel more at home.

THE ETONIANS

Having said this, it is important to realise that the gap is not always as big as it may seem. Those who come across as "posh" on first sight are often, as the student gradually discovers, bright young people from all sorts of homes who went to Britain's few remaining grammar schools. This group makes up over a third of all state school students at Oxbridge.

Many of the privately educated students at the two universities are not the sons of gentlemen farmers anymore either. They are more likely to have fathers who are shopkeepers, lawyers or managers and mothers who work in an office to pay the fees. Quite a few Oxbridge parents are said to be self-employed builders.

These people are not sending their bright kids to public school so that they can look down on others, but in order to ensure that they are taught for longer hours, by more qualified teachers and with more attention to their ability, in short, to give them the kind of education which is free and taken for granted in much of Europe.

There are, of course, some very posh students at Oxbridge. There was one question to which all working class students I eventually met responded in exactly the same way. Asked what they found strangest at Oxbridge, the answer was invariably: the Etonians. There seemed to be a huge number of them about, roaming the place in tightly knit, well-spoken groups, utterly at ease there from day one.

This was slightly puzzling since there are, in fact, relatively few Etonians at Oxbridge today. Britain's most exclusive boarding school, whose intake, in any given year, includes one third landed gentry and at least a dozen boys with aristocratic titles, sends most of its trust-funded pupils to slightly less demanding places. The most popular destinations are Durham, Bristol, Exeter or a nearby agricultural college. Still, Eton is a big school with a big scholarship form and at any moment there can indeed be over 200 Etonians at Oxbridge. All of them, too, seem to know one another or at least someone's younger brother. Most are found at Christ Church, Oxford, which the school has centuries-old links with, so you can, as said, always avoid it.

On the other hand, why should you? Eton does not actually produce monsters of snobbery, but polite, charming young men who wear their privilege lightly. Despite what you have seen in the movies, they don't ever line up to bray at northern lads for wearing elasticated bow ties. They are all male and, when sober, sweetly polite with the female sex, which they have before mainly known as matron. When drunk, they go in for strange tribal singsongs and tend to monopolise the universities wine societies, where they can be rather less charming to outsiders. As the wine societies are almost the only societies that charge, knowing this can save you lots of money.

However, even today over a third of the Oxbridge British student intake comes from various private schools, and it eventually dawned on me that state school students tended to use ''Etonian'' as a generic term for any male students from a private school. This view can be daunting, as well as misleading.

What Oxbridge has, in fact, is a quickly formed fraternity or sorority of people who have never met, but play squash and know what Rugby or Teddy's are (they're boarding schools). Most also live in the same part of the Home Counties or the Green Belt around London.

Once at Oxbridge, all these students indeed stand out by the relaxed way in which they move around their strange new home. There are good reasons for this. The oak beams, stained glass windows and coats of arms on the wall of the college dining hall will be familiar to them from their school, even if that establishment was only launched after the Beatles' first LP. Their teachers too are likely to have worn black gowns over their M&S suits, at least at formal occasions. The Latin names of obscure Oxbridge practices are no mystery to those who survived a decade of compulsory Classics.

Most importantly, perhaps, pupils from the private sector do not arrive at Oxbridge alone. Even the smallest rural establishment which will take anyone who pays expects to send a bunch of pupils to Oxbridge each year. What parent would pay £16,000 a year upwards without at least the distant prospect of a place? The handful of top independents which pick (and expel) pupils on the basis of academic achievement alone may annually send up over fifty students each. This begets the little groups of first years with the plummy voices.

But do they want to stay among themselves? Well, they may initially. In a new place, it is reassuring to be among friends, and so you find clusters of new students swapping fond memories of their housemaster, Mr. Chips, in some distant corner of an Oxbridge playing field. If you went to a comprehensive, this can make you feel excluded, but I wouldn't jump to conclusions just yet. Usually, it's nothing more than a bit of childish nostalgia and the boys will soon drift back into grown-up life.

Asked whether they think it is best to stay among one's own kind, the numerous private school students I have met over the years certainly responded with an emphatic no. They are at university to meet exciting new people, and some would go as far as drop their h's to that end. There is even a better reason that few will admit to: private schools tend to be single sex, so getting to university is at least partly about escaping this hellish state.

FITTING IN OR STANDING OUT?

Still, being working class at Oxbridge can often be harder than expected at the earlier stages, and there are problems which do not go away. Having less spending money than others is one of those. When you first arrive, it can often seem as if all the interesting people go out for a restaurant dinner every night, rather than eat in college. Fortunately, this is not actually true.

Drink is a more serious issue. Binge drinking is now so deeply rooted in student culture that it threatens to not just destroy the livers of a generation, but also any efforts towards integration. Student leaders who are serious about Access should perhaps acknowledge that if the normal student is spending every night at the bar, then many poorer, working class student will invariably be excluded. So, of course, will Muslim students.

Meanwhile, working class students need to be prepared for the fact that Oxbridge is a very middle class world, albeit not one necessarily hostile to outsiders. Many of those I spoke to were quite thrown at first by the extent to which they stuck out. Each one also recalled, without prompting, one thoughtless, hurtful remark. When you are eighteen and new to a place, being jokingly referred to as "our Prole" can really upset you. Of course it's a joke and you should joke back, but that does take confidence.

The most common advice working class students gave was to relax: everybody experiences a bad response once, so there is no point in getting uptight. You are in the modern world, among fellow students. It is crucial to realise that you are not constantly being snubbed. Don't let anyone intimidate you, but don't feel too easily slighted either.

You also need to reach out. As Ruth, the SPS student, put it: "Some working class students don't understand that the way of mixing at Oxbridge is not necessarily by finding similar people, but by doing similar things. They wait for someone congenial to turn up in their year or course, rather than join societies to develop joint interests."

Some students adjust by completely losing their working class manners and accent. "You'd never know he was working class," one girl said of a passing young man with flowing locks, dressed in pure Brideshead. Others play the wide boy for all it's worth, even claiming to be related to the Krays. Others yet again spend far more money than they can afford and have to take a college job to pay their debts. Budding campaigners join *ClassAct*, the Oxbridge student society giving voice to this group's concerns.

Many working class students, though, just look ahead and seize the opportunities with both hands. Some, to their own surprise, simply enjoy the terrific features of the place. Admittedly, it is easier to do this if your parents told you that everybody is an equally worthy human being, and if you are blessed with a sharp wit. It would be even easier if more middle class people taught their young that good manners are not really about holding a wine glass at the stem with three fingers; they are about making the person opposite you feel at ease.

The truth, though, is that in the end both sides adapt a little. Middle class students learn to play darts, working class ones become experts on vintage dry sherry. The bad old days when Oxbridge was a lily that needed protection from the workers are over. If you can persuade yourself that you deserve to be there, you should have three or four great student years.

22
What if they didn't get in?

However, talented your teenager, and however good the preparations he made, the fact remains that more people apply for Oxbridge than get in. There are between three and six applicants for each place, ten for some top courses. Readers can much improve the odds by following the advice in this book, but in the end candidates and parents must also accept that there is an element of luck involved. Young people of equal ability, suitability and amiability compete for the same places every year. It is, therefore, possible that the lad will suffer the disappointment of not getting an offer, or of not getting the grades required to take up his offer.

Being told that the university you chose has not chosen you can come as a nasty shock, even to those who thought they had allowed for it. So, if you don't want your son's self-esteem to be damaged, don't wait until the rejection letter is in his clenched fist. Instead, think ahead and positively consider other options when you are first looking at university prospectuses, or when he tells you about his teachers' recommendations.

This means that you should say good, constructive things about the second and (if possible) third place he is thinking of applying to. You do not need to be a university expert for this. Just point out that the course in University B looks interesting, the staff friendly and young. Talk with genuine warmth about the location of University C even if your own memories of the bleak East Anglian landscape or crowded Central London make your heart sink.

None of this makes you a hypocrite. Students can be deliriously happy in a concrete jungle, as long as it offers them good teaching and a lively campus. Encourage the lad to find out more and perhaps visit the place. Encourage him also to check where his own role models have studied; it may well not be Oxbridge.

What you want is for your son to feel that all the choices he has made are good ones, that he can look forward to his university education, whatever happens.

True, Oxbridge particularly suits some students, being more theoretical and more intense than other places. It is also so much better funded. If the lad goes elsewhere, though, he will reap other benefits, not least the skills to survive in the real world, and he'll learn about much the same academic subjects.

Again, you need not feel dishonest by telling him this. Britain's world class experts studied at all sorts of universities and many still lecture there. Top careers are made by people who have graduated from all sorts of degree courses or none. A great university experience is determined not just by the status of the institution: it can come from the friendships formed and the infectious enthusiasm of one single staff member, plus the kind of bands which the student union gets in for gigs. And this experience, in turn, generates the self-confidence that bolsters careers.

So, do make your son feel from the start that he has a range of attractive options ahead of him. Don't be afraid that unless you turn his getting into Oxbridge into a life or death matter he will rush off to Skate City or the pub, rather than cram for his exams. Firstly, this is not true and, secondly, such brinkmanship will not do him any good. By now he will know from his teachers, his environment and everything said at home that he needs to work to the max. Those with a clutch of strong university choices do so in better spirits and with a lighter heart.

If you follow this advice, the lad will still have something to look forward to, should the Oxbridge offer not materialise. Being rejected always hurts. Without other attractive prospects, your son may well feel cast out into limbo, or appalled at the prospect of studying at a place he has taken absolutely no interest in or treated with scorn.

Nor is being positive about other options merely a fall-back position, as you might think. It is also a great way of enabling your son to impress his first choice. Oxbridge, like the perfect lover, comes to him who is cool - not desperate.

WHAT IF SHE DIDN'T GET AN OFFER?
Faced with a glum boy who picked up the courage to apply to Oxbridge or a tear-stained girl who fell in love with the medieval quads on her school's Outreach visit, the temptation is nevertheless to curse that stupid, snobbish place. Or you might want to mumble about playing the game being more important than winning.

My advice is to do neither. All is not lost yet. If there is real talent here and not just parental pushiness, and if your teenager remains determined, there is always the option of reapplying in the next academic year. The cobblestones of Oxbridge are trodden by a surprising number of students who did just that. However, the steps a student must take depend on the precise situation.

Let's say your daughter was expected to get above-average

grades relevant to the degree subject she had hoped to do at Cambridge. However, as a result of her interview and/or test not going as well as expected, or of some other, mysterious factor, perhaps a tepid reference from her school, she was not offered a place.

If she does not want to go to another university instead, she will have no choice but to wait. Her first wait will have to be for her A-level results. If these are at the top of the range, Oxbridge is still an option the following year. Anastasia Fedotova, a Manchester pupil rejected in 2001 by Brasenose College, Oxford, although she was sitting six A-levels, dealt with this by taking a year out. After receiving her exam results, which were six A-grades, five of them in the sciences, she then applied to Trinity College, Cambridge, and went on to happily read Maths there.

But where should your daughter try next? Theoretically, students can just reapply to another college in the same university, but the dirt among the private Oxbridge tutors is that your chances in these circumstances are vastly better if you try "the other place" instead. In other words, if your very bright daughter was turned down by Cambridge, she should try Oxford next. Apparently, there is a mild form of one-upmanship in taking a good candidate rejected by the competition.

WHAT IF HE DIDN'T GET THE GRADES?

This is quite a different situation. Grades well below those specified in the Oxbridge offer obviously mean that another university offer should be accepted.

However, if your son missed the required grades by a hare's breadth, he needn't give up yet, as long as there were very good reasons for it. Bereavement or a serious illness suffered during the exam period and backed by a doctor's certificate will be taken into account. A bog standard, self-treated runny nose won't.

If the lad's results were due to factors such as emigration, you may feel that he should now resit. This can be the wrong thing to do, as Oxbridge increasingly insists on grades obtained at first try. Check the current rules not just with the university but, especially at Cambridge, also with the college your son is aiming for.

Still, if it is just that one of your son's grades was an A, rather than the required A*, there may be a way forward: he could obtain further qualifications for the desired course. This can mean taking a third science A-level (Cambridge is less keen on applicants with a mix of arts and science subjects than Oxford). Also note that while Oxbridge officially does not take note of AS levels anymore, there is one main exception. An AS-level in Maths can still improve the Oxbridge chances of applicants to certain courses.

Alternatively, your son could court Oriental Studies/AMES by now exploring Chinese or Arab history in depth, or look at Britain's key structures for Geography, HSPS or PPE. Relevant work experience and a willingness to show what he has learnt from it may also increase his appeal in Oxbridge eyes. Alongside this active stuff, determined applicants read and read.

To further improve his odds, a retry student with added qualifications should also pick a different college and perhaps university to apply to. Your son's chances are certainly better if he now lowers his expectations. The top colleges, mostly situated in the centre of town, will be less interested than the less highly ranked ones at the edge.

This can also be the time to target a slightly less competitive Oxbridge course. Determined students now shift from English Lit. to Modern Languages or from Medicine to Biochemistry. It is usually too late to make the more drastic switch from arts to sciences or the other way round.

Before considering such a route, though, look carefully at all the facts. First, be sure that your son is really capable of getting the grade required, especially if it is an A*. Then look at the precise marks he obtained in every part of the A-level exam, which are listed in the certificate. B-grades and A-grades may seem close, but if the document shows that the lad only just scraped his three B's, despite good teaching at a school which regularly sends other pupils to Oxbridge, do encourage him to accept another offer. Cambridge won't consider an Oxford reject with middling grades and the prospect of much the same.

Even if your son's grade results were a narrow miss, though, you need to make very sure he really wants to time-travel back to the classroom. Re-try students usually attend classes at a local authority or private sixth form college. These are places without pack drill or uniforms, but we are still talking about some 20 hours of schooling per week, plus homework. Some of the work may not even be new to the student, even though the syllabus changes every year.

Oxbridge is now an option again, and if your son knuckles down to the work, it's time to cook him his favourite meal or take him fishing. You can also help him achieve his goal by insisting he does more after class than just improve his score in Grand Theft Auto.

Don't be put off by claims that he can't possibly find the

time. Even re-try students have evenings, weekends and holidays; ample time to practice your foreign languages in a tourist hotel, or to scrub hospital corridors in preparation for Medicine. Such activities show that you are a determined, eager young person and might even give you something to talk about at your interview.

What a student hoping for a second Oxbridge chance must do alongside all this, though, is work out where else he and his vast DVD collection could be happy. With the number of Oxbridge applicants steadily growing, re-try applicants do not stand half as good a chance as they did a decade ago.

LAST CHANCE SALOON

Even those who've failed to get into an Oxbridge undergraduate course at all, and this includes some of the brightest and most successful people I know, need not completely give up. If you excel at another good university, you might still be able to take a master's degree at Oxbridge, and eventually perhaps even a doctorate (known as a PhD or DPhil).

This is not a second-rate choice. The Russell Group universities, and especially Imperial College, London, the London School of Economics, University College (London), Durham and St. Andrews are ranked close to Oxford and Cambridge in the academic world. Other universities may have less famous staff, but their approach may be more modern or more down to earth, and this can make their lecturers the academic stars of the future. Also, some students feel more inspired by younger staff, and these are less common at Oxbridge.

If you want to continue an academic career started elsewhere at Oxbridge, what you need, above all, is a First and a very strong recommendation. You will not be looked down upon. After all, many of the great discoveries that constitute the glory of Oxford and Cambridge were made by people who had studied first at less fussy, more accessible universities.

For a student in need of a reassuring example (beyond that of the outsiders who developed Penicillin at Oxford) there is always Professor Bob Edwards of Cambridge. Edwards who, together with the late Patrick Steptoe, invented the fertility treatment which created a million test tube babies, initially studied at Edinburgh.

IF ONLY

It may be too late, but you should be aware of another, somewhat devious route into Oxbridge. The advice given to pupils at more than one private tutorial college has been to concentrate on getting into the course in which there was least competition from outstanding applicants, no matter what course the candidate actually wanted to do. This could mean, for instance, applying for Materials Science, even if you were really an engineer at heart. A week or two after starting his course, so the student is advised, all he needs to do is to confide in his supervisor that he feels he has made a terrible mistake. Materials Science, however worthy a calling, does not suit him. Would it therefore be possible for him to change to his true passion, Engineering?

While the new, almost universal and course-specific pre-interview tests now make it difficult to switch between dissimilar courses, it is still not impossible. The prospective switcher is likely to discover that a college can be remarkably flexible once it has accepted a student. While there are no guarantees, and while switching is most easily accepted between language courses, the request will be considered. Assuming the student has the right A-level grades and subjects, he might even be found a place on the coveted course.

There are, however, three points to remember if your son might wish to adopt this underhand, but not unknown, strategy. One is that the change of mind really has to take place within the first few weeks of starting the course. The second is that the student might find it rather hard to keep up academically with those who gained their Oxbridge place in the conventional way. Thirdly, and most crucially, it is pointless to try this as a bypass road into Medicine. It never works.

23

Best in show

What I have tried to show in the preceding chapters is that Oxbridge students come in all shapes and sizes. It's a miracle some of them don't bang their heads on those low medieval doorways.

There is one group, though, which does have an amazing success rate. What I discovered after interviewing dozens of state school students who had progressed to Oxbridge was that most had one key trait in common. This had nothing to do with their individual character or type of ability. Instead, what linked them was their parents' workplace. To stand a fair chance of getting into Oxbridge from a private school all you need is a parent who can pay (or a scholarship). To get in from elsewhere, a pupil wants a parent who is employed by a school.

To some people this will seem an obvious matter. After all, a teacher is likely to know which areas of the syllabus his son needs to cover to get good grades and will be able to help with homework and projects. That sort of parent will also stress the value of studying, although the poor little swot forced to stay at home and study nonstop by his ogre of a teacher-parent is a figure of the past.

Many of the successful Oxbridge entrants I talked to, whether they were white, Asian or black, had a strong school connection. The majority had mothers who had trained as schoolteachers. A few had fathers who taught at university, but had started their careers in schools. This factor was so common that after interviewing my first three dozen Oxbridge students (past and present) I had to resist the temptation of asking "What does your mother teach?" rather than "What does your mother do?"

But beyond this common feature my interviewees varied tremendously. Some were chatty, others quiet. Some had the kind of curiosity that even an Oxbridge course could not satisfy, while others seemed very focused. Some had well-off middle class fathers and their mothers taught only a few hours a week. Others were raised by a single parent who barely managed to pay the mortgage with the help of her full-time classroom job.

The story, though, does not end here. Lots of these parents taught at primary schools. This meant they were not equipped to explain the A-level syllabus or help with school work. Nor were they in touch with Oxbridge requirements.

Quite a few parents, moreover, did not teach at all. The mother of a young Oxbridge-educated doctor had given up teaching years before her daughter's birth and had, in any case, only ever taught in Pakistan. Another girl, one of very few "real" working class students, had a mother who had been a school dinner lady. Yet another student's mother was a special needs assistant at a junior school. These mothers were in no position to tutor anybody, yet their bright children still made it into Oxbridge.

By the time the proportion of interviewees with school connection had reached around two thirds of my largely random sample, this became deeply puzzling.

BEING SUSSED

By refining my questions, gradually I discovered that there were important contributions even a non-teacher parent who was working at a school could make. Often this had to do with realising that not all schools were equally good. Even the dinner lady, it turned out, had heard enough staff room talk to move her daughter out of a poorly performing school and into a more highly rated sixth form college.

Such parents were also often remarkably clued up about the different career paths pupils could take, or the timetable involved. Words like resit did not flummox them. If the school had certain problems, they would hear about it. They had a positive attitude to teachers, but were not overawed by them.

One former student, the daughter of a school caretaker, recalled that she had received a sympathetic but not actually helpful response from her class teacher when she mentioned an Oxbridge course. Her father, who worked at a different school, advised her to consult another teacher before giving up, and this swung it for her. As she put it to me, her father, although not an educated man, was "very sussed about anything to do with school".

"LIKE A CONVERSATION WITH A TEACHER"

Perhaps the main clue lies in the phrase used by one highly successful Oxbridge graduate, now a research scientist with a big pharmaceutical firm. I had expected the London-born daughter of a South Indian junior school teacher to describe her interview as a highly intimidating experience. After all, many others had done.

Instead the young woman thought for a moment, then suddenly smiled. "My interview was alright," she said. "It was like a conversation with a teacher." In other words, neither the setup nor the adults asking tough questions had felt alien enough to scare her.

The result is, if my impressions are correct, that teachers' children constitute a staggering proportion of Oxbridge students, far beyond their proportion in the general population.

FINDING OUT MORE

So what is wrong about this? Given that these students seemed as talented, varied and likeable a group as one could wish for, it took me a little while to pinpoint the cause of my unease about my - however provisional - findings. The problem is, in fact, pretty obvious. If the Oxbridge Entrance process is working best for one specific group, students whose parents have school-related jobs, then "widening participation" has some way to go.

It is, of course, possible that my findings were a fluke; that actually the majority of state school students at Oxbridge do not share this common trait. Even the fact that many students themselves had noticed the high proportion of teacher's kids in their year or college may still be an accident.

It would take a much larger and more scientifically structured survey (ideally one based on the entire student population) to reach any definite conclusion. I would, however, be very surprised if I was wrong. There is certainly an argument for Oxbridge commissioning such research. While the bright young people I met clearly deserved their university places, we need to understand why students from their backgrounds, more easily than others, negotiate the Oxbridge maze.

My suspicion is that ability is not always enough. Even the brightest students need in-crowd knowledge to succeed in a system not primarily based on scientific testing (though this is since 2018 used by both universities) but also on verbal interviews and top grades. Meanwhile, I suspect that the range of backgrounds within the Oxbridge student body is far narrower than the statistics suggest and the bright "non-traditional" student who gets in is quite often the daughter of a teacher and an engineer.

BE A COPYCAT

But what, you may ask, does this provisional insight do for the student whose mother or father is a bus conductor, cellist or IT manager? The answer is quite a lot: it enables them to improve their Oxbridge chances by copying the strategies that work for teachers' kids.

The most obvious strategy is that of studying hard but in a well-focused way; but there are other, less obvious ones. One is keeping up with a school's changing reputation. The retirement of a good head teacher can send a school into tail spin, while its upgrading to specialist status can dramatically improve results. As parents are unlikely to find out about these consequences from the staff, their local paper or a community news website can be a great source of information.

What also matters is being aware that knowledge about university entrance, and Oxbridge entrance in particular, can be spread out among a number of people in a school. So, if you cannot work out the course requirements, or don't understand the terminology, ask around. If you are a pupil, this can mean consulting not just your subject teacher or the head of post 16, but also perhaps another staff member with some Oxbridge links. Write out a list of things you want to know and take it with you, in case you get nervous.

If you are a parent, don't be shy about asking ''stupid'' questions at parents' meetings, or make a special appointment with one of your teenager's teachers to clarify a point. Not only do entry rules periodically change, but this really is a specialized field. Even the scraps of information you picked up could be out of date. Many parents, for instance, still assume that to get into Oxbridge a pupil needs to stay an extra term at school.

On the other hand, it is important not to be overawed by a teacher's opinion. This is especially true if it conflicts with a student's own. If your dream is to study Japanese (as part of Oriental or Asian and Middle Eastern Studies) but your teacher feels you ought to do a degree in Geography, you need to ask why. If it is because she thinks more highly of her own subject, you might want to stick to your guns, assuming you are doing the right A-levels.

If you are not, it is sometimes possible to change subjects at the start of the sixth form, once a student has discovered the university course of her dreams. School secretaries hate such changes as they have to redraw the time table, but do try to get the sixth form head onboard. You may have to spell out to him that it seems unfair for the girl's entire future to be determined by one, single wrong choice. If the school is really uncooperative, the girl could perhaps take one of her A-level courses elsewhere.

Don't assume that teachers are infallible when it comes to picking Oxbridge candidates. If your son wants to apply, has very good GCSEs and is blessed with some of the key qualities outlined earlier, do encourage him to go ahead, even if his teacher has doubts.

Unfortunately, a few teachers identify only the well-behaved, perfectly polite and mature pupil as an Oxbridge candidate. You may, therefore, have to consult other staff, or just trust your instincts before both of you decide.

A renowned science writer I know recalled with a chuckle that he had (successfully) applied to Oxbridge against all his teachers' earnest advice.

Teachers have a lot of knowledge at their fingertips and the best interest of their pupils at heart, so take advantage of this, just like their own children do. However, not all of them have the time to keep up with Oxbridge rules, especially the unwritten ones. Fortunately, reading this book gives you the best of both worlds.

24
Nailing down the Oxbridge dream

The road to Oxbridge, as you will have concluded by now, is more open than most people believe and can often be opened up further. However, it is just as true that access remains far from equal. So, how can real progress be made? The good news is that further change is not directly up to you, the parent or potential Oxbridge student. You just need to play the ball where it lies. The bad news is that action needs to be taken by two monoliths, Oxbridge and the Government.

Having said this, it is worth pointing out that there is periodic progress anyway, though not always as a result of deliberate action. When the makers of the Harry Potter films decided to shoot part of the first sequel in Oxford, they had no idea of what they were doing for British education. Visiting pupils, who would once have been intimidated by its venerable sites, now squealed with delight as they recognised the Hogwarts library (the Bodleian) and Hogwarts hall (the dining room of Christ Church). The university town with its crenellated walls and medieval towers had become a familiar, inviting place. Applications followed.

Other changes, previously unthinkable, suddenly happen if enough fuss is made. The public outcry which in January 2011 shamed Oxford into upping its Afro-Caribbean student intake was one example. Another is the saga of the Oxford medical entry process, centred on an exam set by the university's own staff. It was this exam which had led to the rejection of Laura Spence in January 2000. Known to work best for articulate middle class entrants who already knew much about medicine, it was crammed for at almost every private school.

Despite this known fact, Oxbridge dons defended the outcome to the hilt. They were backed up by the President of the Oxford Student Union, Will Straw, who wrote in *The Guardian* of 4th July 2003, "there was no prejudice...Spence had applied for a particularly difficult course with very few spaces. Tutors at Magdalen College had interviewed over 40 applicants for five places all with similarly outstanding predicted A-level grades. According to the college principal, Anthony Smith, she had come tenth..."

While Straw still blithely argued that there was nothing wrong with the procedure, Oxford had already ditched it in embarrassment. As previously mentioned, medical candidates aiming for Oxford, Cambridge and University College London were by November 2003 sitting a completely different exam, devised by ability experts rather than medics. The new exam, known as the BMAT, further revised more recently, still includes a college interview, but the procedure is designed to ensure that cramming and cultural factors play less of a role in medical selection. Intakes have greatly changed as a result.

Oxbridge, as said before, is ever changing, and those too eager to defend current practices can end up with egg on their face.

IS THE WHOLE ENTRANCE PROCESS GOING TO IMPROVE?

Despite the above examples, I would not bet my child's higher education savings on this. Past government intervention threats have ended with a hasty retreat. Even the new OFFA powers to check the fairness of a university's admissions process announced in 2008 did not mean it could punish offenders. As a result, previous OFFA head Martin Harris often sounded more like an observer of the Oxbridge entrance process than a regulator. After admitting in March 2011 that progress towards a more diverse intake was "virtually flat," he merely told the universities to spend yet more on Widening Participation (i.e. Access).

Access, though, still primarily focuses on encouraging more students to apply. Tasked to achieve more, Oxford's Head of Admissions, Mike Nicholson, insisted in December 2010 that critics were wrong to "focus on what is happening at eighteen... what really matters is provision at a much, much younger age."

Oxford Chancellor Lord Patten took a robustly anti-interventionist line throughout his tenure. Soon after his 2003 appointment, Patten had argued in an interview with *The Times* that if too few state school and especially working class students were entering Oxbridge, the blame lay with the schools' "spectacular failure in the past 30 years to raise standards...It is outrageous for politicians to blame universities over access."

In his investiture speech on 25th June 2003, Patten spelt out his stand further: "It is insulting to the able, and damaging to the universities that seek to educate them, to make the issue of access a crowbar for social engineers rather than a challenge for educationalists, and it is downright vulgar to allow it to become a populist political slogan." Social engineering, once seen as a worthy public project by public figures and pursued by widening access to educational institutions, was now deemed a sin.

While many dons (and parents) would agree that the school syllabus can be undemanding, that pressurised teachers may "teach to the test" and that basic skills are sometimes absent, Patten's position wrongly implies that Oxbridge has a right to teach only pupils who have already been taught very well. This, in turn, implies that what it is really seeking is not talent but candidates whose school has already taken them through much of their first year university course, as the best private school indeed do.

What this approach disregards, say its critics, especially among teachers, is that the state school standard happens to be the national norm. Even the top national universities, therefore, may have to teach upwards from it. After all, the education that state school pupils receive is meant to equip them for university and so it does. Those who get in cope. More than that, quite a few excel, even at Oxbridge.

In any case, most parents have no option but to send their teenager to the nearest school, which is usually a comprehensive or academy. It would clearly be desirable for all state school entrants to know more grammar, more maths or more science. However, very bright eighteen-year-olds are still capable of learning anything, and in amazingly short time. The Oxbridge way of picking by pre-admission attainment of the highest sort and of numerous kinds contradicts all we know about child development.

This is not a plea to tolerate ignorance. Unfortunately, though, an afternoon talk on an Open Day or a three hour Masterclass, however inspiring, is rarely enough to get a bright but otherwise unsupported student into Oxbridge. Nor have Access projects like shadowing, online tutoring or one-off visits to struggling schools substantially increased its student intake from under-represented groups. It is therefore hard to see why proper transition courses, short or long as appropriate, should not be offered.

What can be achieved has been shown by the success of the academic summer schools. It is good to know that these are now being expanded, but it would be even better if Oxbridge could also hold a few of those in our big cities. With no need for accommodation to be provided, these would reach far more students at a far lower cost. Lovely as the summer schools are, a larger, urban version might widen participation yet further.

Running year-round maths or academic writing clinics staffed by needy postgraduates for struggling Oxbridge first-years might be another option able to take the pressure off tutors.

Meanwhile, the cautious introduction of residential

Masterclasses at Oxford and the new residential STEM workshop in the physical sciences held for female Year 11s and 12s at Cambridge constitute great steps forward.

An even greater step has been the small but highly successful Foundation Year launched by Lady Margaret Hall in 2017. Less of an Access course than a US-type freshman year, it was designed for highly able students who, due to adverse circumstances, did not reach their potential. Its adoption by other colleges would be a great step forward towards equalizing opportunities. Yet another option might be a bridging course held in the pre-admission summer holidays, something being trialled by New College at the same university

Dons to whom I have put such bridging proposals have been less than enthusiastic. "Surely, we cannot now also be expected to teach remedial courses," one scientist remarked, his facial expression implying that I might as well have suggested a spot of child abuse. Others politely said that if the Government really wanted to safe-guard their world-famous research standards, a smaller teaching burden, rather than an even bigger one, would be very nice, thank you.

While it is hard not to sympathise with the last point, too many bright state school students have not been taught up to Oxbridge entrance standard, and it is hard to see how student proportions can change if the private sector, or rather the top of the private sector, continues to set the pace.

A FEW MODEST PROPOSALS

All this suggests that at least part of official Oxbridge might be happy to passively wait until state education improves, thereby punishing at least some bright pupils for their education authority's failures.

As mentioned earlier in this book, the situation at both Oxford and Cambridge is somewhat better. Admissions departments endeavour to attract able student from a wider social range than before and continuously devise new types of Access events. Colleges now share information about candidates and use standardised aptitude tests alongside the interview. Most dons have also greatly improved their interview techniques to reassure non-traditional students.

Both universities, moreover, have started to contextualise applicants' GCSE grades. The A* grade now attainable at A-level may yet pinpoint braininess in all kinds of students, at least if all kinds of schools were to teach towards it.

Having long claimed that "what really matters is provision at a much younger age," each university also has started to run Access events for pupils in Years 9, 10 and 11. This, Oxbridge hopes, may yet raise its state school proportion beyond the current, record level of 64 per cent. While testifying to both good intentions and valiant efforts, this figure certainly does not yet reflect the fact that 86 per cent of UK sixth formers attend state schools. Those left out, moreover, are often black and working class students.

It is worth recalling that there has also already been action at government level too. Its departments have in recent years sunk millions into a myriad of new, well funded initiatives aimed at students, teachers, parents and university departments. Change, in other words, has become a key feature of the entrance process. Progress, too, has been made. If the Oxbridge student balance nevertheless still fails to reflect the national one, this is because encouraging change is not the same as having an effective strategy or binding targets. It therefore seems important to list some specific measures which could at least create a more level playing field, preferably before the Harry Potter craze fades. Below are the most urgent ones.

WHAT THE GOVERNMENT SHOULD DO
1. Spend its money more wisely

Successive governments have accepted the Oxbridge view that fairness merely requires it to increase applications through Access projects. The assumption behind those, however, is that the key problem Access is confronting remains students' low self esteem. In fact, applications from a steadily more self-confident British public have been growing for years. The major 2011 fee hike, therefore, shocked thousands of families from a wide range of socio-economic backgrounds.

As the hike was due to sharp government cuts in Oxbridge funding, the job of defending it was left to a few sympathetic media editors. One such pin-striped soul blithely advised the public not to worry, as fee loans were just like mortgages, "but offered on better terms". Unlike his readers, he seemed unable to grasp that graduates would have to take out real mortgages alongside these bargains.

So, if admissions are to become fairer in these leaner times, government cash currently topping up the Access expenditure of Oxford and Cambridge urgently needs to be channelled towards different aims. The main one must be to reverse the 2010 cuts in the universities' funding, so the universities can lower their fees. This will be far more cost-effective than just pouring new money into endless Access schemes. We know now that when the new fees came in, the number of Oxford's state school applicants, which until then had been steadily rising, fell quite dramatically by 240.

Almost a decade later, it is time for the government to admit that Oxbridge Access in its present form is poor value for money. Its varied, numerous and friendly events, funded to the tune of altogether some ten million Pounds a year, are raising the number of state school students far too slowly, with too many years of stasis or setbacks in between. Worse, Access did not result in the admission of significantly more applicants from poor and black minority ethnic backgrounds, who remain hugely under-represented. So are students from England's less prosperous North East, North West and Yorkshire. Proof of this can be found in the official admissions figures, and the rest in the data released by the Sutton Trust or accessed by David Lammy under the Freedom of Information Act.

Clearly, spending ever-more money on encouraging applications from an ever-a wider group of students is not the answer. Even the otherwise highly sympathetic Sutton Trust criticised Oxford and Cambridge in a 2016 report for their "funding of unproven or ineffectual schemes" and for not evaluating their activities. It suggested that the government should only "support those projects that have robust evidence of impact."

By 2018 Sam Freedman, the Executive Director of *Teach First*, a charity which sends graduates of top universities into struggling schools to raise both standards and aspirations, was urging Oxbridge to scrap ineffectual schemes. Meanwhile, its failure to do so is having a negative effect: it is setting teachers, parents and pupils at different types of state schools against one another.

As Access money mainly goes to new projects, efforts are becoming increasingly fragmented. There are now Access projects directed at mining areas and rural schools, at further education colleges and at schools which have never sent a pupil to Oxbridge, at ethnic minorities and children in care. Young people all over the country are told that if they work hard and attend an Oxbridge event, they stand a good chance of getting in.

Given that the share of the cake allocated to the state school sector, although growing, remains unrepresentative in terms of its student numbers, this inevitably multiplies disappointment, and not just among pupils. Let me give you an example from a very mixed area of London.

The story starts at a comprehensive, renowned for the quality of its teaching and its excellent Ofsted reports. It is also part of a sixth form consortium which achieves some of the inner city's best state school exam results. Proud of its orderly atmosphere, anti-bullying policy and highly qualified teachers, the school attracts a wide range of pupils. Some, including children from ethnic minorities and asylum seekers, come from the poor neighbouring housing estates. Many others come from the opposite end of the spectrum; they are the children of doctors, lawyers, university lecturers, journalists and civil servants.

In this top-university orientated school, pupils are helped to prepare by teachers who regularly attended Oxbridge seminars. Students are encouraged to participate in every sort of Access event. Usually, out of a sixth form of some 370 pupils, five to eight succeeded in getting in.

Not that long ago, the school confidently sent off twelve of its pupils to be interviewed. The results were unexpected. Only one pupil, a middle class boy whom the school had not actually picked as a high flyer, received an offer. As the head of sixth form put it: ''There is not really much point in our overworked staff putting weeks of effort into encouraging, persuading and preparing pupils for Oxbridge, just to see a single one getting in. All Access has done to build up our kids' expectations, only to dash them again.''

Meanwhile, a few miles away in the same area, the staff of the area's largest sixth form college were equally bewildered. The college, whose devoted, well qualified teachers have changed lives, had thought that their pupils were just what Oxbridge wanted now. Most were, after all, working class, or from disadvantaged minorities.

Not that the teachers had ever relied on such assumptions. Over the years, they had instead built up links with six colleges, two in Oxford and four in Cambridge. They also ran enrichment activities which gave pupils experience in journalism and poetry. The college had invested time and expertise in Oxbridge preparation, and this seemed to pay off. Out of a sixth form of 280 pupils, it would annually send up a dozen interviewees. Between three and five of these would be made a conditional offer. The grades stipulated in the offers remained inappropriately high, but two to three pupils a year were getting in.

When the replies to the applications dropped through the doors, though, the news was really bad. Not one college pupil had even received an offer. Some of the teachers' comments were not printable, but a veteran Maths teacher expressed what many others clearly felt: ''It's back to the same old thing. The ones we send are really exceptional, but Oxbridge won't see that.''

The college teacher also got on the phone to colleagues in order to find out where ''their'' Oxbridge places had gone. A chat with a friend teaching in a well-known private school situated between the college and the area's comprehensive revealed that they had not gone there. The private school, which has a sixth form of 90 pupils and prides itself on accepting pupils of all abilities, had received the same number of offers as usual – fourteen.

It was a teacher whose sister taught in a small town with a high unemployment rate who finally came up with an answer. For the first time ever, her school had received an offer from Oxbridge. So had another school in the same town, targeted by Access under the "Widening Participation" scheme.

In other words, Access had "worked", but not as most people naively thought it was meant to. Faced with an unprecedented number of "good" state school candidates, an outcome Oxbridge had mysteriously not foreseen, it had decided to redistribute its places within the state school group.

The college teacher, who has an English degree from a good university, found no difficulty in expressing how he felt. "Perhaps they should rename 'Widening Participation' something more appropriate. How about 'Thinning the Soup?'" he said.

On the parents days of some urban comprehensives, the talk can be uglier than that. "Just as our school got itself sorted out, they take it all away and give it to the kids of people who don't even pay taxes," said the mother of a girl put on her school's gifted and talented list, but rejected by Oxbridge.

Unless Access has been created to sow despondency and discord, the Government really needs to restructure its spending on it now. The bulk of its money needs to go on learning projects which raise prospects, rather than hopes. Or perhaps funding for all Access projects should initially come from Oxbridge itself, which would be repaid pro rata by the Government if a specific project resulted in an acceptance rate of, say, 30 per cent.

2. Become an enforcer

There is, of course, a far cheaper alternative. The government could simply enforce the 75 per cent quota for state school students announced by its own officials in 2006. Half-heartedly set and unenforced, it had never been accepted by Oxbridge. Instead, state school proportions were allowed to remain almost static for years.

Suggestions of reform rarely went down well at Oxbridge. Jane Minto, the director of the Oxford admissions office, spoke for many of its academics when she told journalists on 6th March 2003: "We don't subscribe to quotas at Oxford...Students should be selected purely on academic merit." At Cambridge, her counter-part Susan Stobbs took a similar line. When the government in 2008 dared to again suggest an entrance quota, Cambridge Vice-Chancellor Alison Richard angrily dismissed this as "meddling".

As recently as February 2016, one of Oxford's most senior university officials responded to a critical report by the Sutton Trust with the astonishing claim that a commitment to Widening Participation did not necessarily mean it had to take in more state school students.

Such knee-jerk responses do leave the listener with a nagging question. How come academic merit can manifest itself in quite such a static way among Oxbridge applicants, and among them alone? Surely, different cohorts of young people from different schools should produce different proportional intakes? Alas, it does not, and none of my academic interviewees was prepared to comment on this staggering coincidence. In fact, cooperation quite often suddenly dried up at this point.

Nevertheless, the matter remains puzzling for those who understand the rules of mathematical probability which, I am sure, includes many Oxbridge academics. It is as if two roulette wheels, once spun, would always land on one of the same narrow range of numbers between, say, fifty and sixty. Magic, or what? Please don't try this at your nearest casino.

The reality, of course, is different. There has always been a quota. In fact, there are several. Most Oxbridge colleges divide their places on an individual, pre-set basis between state school and private school candidates, no matter how many applications they actually receive from each group, and this balance may annually change by just one or two percent. A handful of colleges, committed to a more representative university intake, aim to steadily increase their own state school intake and manage to do so almost each year.

Some faculties, notably Oxford Medicine, accept the same proportion of candidates from each group, usually 20 per cent, but since the state school group is larger, this results in rather more of its students getting in.

Ultimately, all these decisions are coordinated at Oxford and Cambridge during post-interview meetings of admissions tutors and senior leaders until the desired balance has been reached. In response to public and government concerns, the state school proportion has gradually crawled up, but it took fifteen (!) years to move from 47 per cent in 2002 to 64 per cent in 2017.

There is what some may regard as a benevolent explanation for this process. Several dons I spoke to hinted that they made allowances for state school candidates. If they were to go purely by evidence of ability alone, so they suggested, their proportion would be even lower than it is now. Instead, the number of state school candidates accepted was regularly rounded upwards, up to a point.

There are two not so small problems with this explanation. One, as already suggested, is the implicit assumption that state school candidates are not only less intelligent than private school ones, but also that all of them are less intelligent year after year. The other problem is that this intellectual difference is assumed to exist despite the fact that both types of candidates obtain similar A-level grades. So, it may just be possible that the interview, which is based on a highly educated middle class discourse, does not work as well for applicants from other backgrounds, as suggested earlier, and this would be a strong argument for downgrading its importance.

On the other hand, the whole differential ability claim can just be dismissed as nonsense. Churchill, which has the second highest state school intake in Cambridge, has consistently been in the top quarter of the university's Tompkins table: in fact, it came fifth out of 29 colleges in 2017. Clearly, state school pupils can do as well as the rest if given the chance.

It certainly seems hard to think of a strong argument against a representative quota. The only real question is how high it should be. The original government target, 75 per cent, is one option. The two universities almost a decade ago set their own benchmark at 62 per cent, planning to reach it within five years. Oxford by 2016 had not even come near it, though Cambridge reached it in 2012. It then stayed there for another four years. Only in 2017 and after more public criticism did both reach a new, shared summit, 64 per cent.

But what would the right percentage be? Given that the Government funds 70 per cent of Oxbridge expenditure, the proportion of students it accepts from the state sector should perhaps be identical, at least for a while. This would leave the private sector, which educates 7 per cent of pupils, with 30 per cent, still a high proportion but one that acknowledges that it nowadays educates many talented young people as non-paying sixth form scholars.

To instead maintain that "we're not looking to do any social engineering", as Oxford's previous Head of Admissions, Mike Nicholson, did, now seems bizarre. Oxbridge is the country's main social mobility route, as well as a great place of learning. The degrees it bestows, even in the most obscure subjects, open avenues to job satisfaction, power and wealth. If there is a recession, they might become one of the few ways of getting any job at all. This does entail some social responsibility.

3. Make schools more equal

One major obstacle to a more representative Oxbridge intake remains the inequality among state schools themselves. Rather than creating ever-new categories of secondaries, the government must now close the gap among the existing ones. A sixth former doing science A-levels should be taught by someone who has a degree in chemistry, physics or maths, irrespective of whether she is attending a state grammar, academy, free school or bog-standard comprehensive.

The current situation, in which a third of all of physics teachers in state secondary schools (and 70 per cent of all those teaching physics) are unqualified in the subject, is a real outrage. So are Britain's class sizes, which are the largest in the developed world. How can a pupil taught in a state sixth form of twenty-eight possibly compete with someone from a private A-level class of twelve?

Nor should the location of a school make a difference. Merely living in a British city can condemn you to an inferior education. While the academic performance of the lowest achievers among London's pupils has greatly risen in recent years due to public and private cash injections, the results for more able ones have not. Unsurprisingly, the capital's state schools hardly ever feature among the country's top 500. In Birmingham and Liverpool things are even worse.

Given that our famous cities attract the most motivated, able people, the fact that their children achieve educationally less than those in small farming towns should not be blamed on the parents. True, some urban areas are struggling with the loss of manufacturing jobs, but this is surely yet another argument for sending in more, better qualified teachers. Creating a larger teaching staff, moreover, can mean shorter working hours for teachers, which might reduce their shocking drop-out rate.

This situation does tempt many Oxbridge admissions tutors to pick their state school students from a small range of academically strong schools in cosy suburbs. According to a 2007 study by the Institute for Public Policy Research, one hundred elite schools, constituting less than 3 per cent of 3,700 schools with sixth forms and sixth form colleges in the UK, accounted for a third of admissions to Oxbridge during the previous five years. The group was composed of 80 private schools, 18 grammar schools, and two (!) comprehensives.

Four years later, this situation had got even worse. According to a Sutton Trust report published in 2011, four private schools and one Cambridge state sixth form college got more students into

Oxbridge between them than 2,000 schools and colleges across the UK, despite the Trust's own huge investment in Oxbridge Access schemes. Current data on this are not available, but it is clear that the gap has been considerably reduced. However, when applicants from previously unrepresented schools do get in, it sometimes still seems to be at the expense of state schoolers elsewhere.

While Oxbridge may feel an understandable duty not to over-burden its academic staff, given that these are also expected to produce top level research, government has a duty here too. This is to ensure that our most able students can access our most outstanding universities, if necessary by funding transition facilities.

4. Modernise

Lastly, the Government must take the lead in defining what the Oxbridge debate, fiercely fought already within Government departments, in the media and among parents is really about.

Those who wish to preserve the Oxbridge entrance structure largely unchanged define this, in the words of Anthony Smith, the President of Magdalen College, Oxford, as "a matter of autonomy". The two universities, as seen from this angle, must be allowed to stick with their current system if they so wish. Nobody else is allowed to impose anything on them because they are autonomous bodies in law.

The problem with this argument is that the autonomy enjoyed by Britain's higher education sector is mainly designed to cover what its academics teach, and nobody is proposing to change this.

Admission, though, is a different matter. Legislation, or the threat of it, gradually compelled the universities over the last 130 years to accept Jews and Catholics, Dissenters and women. A-levels too became a universal entrance requirement only because Government wished it, although the pupils of Britain's seven top public schools (Eton, Harrow, Westminster, Rugby, Winchester, Charterhouse and Shrewsbury) were exempted until the mid 1960s.

Usually, such changes are imposed by means of the carrot and the stick. The government or the Department of Education says what it would like to see happen, and Oxbridge refuses until threatened with funding cuts. At this point, internal reform kicks in.

This certainly explains the unprecedented 6 per cent jump in state school proportions, proudly announced in early 2018 by Oxford. The same is likely to be true about the sudden Cambridge announcement of May 2018 that the university would from now on lower its entrance requirements for students who had experienced "significant educational disadvantage", a move it had always opposed. Both reforms are said to have been prompted, amongst others, by suddenly growing government nudging, especially from the new Universities Minister, Sam Gyimah. The son of Ghanean immigrant parents, Gyimah had got into Oxford from a state academy in Hertforshire.

Interestingly, Oxbridge itself rarely offers any reason for changes in its state school intake or admissions policies. One such reason the government might want to embrace was offered by the President of the National Students Union, Mandy Telford, when she stated that the universities needed to reform their entrance process for the sake of opportunity. In a modern society, she argued, a small group should not be allowed a disproportionate hold over this.

In the end, though, it would be easiest if the Government looked at Oxbridge entrance in terms of simple justice. If this is indeed the best place to develop certain types of knowledge and to acquire certain skills, then those who can be scientifically shown to be most suited for this endeavour should be allowed in.

As said before, this may require ongoing improvements to Oxbridge tests and interviews, making them more socially neutral and less focused on knowledge and skills not imparted by most of our schools. If there are crucial knowledge gaps between the National Curriculum and Oxbridge expectations, the universities should also be expected to provide formal bridging facilities, either just before or during students' first year, as America's top universities do.

First, though, both universities should be made to more openly acknowledge the extent of student preparation required in order to succeed. This is essential if the proportion of state school sixth formers admitted to Oxbridge is to more accurately reflect their general proportion within Britain's sixth formers.

In the same spirit, the Government may want to impress on Oxbridge that the huge but little-known gap between the handful of their colleges which consistently admit a majority of private school students and another handful which admit mainly state school ones is unacceptable today. In other worlds, with a little more Government intervention Oxbridge could remain the impressive, unusual place it always was, but also finally embody the values of our age.

WHAT OXBRIDGE SHOULD DO:
1. Ask for realistic grades
One of the most positive Oxbridge developments has been the shift towards gathering what it calls "contextualised data". Admissions

tutors can now tell if a candidate has achieved high grades despite attending a low achieving school, if she has been in care and whether her post code is that of a disadvantaged neighbourhood. The latter may not always help, as urban neighbourhoods are often socially mixed, but the combined data have their uses.

Unfortunately, one use these data are almost never put to is to make contextualised grade offers. Students who fit the criteria are often encouraged to attend specially targeted Oxbridge events. They may also stand a better chance of getting an interview and, if so, be questioned just a touch more gently than others. However, most still need the standard course-specific A-level grades of AAA, A*AA, A*A*A or even A*A*A* to actually win a place.

The even greater emphasis on a high proportion of top GCSEs harms especially students from non-university homes. Few realise that exams taken at the hormone-ruled age of fifteen may determine their future, no matter what grades they achieve later-on.

Inequality increases further at the A-level stage. Given that grades are partly determined by a school's standards or by a parent's ability to pay for tuition or private schooling, factors over which a student has no control, this can mean that a B-grade applicant may be considerably smarter than one with three A*s.

Teach First's Sam Freedman, who used to be a policy adviser to the then Education Secretary, Michael Gove, has no doubt that asking students from different homes and schools for different grades would be both fairer and cheaper than the current system. "It is ridiculous to suggest," he says, "that three A/A* s at A-level is the sole valid signifier of academic ability."

There are also still no allowances made for poor or working class students not living in a known slum, not destitute or not attending a failing school. As these don't fit the 2017 "contextualised" admission criteria, they are still expected to have the same grades as private schoolers. Given the gap in educational, parental and financial resources, this is absurd.

Even the 2018 Cambridge announcement that the university was now set to lower entrance requirements for students who have experienced "significant educational disadvantage" (a term yet to be publicly defined) does not hit the spot quite yet. What is needed are clearly spelled out, different grade rules for different kinds of applicants. Knowing about parental occupation, data available but not used by Oxbridge, would also help dons to make a fair choice.

The iron grade rule, meanwhile, makes the rest of the admissions process, notably tests and interviews, fairly pointless.

Letting a student from a low income home and non-Oxbridge geared school who has successfully navigated the rest of the admissions maze then fall at the grade barrier seems a shocking waste of resources. It also makes the Oxbridge claim to a "contextualised admissions process" meaningless. For those of us working with students identified as outstanding by their school it is heart-breaking to see such an applicant rejected after successfully navigating the rest of the admissions maze because she has narrowly missed one of the required As or A*s, sometimes not even in a course-related subject.

Admissions tutors ought to also take more account of the difference between subjects. Some are considerable harder than others. If an A-level student is not aiming for a degree in Maths or Physics but picked it at school because the subject intrigued her, a B grade in it should not automatically imply that she won't be able to keep up in a history course. This practice, too, disadvantages many state school pupils unable to think strategically at age fifteen.

The outcome, of course, does not just matter for personal reasons. Social scientists at a 2018 academic conference organised by the think tank *Reform* under the heading "Diversifying the elite" argued that a more flexible Oxbridge approach to grades was essential for social mobility.

The Oxbridge belief in the supreme value of top A-level grades is not, in any case, born out by statistical facts: a 2013 *Guardian* report revealed that state school applicants gaining the top A-level grades of A*A*A* grades were still 14 per cent less likely than private schoolers to end up with an Oxbridge place. Unsurprisingly, then, 80 per cent of Oxbridge students between 2010 and 2015 had parents in professional or managerial roles, as against 30 per cent of the population. Collecting more educational and socio-economic student data, as Oxbridge has recently done, is a great step forward, but unless these data are used to make more differentiated place offers, state school students will never be properly represented there.

2. Reconsider the interview

The change that would have the greatest impact would be for dons to acknowledge that the interview, which remains central to the admissions process, is not an effective ability test. This is not to query the good intentions of those administering it. Contrary to the widespread impression that dons just seek to pick out posh students, Oxbridge is almost obsessed with finding the most able ones.

One elderly science don, determined to get more gifted

working class students into his renowned college, once confidently told me that he had solved the problem. "The way is to dive straight into the subject questions at the interview, if you want to get the measure of their abilities. Being talked to about this and that for the first few minutes only confuses them," he told me in a firm voice clearly used to imparting universal wisdom.

For a moment I wondered if I should also ask him for the secret of composing music or of writing a great novel. Clearly a man so sure of his expertise in a field not his own could provide the answer to everything. He had certainly created a new scientific truth: all working class candidates were alike, and those who didn't sparkle in response to his majestic, well-spoken approach were just not bright.

The scientist was not alone. Other tutors seemed equally certain that they had found the philosopher's stone, albeit a different one. A mathematician sought to relax all male candidates by initially mentioning sport. One engineering don seemed certain that only through disorientating a candidate by remaining silent could he identify brains, while another relied on discussing a subject miles from a student's interest area. A historian would confess, after defending the interview process, that she spent a lot of her time thinking up ways of further perfecting it, of making it even fairer.

Listening to this as I did my initial 2002 research, I sometimes felt as if I was in the presence of a very bright but unworldly child. After all, the question of how to identify giftedness had been professionally pondered for decades. The people who devise scientific ability tests are called educational psychologists. Their research has given us ways of spotting talent irrespective of class and methods which reduce cultural bias. They have worked out which background data can be relevant and how to weigh results accordingly. These experts produce journal pieces and books which, as their authors tend to be non-Oxbridge, never seemed to impact on it.

This, fortunately, is no longer true. Interviews, certainly, have become far more subject-focused. The raft of newly devised tests described earlier has also provided dons with yet more tools for identifying ability. Almost all are now using one of those. The combination of interviews and scientific testing is certainly a positive development. A gifted but jittery interviewee should be much less likely to fail these days. Sadly, quite a few still do, and far too many admissions tutors cannot see the reason for this. One of the latter was actually heard to say that he could not understand why interviewees so often did poorly in their first interview, yet much better in the second.

This is no accident. Unless the role of the interview in ability testing is now down-graded, students used to discussing challenging topics with well-spoken adults will enjoy a continued advantage. Tests, too, need to be updated if it is found that schools can cram their students for them. As private school students start preparing for Oxbridge years before state schoolers do, this is a real problem.

What neither interviews nor tests can do is solve the problem of extremely bright students being rejected because they know too little. High academic ability is more evenly spread than good schools with small classes, but it needs building on. Oxbridge transition courses, long or short depending on student needs, thus ought to become standard.

What this also means, though, is that Access expenditure should be concentrated. By getting rid of largely ineffectual schemes like shadowing or one-off visits to distant schools designed to just encourage applications, Oxbridge will be able to afford long-term projects which increase the success rate of state schoolers from all backgrounds. Failing to do so is to perpetuate a zero-sum game. If the admission of a farm worker's daughter from a struggling school in the Welsh Valleys just comes at the expense of a welder's son at an outstanding Leeds academy then nothing has changed.

Alternatively, Oxbridge might want to fund a few Saturday schools teaching science and mathematics to academically able pupils in Moss Side or East London. Teenagers would flock to them if the classes were cheap. Raiding the Oxbridge Access pot for such projects may turn out to be wise as well as fair. One of these rough diamonds may one day find a cure for the common cold.

The good news is that both Oxford and Cambridge are steadily making changes. That they embarked on most of them shortly after the Government-commissioned 2004 Schwartz report sharply criticized the university entrance process (and soon after the first edition of this widely rad book appeared) was pure coincidence, perhaps.

2. Watch its language

While standardised, written tests constitute progress, they are not, as yet problem-free. Comprehensive school heads bitterly complain about their terminology and phrasing. Too much of this, they feel, favours students from genteel, educated homes. "Students from working class backgrounds" one London head told *The Oxbridge Student*, "need to learn the language as well as the skill. Maybe a few less Latinate terms and a few more rooted in Anglo-Saxon?"

This mirrors teachers' complaints about the verbal interview. Good talk, like a good test, requires comprehension. University speak is normally learned at university; you can't pick it up by walking into a don's room. Some interviewers are able to conduct an intellectual cross-examination in colloquial English, but others have communicated in upper middle class, academic language all their lives and are unable to change. So, a student unfamiliar with elaborate wording or vague, open-ended questions may not come across well.

This seems to be a particular problem in the case of one very popular course, Law. Applicants do not require specific A-levels for this subject, but they do need very well-developed writing and verbal skills; these are more easily attained by students growing up in wealthy or highly educated families. Probably as a result, at Cambridge the 2015 success rate of state school applicants was 23 per cent, but 36 per cent for private school ones. At Oxford the same year, it was 17 per cent for the former, but 25 per cent for the latter. By 2017 and following some governmental finger-wagging, these figures had somewhat changed: the Cambridge success rate for state school students was now 17 per cent, but 23 per cent for private school ones. At Oxford, too, it was 17 per cent for state school students, but 20 per cent for private school ones.

In other words, the gap has narrowed, but students from fee-paying schools are still seen as more able. Such gaps continue from year to year, if modified slightly, and they matter. An Oxbridge Law course, for instance, is not just a route to high pay. It is also a production line for the top of Britain's legal sector and especially its judges. Do we really want a judiciary whose practitioners do not know the price of milk? Well, we've got it.

Moreover, the precise role of the tests has been left open. Neither Oxford nor Cambridge are willing to reveal how much even a top result in the BMAT, LNAT, TSA, ELAT or any other candidate test actually counts for. Teachers have been shocked to discover that a 90 per cent test score may not compensate for a stumbling interview performance by a nervous inner city student. Verbal skills still seem decisive.

Test were ostensibly introduced to solve this problem, but they cannot do so if they are obscurely worded or accorded little weight. True, brain testing has not yet been perfected and intensive coaching can produce misleadingly good results, but education experts can usually refine questions to minimize this. Oxbridge should ensure this is regularly done, since written tests are at least familiar to most students. As the warden of New College Oxford, Alan Ryan, has pointed out, they also more accurately reflect academic reality: "What students do at university is write."

3. Join the youth club

The well-publicised Oxbridge renunciation of extra-curricular activities as a selection factor will improve many students' admissions prospects. A sign of the commitment to widening participation by the universities, it also reflects the changing social origins of its dons. Around half of them now come from state schools and so know more than their predecessors about how ordinary people live. They are aware that most families don't go to church, that teenagers often hate school sports and that modern music lovers tend to indulge this passion by down-loading iTunes.

We can glimpse just how resourceful many past state school candidates really were from the fact that they managed to assemble that old, slightly sad parcel of spare time activities. Not only was it a century removed from today's youth culture, but it was also so much easier to fill if you had cash.

Moreover, what sixth formers do determines how they speak and what they understand. This means not just that interview questions should not be worded in ways that are hopelessly incomprehensible to them. It also means that bright students who use everyday or even street culture language are not be quite so easily dismissed as non-academic. As long as they have a library card, they too might well be "interesting young people".

Family data could also be made use of more. UCAS is now able to tell universities whether either of an applicant's parents has a graduate job or is working in a manual field. There is no longer any need for guesswork. Knowing such things would enable Oxbridge to make allowances for educational disadvantage, even in the case of students not quite poor enough to qualify for any special support.

Sadly, both Oxford and Cambridge have announced that they will disregard this information as "uncorroborated data". Some admissions tutors openly say that they fear applicants might lie. Oxford does not itself collect similar information. Neither does Cambridge, but its *Supplementary Application Questionnaire* and *Extenuation Circumstances Form* add detail and could be a factor in the traditionally somewhat higher success rate of the state schoolers applying there.

Meanwhile, it would be nice if the existing entrance criteria were applied with more care. Before insisting, yet again, that "we're just not getting the applicants" as almost every admissions tutor I ever spoke to did, Oxbridge may want to look at the characteristics of those it rejects.

Returning from an Oxbridge day school to his inner city comprehensive, one frustrated teacher summed up his feelings to me: "Now that we've learnt all we can about the admissions process, maybe their admissions tutors should get some training. We need to train Oxbridge; our students cannot conform to their criteria, but they are bright young people and will achieve."

Anyone doubting his words only needs to look at the final twist in the Laura Spence saga. The working class girl who was rejected by Oxford in 2000 went on to excel in the Harvard entrance test, winning not just a place but a £37,000 scholarship. At Harvard, Laura became one of only five women named "All-Ivy" for her academic achievements. Returning to Britain with a top Biochemistry degree, she then applied to the small, hugely contested Cambridge postgraduate medical course. She got in, you will be glad to hear, but there must be a faster, easier way of proving your worth.

4. Learn to love teachers

One of the most important things which a university that wants to be sent lots of good, enthusiastic candidates does is to cultivate their teachers. This is a relationship that Oxbridge has yet to build, at least with regard to state school teachers. Quite a few Oxbridge dons seem to regard them as unreliable suppliers of goods: they don't answer Access circulars, I was told; they don't send enough candidates or send the wrong ones. There was a distinct sense of impatience, almost as if the teachers were not really doing their job.

The most serious crime, and indeed one I often heard state school teachers accused of, was anti-elitism. Pushed a little further, some dons spelt out to me what they meant. "There's a lot of left-wingers, of course, among the teaching profession. People thinking that Oxbridge is a posh place, so one mustn't encourage pupils to go there," I was told by an elderly male don, educated at a famous school, in the quiet, confidential tone used by gentlemen to imply that one's butler may have been at the gin.

In the course of writing this book, I went to great lengths to test this assertion. That there are many left-wingers among state school teachers is undoubtedly true. The kind of people who opt to develop the potential of children whose family has never earned more than the minimum wage tend not to be on the right in their political sympathies. Neither are those who see potential in a scruffy boy with battered trainers.

But does this mean left-wing teachers are against Oxbridge? To find out, I deliberately arranged in-depth interviews about Oxbridge entrance with sixth form and careers teachers I knew not just to be vaguely on the left, but politically committed. Some were active in leftwing branches of the Labour Party. Several were Trotskyites, members of Britain's Socialist Workers Party. Others defined themselves as Anarchists or Communists.

They had a lot in common. All were fully clued up about the technical requirements for Oxbridge entry. Most had read the piles of online bumph emanating from there, on top of other university entrance publications. Some had been on college visits; others were booked on yet another Oxbridge teachers day.

All this required massive form-filling and a rearrangement of the school's timetable, because their kind of school was always short-staffed. The teachers would have to take home papers for marking to compensate for the time lost. All had sent pupils up for interviews after preparing them to the best of their abilities.

By the end of the year, though, almost all of them also had failed to get even a single Oxbridge offer for a pupil. You might have expected them to proclaim that, as enemies of the people, the two universities should be burnt down, or at least picketed. Instead, the teachers were downcast as well as fearful that I might identify them or their schools.

"It's not an effective use of my time if nobody gets into Oxbridge, yet I don't send a student who I don't think is really good," one teacher in a battered leather jacket sighed. A colleague wearing a Stop-the-War badge nodded, adding with quiet understatement: "We despair a little after having spent so much time and effort on Oxbridge, yet middle class applicants still do much better."

These teachers were, nevertheless, prepared to soldier on. Next year things might improve was their hope, at least if the Government intervened. What set them apart from others was certainly not any hostility to Oxbridge, though they were scathing about its selection criteria.

These were not people who thought of the two universities as precious national heritage institutions with mysterious, unfathomable ways, unlike quite a few other teachers I had met. Oxbridge, to them, was just top of the Russell Group, to whose universities they directed their very best pupils.

But that's left-wing teachers. What my research suggested is that Oxbridge is doing no better with teachers holding more mainstream political views or none at all. These are people who unreservedly admire the two universities, yet would wistfully say: "We thought we had built a relationship with Oxbridge." Usually, this meant with one of the universities and two or three of its colleges. These teachers had talked to dons, trying to explain their students' backgrounds and strengths. They'd had tea, dinner at high table, promises of consideration.

The problem, so they told me, is that most of this relationship does not bear fruit, at least not on an annual basis. A college which used to take two or perhaps three students out of a sixth form of almost 400 kids suddenly stops. Another college keeps taking one student every other year, but the applicant mustn't be too black, it seems, whatever his other qualities. Or there is a sudden, unexplained, several yearlong gap.

Somehow, an Oxbridge college's relationship with a private school never breaks down. The school may only have a sixth form of 80 and may admit students on the strength of parental funds, not students' talent, but it will be going steady with the college.

The state school, on the other hand, can have quite a different experience. It may only find itself taken out for a whirl ever so often if the Government has recently made a fuss; if priorities have not shifted to another part of the state sector, say rural comprehensives; if it is compatible with the quota which is blatantly there but never admitted to. The state school is like the girl you can take for granted, the girl who will put out even if you won't elevate her to girlfriend status or show her respect. No wonder state school teachers feel hurt.

To make things harder still, all those teachers were, by choice, working in large urban schools, and this created constant dilemmas. As one sixth form head put it: "You know, it can take up to 20 hours to prepare a kid for Oxbridge, but we do it. Sometimes it's hard to decide. I had a student living on a really bad estate. He was not a genius, but still a capable kid with a potential for higher education. I could either spend lots of time getting him into some former Poly in another town, away from his criminal environment. Or I could concentrate on getting a kid from a safer, more stable home background into Oxbridge. What would you done?"

In the event, the committed professional did a bit of both. Unless such efforts are regularly rewarded at the Oxbridge end, it would be hard to blame him if he slackened.

5. Stop the nostalgia
When discussing student proportions at Oxbridge, dons almost invariably launch into a nostalgic account of how much better things

were when the grammar school system was still operating all over Britain.

Despite the heartfelt emotion, the statement is factually wrong. There never was any golden age in which Oxbridge threw open its gates to those outside its traditional catchment area. In 1955, the proportion of students who had fathers in manual work was 9 per cent in Cambridge, the same as in 2002, and 13 per cent in Oxford, compared to 10 per cent in 2002. In 1963, the heyday of the grammar schools, 25 per cent of Cambridge students and 39 per cent of Oxford ones came from state schools (compared to over 60 per cent now).

In fact, the pre-comprehensive school figures are even worse than they look, because the proportion of manual workers among the public was far higher than today. Also, the number of children at private schools was half what it is now. Meanwhile, the vast majority of children were attending secondary moderns, schools that led nowhere in education terms.

Still, the nostalgia persists because among those bright grammar school kids fortunate enough to then enter Oxbridge were many of today's dons. Ultimately, there is something cranky about the way in which today's top educators go on about a system that was abolished more than forty years ago. It is as if they feel no duty to relate to current reality, which is that most children in Britain are schooled in comprehensives or academies.

There is indeed a great deal wrong with these schools: they are shamefully underfunded and short of teachers and equipment. Some are quite brilliant, but education standards vary to a shocking extent, often in the same catchment area.

Many comprehensives also cater poorly for both slow and fast learners. Keeping students of all levels in the same class, right through their A-levels, is often seen as a measure of equality. However, this can mean that the more challenging, more academic aspects of a subject are not explored.

As a result, some would now like to see very able teenagers educated separately from a certain age, at least if there was a way of identifying ability irrespective of class; it is not a job the old grammar schools did well. The change would certainly be welcomed by many families considering Oxbridge. Those in favour are likely to include thousands of middle class couples crippled by school fees.

Different solutions are being tried by struggling schools. London's Holland Park Comprehensive is working its way up by "setting, banding, personalised learning plans" and teaching Latin. Some academies founded to replace under-performing schools are using academic mentoring schemes or putting students on online science courses. Schools in the Midlands send their gifted students to Warwick University for enrichment schemes.

Others focus on students' social concerns. In 2011, one Hackney academy spent over £10,000 on creating a perfect facsimile of an Oxbridge don's study, complete with Persian rugs and 18th century furniture, on its premises. After past failures, teachers wanted its disadvantaged pupils to feel at ease in the interview setting.

All these initiatives may, in time, create a new pool of Oxbridge applicants. Meanwhile, though, comprehensives remain the nation's main secondary schools, even if their name has been changed to academies, specialist schools, community colleges or whatever. So, top universities really must pick more of their bright students.

That many dons would genuinely like to do so I have no doubt. That they often don't because they've failed to grasp just how bright and resourceful a state school applicant often needs to be in order to merely get interviewed is equally true. Fortunately, the detailed preparation offered to pupils by this book should make the two universities' selection job much easier.

25
At the gates

If you have been able to put your video games, or the housekeeping, or your employer's demands on standby for long enough to read this book, then your family dream of Oxbridge has become an actual possibility. You now know the real rules of the entrance process, a prerequisite for effectively competing in this snakes and ladders game. Knowledge, in turn, tends to raise a person's confidence, and confidence is yet another ingredient of Oxbridge success.

You will also be able to distinguish between the two universities' present reality and their past. No longer are talented young people automatically excluded just because they didn't go to public school, or don't have middle class parents, or are not white. Nor need such students expect three years of humiliation if they get in. True, all those things were a feature of Oxbridge history for hundreds of years, but so were outside lavatories.

Meanwhile, though, university reforms and new types of schools have changed Oxbridge so much it would be unrecognisable to those fighting for its "lily-whiteness".

This is not to say that today's entrance rules are equally fair to all bright students, and this book has no magic formula to offer which would alter this. What it can do, primarily, is to provide you with the tools to achieve the best possible outcome. It can also point out which aspects require further change.

Many self-help books give the impression that everything desirable will come to those willing to take just a few quick, easy steps. "Everyone can be a millionaire," "Think yourself thin," or "Be the person you always wanted to be" are the mantras of their optimistic authors.

Unfortunately, the real world can be less flexible than these books imply. Powerful forces may thwart even the most determined. There are still Oxbridge rules which prevent some of the best students from getting in. Hardly ever talked about, they remain in place alongside all those friendly invitations, worthy proclamations and jolly Access websites produced with the taxpayer's help.

Some of the obstacles created by these rules are unintentional, I am sure. Others are based on surprisingly sloppy thinking by academics paid to do rather better. Lastly, there are a few obstacles whose continued existence can only be due to a determination to keep student proportions roughly as they are, often by people who have invested a great deal of money to gain a lifelong advantage for their family or group.

On the other hand, my research showed that not all dons are happy with the status quo. Younger, state-educated ones would like to see the Oxbridge intake reflect the modern world. Quite a few older academics feel that, in the age of the human genome, Oxbridge will miss out on its intellectual lead if too many fine minds are snapped up by Imperial College, the LSE, UMIST or Harvard. Lastly, the fear of government sanctions concentrates many a don's mind.

Student intake proportions, though, will not automatically become fair as a result of some academics' good will. Nor can a young person's talent alone turn an obstacle course into a level playing field. Change will almost certainly require both further adjustments to Oxbridge selection methods and a representative, government-enforced entry quota.

The good news is some of the former is already happening: having argued for decades that its admissions process is already perfect and its outcome unchallengeable, Oxbridge has, in fact, greatly improved it in recent years, notably by adding standardised, written ability tests. Both universities now also acknowledge that "more support is needed at the pre-application stage" if students from currently under-represented groups are to stand an equal chance of success.

The problem is that while this had an impact, it clearly is not enough. Having last year announced a new "contextualised" approach to student admissions, Oxbridge continues to demand the same A-level grades from the children of Dukes as from the children of dustmen, from those taught in classes of ten and those taught in classes of thirty and from those having after school tuition to those having after school jobs.

The result has been that while this has raised the general state school proportions at both universities, it still leaves two (often overlapping) groups, working class students and black students, badly under-represented. Middle class parents outside the private sector also complain that many dons seem to have an ongoing preference for applicants who are very intensively and expensively taught, thus enabling Oxbridge to set academic standards which even very bright students attending good state schools cannot meet. As the state school proportion at Oxbridge remains about 20 per cent below the proportion of UK sixth

273

formers in general, these parents may well be right.

None of these problems will disappear simply because this would make life fairer for bright students. Instead, change depends on strong, ongoing pressure from several directions. So, if you're a potential candidate, a parent or a teacher at a school whose best pupils fail to get in, don't keep silent: contact the media, the Government or your MP. High-achieving but rejected applicants may also want to publicly share their experiences of the admissions process.

It is initiatives like these which played a big role in moving Oxbridge into the 21st century, to its own and wider society's benefit. Without those, the proportion of state school students at the two universities would never have risen from 47 per cent in 2003, when dons still argued that "there is just no more talent out there," to a more realistic 64 per cent in 2017.

This increase has already transformed social life at both universities, as well as broadening the academic topics explored there, something students reluctant to consider Oxbridge should be aware of. There is still some way to go, especially given the disproportionately low number of black, working class and northern students at both universities, but addressing this is now officially an Oxbridge ambition.

Those describing such initiatives as "anti-Oxbridge" are badly out of touch. Academics at many colleges will tell you, off the record, that they would actually welcome a state school quota set by the regulator, as it would rein in colleagues rather too set in their ways. If the ambition became a duty they would certainly cope, most claim, at least if helping a student to catch up was not entirely left to her poor, over-worked tutor.

That the admissions process should be a matter of public interest is beyond doubt. Given the career boost generated by an Oxbridge degree, there is more than "just" education at stake here. What happens at Oxbridge affects British society as a whole: if Oxford and Cambridge only feel able to admit Economics applicants with excellent maths, we get politicians who argue that it is mathematically possible for people to survive on zero hours contracts at the minimum wage. If both universities only take students from problem-free schools, there can be no real social mobility. So, you are entitled to air your views, irrespective of whether they are based on personal experience or broader concerns.

Pressure has already started, perhaps due to economic strains. More and more people ask whether it is right that state school students are less likely to get into Oxbridge than privately educated ones, given that Oxbridge graduates get the best jobs.

Critics of the two university's admissions process have included Andrew Neil, founding chairman of *Sky* and a former *Sunday Times* editor, and other establishment figures. Conservative Universities Minister Sam Gyimah told journalists in May 2018 that he struggled to understand how Oxford and Cambridge could regularly produce Nobel prize winners but could not "crack the issue of admissions". By June 2018, even the Daily Telegraph, historically the most ardent defender of Oxbridge, declared itself shocked at the low number of black students admitted.

The social impact of Oxbridge admissions policies is also becoming more widely acknowledged. BBC Director-General Mark Thompson (educated at a top private school and Oxford), made news by declaring himself "disturbed" by the high proportion of Oxbridge graduates in his organisation. *The Guardian* is testing new staff selection methods which might give non-Oxbridge educated applicants more of a chance.

Some dons have argued in response that the two universities are not to blame if top employers prefer staff with an Oxbridge degree although there are other fine universities, but this seems a little disingenuous. By telling Oxbridge students and the world that it picks the "brightest and best", it is holding back progress towards a fairer society as long as too many of its "brightest and best" come from too few schools. What Oxbridge has achieved academically is indeed great, but if it also wants to be loved, it needs to reform.

Meanwhile, though, you must be willing to take the emotional risk of applying or to encourage your teenager to apply. If she is bright and original, if he is focused and hard-working, the process, despite its flaws, could well result in success.

All this is hard work, and some of you may be tempted to give up on Oxbridge instead. Together with many of its devoted students and graduates, I would advise you to persist because the rewards are so great. Oxbridge is that rare, amazing thing in today's Britain, a well-funded, top-level, stunningly beautiful public education facility. It is already enjoyed by thousands of state school students every year, and if public opinion can be hitched to individual effort, might yet welcome more.

Contact list

UNIVERSITY OF CAMBRIDGE
https://www.undergraduate.study.cam.ac.uk/
Call 01223 333308, or email admissions@cam.ac.uk

UNIVERSITY OF OXFORD
https://www.ox.ac.uk/admissions/undergraduate?wssl=1
Call 44 (0) 1865 288000, or email study@ox.ac.uk.

CAMBRIDGE OPEN DAYS
https://www.undergraduate.study.cam.ac.uk/events/cambridge-open-days

OXFORD OPEN DAYS
https://www.ox.ac.uk/admissions/undergraduate/visiting-and-outreach/open-days?wssl=1

CAMBRIDGE AND OXFORD STUDENT CONFERENCES
https://www.undergraduate.study.cam.ac.uk/events/student-conferences

CAMBRIDGE MASTERCLASSES (s.a. OUTREACH)
https://www.undergraduate.study.cam.ac.uk/events/masterclasses

OXFORD SUBJECT TASTERS
https://www.cs.ox.ac.uk/FurtherMathsWhatNext/

OXFORD INFORMATION PAGES FOR TEACHERS
http://www.ox.ac.uk/admissions/undergraduate/applying-to-oxford/teachers

CAMBRIDGE SUMMER SCHOOL (SUTTON TRUST)
https://www.undergraduate.study.cam.ac.uk/events/summer-schools

OXFORD SUMMER SCHOOL (UNIQ)
http://www.uniq.ox.ac.uk/

CAMBRIDGE SCIENCE FESTIVAL
https://www.sciencefestival.cam.ac.uk/

iF: OXFORD SCIENCE AND IDEAS FESTIVAL
https://www.if-oxford.com/

TARGET OXBRIDGE (supporting black applicants)
https://targetoxbridge.co.uk/index.html or call 020 3846 0350

CAMBRIDGE GEEMA (encouraging BAME students to apply)
www.becambridge.com/events/black-asian-and-minority-ethnic-students/

OXFORD AFRICAN &CARIBBEAN SOCIETY
http://www.ox.ac.uk/admissions/undergraduate/visiting-and-outreach/outreach-events/events-students/oxford-african-and-caribbean-society-conference

CAMBRIDGE EVENTS FOR CARE LEAVERS
https://www.undergraduate.study.cam.ac.uk/events/care
Email realise@admin.cam.ac.uk, or call 01223 766872

OXFORD INSIGHT EXPLORE (for Year 10 and 11 students)
http://www.undergraduate.study.cam.ac.uk/find-out-more/widening-participation/insight

CAMBRIDGE SUBJECT MATTERS
(subject tasters & advice on A-level choice for Year 10s and 11s)
www.undergraduate.study.cam.ac.uk/events/subjectmatters

OXFORD PATHWAYS PROGRAMME (student taster days)
https://www.pathways.ox.ac.uk/

HE+ CAMBRIDGE POST-16 SCHEME
https://www.undergraduate.study.cam.ac.uk/find-out-more/widening-participation/he-plusExtension programme for able students in regional school consortia.

OXFORD EVENTS FOR TEACHERS
http://www.ox.ac.uk/admissions/undergraduate/visiting-and-outreach/outreach-events/events-teachers

CAMBRIDGE EVENTS FOR TEACHERS
https://www.undergraduate.study.cam.ac.uk/events/teachers

CAMBRIDGE AREA LINKS SCHEME (with schools)
https://www.undergraduate.study.cam.ac.uk/colleges/area-links

OXFORD UNIVERSITY STUDENT UNION
enquiries@ousu.org / www.ousu.org

CAMBRIDGE UNIVERSITY STUDENT UNION
https://www.cusu.co.uk/about/contact-us/

OXFORD ClassAct (Oxford working class student group)
https://www.oxfordsu.org/campaigns/classact/

UNIVERSITY TASTER COURSES
(list of nationwide course tasters for sixth formers)
https://www.ucas.com/events/exploring-university/learn-about-uni-taster-course

ROYAL INSTITUTION
(runs the Annual Christmas lectures and science workshops for teens)
http://rigb.org/about

INSPIRED
(Government-funded body helping young people find volunteer jobs.)
www.vinspired.com/

STEM NETWORK
(helps schools create and run science, engineering and maths clubs)
 http://www.stemnet.org.uk/

KHAN ACADEMY (free online academic learning site)
www.khanacademy.org/

MENSA (runs some annual events for high IQ teenagers)
https://www.mensa.org.uk/

POTENTIAL PLUS (supporting gifted children and their parents)
http://www.potentialplusuk.org/